〈16〉

［繪本〕

童話中國

白兔姑娘

侯維玲❖文

葉慧君❖圖

遠流出版公司

在中國的西北方，有座麥芽山，山後有個小村莊，住著回族。這裡的土壤不肥沃，村人只好養些羊，喝羊奶吃羊肉。

回族人信仰回教，他們每天念經祈禱，更愛到清真寺，聽阿訇講可蘭經。大家都說，阿訇是天神阿拉的使者，他講的經要聽，他說的話要信，死後才能上天堂，跟阿拉過好日子。

但是阿訇很貪心，他愛吃烤羊肉，便要村民捐肥羊，說是獻給阿拉。村裡有個女娃兒名叫艾伊莎，聰明又漂亮。她的媽媽想捐出肥羊，艾伊莎擔心的問：「媽媽，我們以後要靠什麼吃飯？」媽媽笑著說：「傻孩子！阿拉會保佑我們。」艾伊莎只好和媽媽趕著羊到清真寺。

　　清真寺，廣場大，羊比人還多。阿訇看了笑得嘴都合不攏。阿訇今年七十多，不但貪吃，還很好色，他看艾伊莎長得活潑漂亮，便對艾伊莎的母親說，要在一個月以後娶她。老媽媽心想：艾伊莎當阿訇的新娘，便能接近阿拉，一定會過得幸福快樂，說不定自己也會長命百歲呢！於是一口答應。可是艾伊莎並不想嫁給老阿訇，她哭哭啼啼的跪著求母親，卻被母親大罵一場。

艾伊莎天天嘆氣，阿訇卻高高興興的每天烤羊肉、涮羊肉、燉羊肉、清蒸羊肉……吃個不停，沒想到吃壞肚子，生了大病，躺在床上爬不起來。阿訇知道自己快死了，連忙叫艾伊莎的媽媽來，說：「阿拉喜歡我，要我去陪他。至於艾伊莎，千萬別把她嫁掉，我會來接她上天堂。」

兩三天後，阿訇死了，大家都說：「艾伊莎能隨阿訇上天堂，真幸福。」老媽媽決定把艾伊莎關在山腰的小石屋裡，不准她出門，要她每天誦經祈禱，等著上天堂。

艾伊莎被媽媽關在石屋裡，連個說話的人都沒有，只能站在窗口發呆。

有一天，一隻黑兔子鑽過小窗口，咕咚咕咚跳進來。艾伊莎見了說：「黑兔，黑兔，你是來和我作伴的嗎？」她把飯菜分給黑兔，和牠一起睡。心煩的時候，就對黑兔說說心事。

一個冬天的晚上，黑兔啣來一張兔皮，開口說起話來：「艾伊莎，你想不想逃出去呢？」艾伊莎流著淚說：「想啊！但是媽媽把門鎖上，怎麼出去？」黑兔說：「穿上這件兔皮，你就能變成一隻白兔，帶著這粒絨線球，向南挖地洞，絨線球滾完的時候，你就可以出洞了。老媽媽叫你吃飯時，脫下白兔皮，就會變回小姑娘。」黑兔說完一眨眼就不見了。艾伊莎好奇又害怕，為了逃出去，還是鼓起勇氣，穿上白兔皮……。

艾伊莎不怕苦，不怕累，天天穿上白兔皮，辛苦挖地洞。老媽媽送飯時朝著屋裡叫：「吃飯啦！吃飽好念經祈禱！」艾伊莎就連忙跳回來，脫下白兔皮，大聲回答：「知道了！」

有一天，艾伊莎挖到一罐金子，她把金子拿回屋裡藏好，仍然繼續往前挖。冬天過去，春天來，艾伊莎的手都磨出血，還是拚命往前挖。挖呀挖，秋天走了，冬天來。

絨線球越滾越小。　第三年冬天，　絨線球終於滾完了！　艾伊莎好興奮，　也不管自己有多累，也不管雙腳已經發軟，　開始拚命向上挖。　挖呀挖，　忽然一道光線射進來，　黑黑的地洞，　一下子變得好亮。「哇！　打通了！　打通了！」艾伊莎高興的說。　她使出全身的力氣，　跳到洞口。　洞口外是一堆柴，　艾伊莎躲在柴堆後，　張著一雙大眼睛，　東看看，　西瞧瞧。　原來這是間廚房，　一個老媽媽，　一邊和麵粉，　一邊唱著歌：「我的兒子阿布多，　今年已十九，　天天忙趕集，　大城小鎮都走過，　孝順又能幹，　可惜還沒討老婆。」

就在這時，門打開了，一個青年走進來，笑咪咪的對老媽媽說：「今天進城趕集，給你買了白蓋頭。」老媽媽笑呵呵的說：「謝謝你啦，阿布多。自從搬出村子，住到麥芽山前來，沒有阿訇欺負，日子過得雖然辛苦，但是快樂多了。」阿布多點點頭說：「只要我們天天祈禱，記住可蘭經的教誨，阿拉就會保佑我們的。」

艾伊莎聽了點點頭，想：「要是媽媽也能這樣想就好了！」以後艾伊莎天天都來，躲在柴堆後頭，聽阿布多說哪座城市最美麗，哪裡的人最有趣，還有個皇帝，比阿訇還大，住在高高的城牆裡。

　　白天阿布多出去工作，　老媽媽忙著放羊，　家
裡沒人，　艾伊莎便跳出來，　脫掉白兔皮，　打掃
屋子，　洗洗衣服，　餵餵雞。　老媽媽一回來，　看
見衣服洗好，　飯也煮好，　覺得很奇怪。

　　一天，有個官差到阿布多家，拉著阿布多的
驢子說：「快帶著你的驢子跟我們走，幫我們載
些貨。」

　　阿布多不敢抗拒，只好跟著官兵走。

天正下著大雨，山路又滑又窄，驢子背著重重的貨，一不小心跌一跤，掉到山谷裡。

　　沒了驢子，　沒了銀子，　老媽媽愁得生了病。
艾伊莎看了，　心裡也著急。　忽然她想起挖到的
金子，　趕緊跑回家，　拿來一個金元寶，　偷偷放
在桌上。

　　連續兩三天，　桌上都冒出金子，　阿布多和老
媽媽覺得奇怪，　他們決定查一查是怎麼回事。
於是老媽媽裝睡，　阿布多假裝出門，　躲在窗子
外偷看。　不久只見艾伊莎一蹦一跳的跑出來。

　　艾伊莎脫掉兔皮，　變成一個漂亮的小姑娘。
阿布多看見，　連忙跑進來，　一把抱起白兔皮，
這時老媽媽也下了床，　緊緊拉住艾伊莎，　兩人
央求著：「神仙別走。」艾伊莎說：「我不是神仙，
我是人。」艾伊莎說出自己的遭遇，　老媽媽和阿
布多聽了，　又難過又生氣。　老媽媽說：「如果你
不嫌我們窮，　請你留下來，　嫁給阿布多吧！」

麥芽山的另一邊，石屋空空沒人住，艾伊莎的媽媽不知道，還是天天送飯菜來，送了一個月，喊話沒人回答，屋裡還飄出飯菜壞掉的臭味。媽媽找來新阿訇，喚來全村人，一齊將鎖打開。門開了，大家睜大眼睛一看，艾伊莎不見了！村人全都跪下來，大家高興的說：「艾伊莎升天了！艾伊莎升天了！」

誰知在麥芽山前，阿布多和艾伊莎，帶著老媽媽正要趕往銀川市，開始新生活。

侯 維 玲

1970 年生於台南市，淡江德文系畢業。累積自小對故事書喜好的經驗，奠定了創作童書的基礎，期許以豐富的想像空間，取代傳統教條式的語言。

葉 慧 君

1966 年生於台灣彰化。國立藝專美術工藝科畢業。現任教於台中明德家商室內佈置科。畢業後開始從事兒童插畫的工作。作品有《小木偶與金鑰匙》（遠流）《三字經》等。

The Rabbit Girl

Retold by Wei-Ling Hou; Illustrated by Hui-Jun Ye

Copyright © 1993 by Yuan-Liou Publishing Co., Ltd.

All rights reserved.

7F-5, No. 184, Sec. 3, Ding Chou Rd., Taipei, Taiwan, R.O.C.

TEL：(886-2) 3651212　FAX：(886-2) 3657979

Printed in Taiwan

Summary:

The kind-hearted Iessa received a gift from a black rabbit.

This wonderful gift was a piece of rabbit skin.

The skin, magic, helped Iessa escape from a disaster.

繪本童話中國⑯

白兔姑娘

文／侯維玲　圖／葉慧君

主編／郝廣才　責任編輯／張玲玲　劉思源　徐美慶

美術編輯／陳春惠　封面設計／石某

發行人／王榮文　出版者／遠流出版事業股份有限公司

地址／台北市汀州路 3 段 184 號 7 樓之 5　郵撥／0189456-1

電話／886-2-3651212　傳真／886-2-3657979

1993 年 3 月 20 日初版 1 刷

行政院新聞局局版臺業字第 1295 號

製版／國光彩色製版公司　電話／(02)2212499

印刷／偉勵彩色印刷股份有限公司　電話／(02)2183605

裝訂／裕成印製廠股份有限公司　電話／(02)9857888

© 1993 遠流出版公司　著作權所有・翻印必究

本書若有漏頁或破損・請寄回更換

ISBN／957-32-1737-6

定價 250 元

MERCHANT SAILING SHIPS
1815~1850
SUPREMACY OF SAIL

David R Macgregor
MA, FSA, FRHistS

NAVAL INSTITUTE PRESS

FRONTISPIECE

In this photograph of the Eleanor Dixon, *she is equipped with Cunning-*
ham's roller-reefing topsails and so the picture was taken between
c1855–65. On the main topsail yard, the chafing spar can just be made out
below the yard around which the sail is rolled. She was built at Belfast in
1848 as a full-rigged ship of 454 tons nm for Dixon & Co of Liverpool.
Here she is rigged as a barque. The old-fashioned wooden stock anchors at
*each cathead must be her original ones. (*Nautical Photo Agency*)*

By the same author

The Tea Clippers (1952; reprinted 1972)
The Tea Clippers 1833-1875 (1983, enlarged and revised edi-
tion)
The China Bird (1961)
Fast Sailing Ships 1775–1875 (1973)
Square Rigged Sailing Ships (1977)
Clipper Ships (1979)
Merchant Sailing Ships 1775–1815 (1980)
Schooners in Four Centuries (1982)

Plans drawn by the author
Additional drawings by Paul A Roberts, T W Ward, James
Henderson and others

First published in 1984 by Conway Maritime Press Ltd,
24 Bride Lane, Fleet Street, London EC4Y 8DR

Published and distributed in the United States of America and
Canada by the Naval Institute Press, Annapolis, Maryland
21402

Library of Congress Catalog Card No. 83-46116

ISBN 0-87021-941-3

CONTENTS

To Basil Greenhill

who did so much to foster my early interest
in merchant sailing ships

Dr Basil Greenhill CB, CMG, PhD, FSA
Director of the National Maritime Museum 1970–1983

PREFACE

The present volume is another one in the series I have called *Merchant Sailing Ships* and advances the story another thiry-five years up to the middle of the century. Like the previous work, this concentrates on the design and construction of cargo-carrying vessels and excludes warships, yachts and fishing boats, apart from occasional references to them where comparison seemed desirable. The period from 1815 to 1850 contains no great excitements and no major wars but the development of ship design provides much lively interest as does the introduction of iron as a shipbuilding material.

As in the previous volume and in my earlier book, *Fast Sailing Ships*, ship plans have formed the backbone of the work and analysis of them has sometimes resulted in the concentration of several paragraphs on a single ship. But I have deemed this in-depth study preferable to a brief perusal of a greater number of ship types. Where I have not had the time to draw plans myself, I am greatly indebted to the services of James Henderson, Paul A Roberts and Frederick A Claydon who have generously provided me with the necessary drawings. James Henderson has helped significantly with data on Aberdeen shipping. Some of William Ward's perspective drawings are reproduced here and his study of the brigantine *Violet* is exceptionally good.

William Salisbury and I spent a remarkable week in north-east England in 1958, studying plans and models in the Whitby Museum and also taking off the lines of the large model of the *Blenheim* at Middlesbrough. It took the pair of us two days to record her hull lines and deck fittings. William Salisbury's drawing of the *Blenheim*'s lines is given here and so are his plans of the brig *Black Prince* which are reproduced through the courtesy of Michael Stammers of the Merseyside County Museum.

Michael Stammers is only one of several museum staff who have helped by providing access to models and archives. In this connection I should also like to acknowledge the help of Basil W Bathe, when he was Curator of Shipping at the Science Museum, London; of David Lyon in charge of the Draught Room at the National Maritime Museum, Greenwich; and of Dr Henning Henningsen when he was Director of the Maritime Museum at Kronborg Castle, Elsinor.

Others who made plans available to me included Michael Costagliola for ships built by William Webb, John C G Hill for the Hilhouse collection, and the late Howard I Chapelle for plans of American ships generally.

The search for illustrations and especially for pertinent and, where possible, previously unpublished material has been aided by many private collectors, several of whom are acknowledged in the text. In particular I should like to thank Ian Barling, James Fairweather, Reece Winstone for Bristol photographs, Mrs Anne Gillis for access to the Richard Gillis Collection, and Peter Barton. Of course, I have been an avid collector myself for many years.

Staff at several museums have given much help, especially Dennis Stoneham of the Photographic Department at the National Maritime Museum, Greenwich; Dr B Friise-Meyer of the Altonaer Museum, Hamburg; the Curator of Maritime History at the Peabody Museum, Salem. In addition, I received unstinted assistance from Bertram Newbury of the Parker Gallery over many years. Frank Sabin of the Richard Green Gallery and Paul Mason of the Paul Mason Gallery provided illustrations.

Amongst others who have helped in various ways, I should like to thank Brian Dolley for translating a long French caption from Adml Paris, Malcolm Darch, Robert S Craig, Dr Basil Greenhill for making the painting of the polacca brig *Newton* available, and the directors of Alexander Stephen & Sons for allowing me access to their records.

In the matter of checking the proofs, I am grateful to my wife and my cousin Catherine Oliver. For carefully photographing the plans, my thanks go to John Mayes of Kingprint.

The larger format of this second work in the series will do better justice to the plans, and I am grateful to my Publishers for adopting this format and for agreeing to complete the series.

David R MacGregor
Barnes, London 1983

1

THE SHIPPING INDUSTRY 1815-1850

Fig 1. Steam power may have been all important ashore, but in everything to do with ships it was manpower that counted. (From Jean Baugean, Recueil de Petites Marines, 1817, pl 81)

Baugean del et sculp.

PROTECTION OF TRADE AND SHIPPING

British overseas trade and commercial expansion had thrived throughout the eighteenth century and towards its close there had been a move for freer trade; however, the outbreak of war with France in 1793 curtailed this. The work of tariff review had barely been resumed at the Board of Trade and also in Parliament when William Huskisson was appointed President of the Board in 1823, a post he was to occupy for four years. Greatly interested in shipping and trade, he worked actively for a new mercantile code and for treaties of reciprocity with various countries to alleviate the onerous Navigation Acts. This policy was continued by the Government and the Board of

Trade for the next thirty years. The British manufacturer benefitted by this freer trade at the expense of the ship-owner who lost a certain amount of protection from competition when the various reciprocity treaties were signed, and in particular he lost trade to America, Germany and the Baltic countries.[1]

The outstanding feature of the period up to 1850 was the harnessing of steam power for use in factories, railways and shipping and its application allowed larger and more efficient machines to be employed with a noticeable reduction in the cost of manufactured goods. Inventors were working hard to patent new ideas, although many of these were whimsical and sheer flights of fancy. Many of the machine tools in use at the end of the century were developed in these years. Unfortunately the training of engineers in Great Britain lagged behind the practice on

Fig 2. The Cape of Good Hope was increasingly the meeting place between traders, where outward-bounders met those returning with goods from India, China and the East. Here, in 1837, the anchorage at Table Bay is full of shipping, with the Dutch frigate Bellona *in the foreground preparing to go about. (Elliott Collection, Cape Archives)*

Fig 3. Ships loading guano off the island of Ichaboe in 1844. (Mac-Gregor Collection)

the Continent, because it was held that practical training was more important than that of a theoretical nature and it was not until 1875 that a department of engineering was established at Cambridge University. On the other hand, the incredible rapidity with which the railways were developed largely contributed to the growing awareness among the public of the new industrial age.[2]

In due course the growth of new industries resulted in the deployment of capital and enterprise into the shipping industry. Manufacturers needed markets abroad and industrial growth throughout the world required the carriage of bulk cargoes. Added to this, home-produced food could not keep pace with a growing population and the regular import of foodstuffs became the only remedy. Imports of food and raw materials grew quickly while exports advanced more slowly until the 1840s, hence the balance of trade was important.[3] Two of Great Britain's largest exports were coal and textile goods; in 1850 the value of the latter was £46 million compared with £46,000 a century before.[4]

After 1815 there had been a minor rush to re-route large British ships to the eastern trade, following the abolition of the East India Company's monopoly with India, but the over-supply of tonnage inevitably reduced the freight rate to such an extent that the large profits expected by the operators did not materialise, and after 1820 the trade settled down to normality again. Business gradually improved, particularly after 1834 when trade to the east was finally freed from restrictions, so that by 1847 it was reckoned that the tonnage in the India trade was ten times greater than it had been in 1816.[5]

The breaking of Spanish control in Central and South America permitted the development of considerable trade with the newly formed states which was symptomatic of a growing world-wide expansion in trade. Another important development was in passenger traffic which was at first concentrated in the growing exodus of emigrants from Europe to America but was later extended to international proportions, particularly in the days of the gold rushes and after.

The period from the close of the Napoleonic Wars to the repeal of the Navigation Acts (1849) was one of depression, although there were several years when the business outlook brightened. British shipbuilders met with a good demand for their products in the early twenties but after 1825 the demand slackened off until about 1836 when it began to revive, and there was another burst of building activity between 1837 and 1841. This in turn was followed by severe depression and depreciation in shipping values which was largely brought about by the over-supply of

tonnage. In 1843 when the picture looked blackest and the British shipping industry was appealing to the Government for aid, guano was suddenly discovered on the island of Ichaboe off the coast of West Africa and all idle shipping was taken up for this short but remunerative speculation.[6] By 1845 almost 220,000 tons of shipping had been absorbed which had the result of removing the surplus tonnage and thus lifting freight rates throughout the world. The Irish Famine of 1845 assisted the repeal of the Corn Laws in 1846 and foreign ships were permitted to bring in additional grain through a temporary suspension of the Navigation Acts.

But this trade expansion was small compared with that made by America whose total registered tonnage of 3,486,000 in 1850 was almost treble the figure of 1830; the figure for Great Britain had advanced by barely half to 3,565,000 tons. These figures show the challenge being made by America for the carrying trade of the world.

Against such competition the British shipping industry appears to have attempted the enlistment of Government aid for a return to fuller protection rather than for the improvement in the quality of their ships and the economic background against which they operated. Many of the ships were excellently run by intelligent owners but there is much evidence to show that a large proportion of the merchant marine was negligently operated and that the ships were badly constructed and unseaworthy. A Select Committee was appointed by the House of Commons in 1836 to inquire into the large number of shipwrecks and the reasons for them; its uncompromising findings brought the matter to public attention. The more important causes for shipwreck were attributed by the Committee to the imperfect classification of ships by Lloyd's Register before the amalgamation of 1834 (see section on Lloyd's Register below); the ships' poor state of repair and their defective construction; inadequacy of equipment; over-loading; bad design arising from ill-conceived tonnage measurement; shallow harbours where ships lay aground and were strained; incompetence of masters and mates; intemperance of masters and crews; the system of marine insurance; lack of harbours of refuge; imperfection of charts. Some years were to elapse and several more enquiries to be held before this stigma could be removed.[7]

It may well be conjectured whether any of the ships of which plans appear in this book come under the description of defective construction or inadequate equipment but it would be invidious to suggest this, although Ballingall commented unfavourably on the *Thalia*, as quoted in *Fast Sailing Ships*, page 67. Nevertheless, as the plans presented here are a fair sample of the sort of ships built, so they may fairly represent something of the best and worst to be found in the shipbuilding yards of the period.

4

5

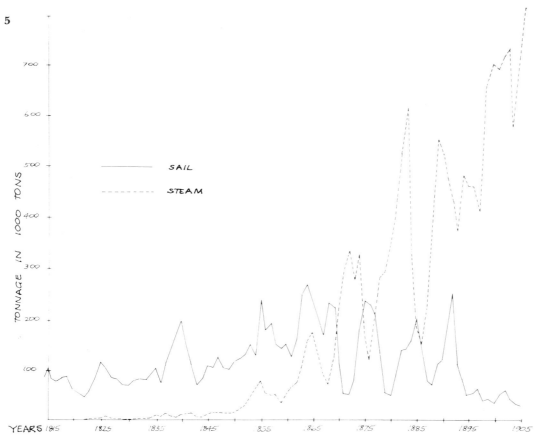

PROTECTION OF SHIPBUILDING

Protection from foreign competition resulted in British ship design of 1845 differing little from the style to be found in 1815 for the majority of shipping, and it was this majority which comprised the carriers of the nation's raw materials and manufactured goods. Unrealistic tonnage measurement practised until 1836, in which the ship's length and breadth only, and not the depth, were included, had assisted this state of affairs, and even after that date comparatively few vessels were influenced by the new method of measurement, although there was a trend in the late forties towards longer ships. Statistics confirm the overall stagnant nature of the British shipbuilding industry in the thirty-five years before 1850. In 1819, 1824, 1827, 1832 and 1844 the total tonnage of sailing ships launched was roughly similar in each of these years, namely in the region of 87,000–90,000 tons.[8] The annual tonnages have been plotted on figure 5 which reveals the cyclical nature of the industry.

The general course of the shipbuilding industry is discussed in individual chapters, but the important part played by Canadian shipbuilders may not be apparent unless specifically mentioned. Throughout the nineteenth century, the output of Canadian shipyards increased so rapidly that in 1847 and 1849 the total tonnage constructed in the colonies, of which Canada was the principal source, actually exceeded that turned out by Great Britain, and in 1847 colonial-built ships comprised one-sixth of the tonnage owned there.[9]

The following figures, compiled by Richard Rice, illustrate the increasingly dominant position Canada was to have in British shipbuilding and in particular the emergence of the ports of Saint John and Quebec as shipbuilding centres.[10]

Year	Total tonnage built in Canada	Tonnage built in Saint John & Quebec	Amount of tonnage built at Saint John & Quebec registered in Great Britain
1790	7775	4354	no record
1800	15,340	7839	862 (from Quebec)
1810	not available	8478	4468 (from Quebec)
1820	15,958	5330	4299
1830	25,939	11,647	7874
1840	128,211	67,439	48,669
1850	95,125	57,646	52,109

Fig 4. *Although still upright on the beach at Scarborough, the partially dismasted* Lily *is in a dreadful mess, but this was a frequent occurrence in days when small sailing vessels were numbered in hundreds, and it gave constant work to the sailmakers, shipwrights and other trades at every port along the coast. The* Lily *was built at Guernsey in 1840 and was of 192 tons.* (Nautical Photo Agency)

Fig 5. *Annual Tonnages of Ships Built and Registered in the United Kingdom 1815—1905. Compiled from figures in B R Mitchell, Abstract of British Historical Statistics (1962).*

For the period 1787–1855, (excluding the years 1809–13, 1842, 1844–45 and 1852) the total tonnage built in Great Britain totalled 5,974,140, while that built in Canada totalled 2,598,797. In 1840, the total tonnage built in Canada exceeded that built in the United States of America for the first and only time.[11]

The Canadians held the great advantage of unlimited supplies of timber but lack of manufacturing resources meant that they had to import copper bolts, sheathing, finished iron fittings, anchors and cables. It was stated that at the end of the thirties, ships could be built of hackmatack (a form of larch) at £5 per ton for the hull, masts and iron fastenings but that a further £4 10s would be required for the rigging, sails, coppering, anchors, cables and to fit them for sea.[12] The Secretary to Lloyd's Register of Shipping stated in 1847 that the type of wood used in the construction of colonial ships had improved and so had the method of building.[13] The use of hackmatack could give a maximum classification by Lloyd's Register of 6 A1, according to the schedule issued by that society in its rules.

Care must be exercised when comparing building costs between one country and another: unless the specification or classification of corresponding ships are known, false impressions can be gained. The evidence before the Select Committee set up to inquire into the Navigation Laws contains conflicting evidence on whether or not British shipbuilders were more expensive than those abroad and whether they would be ruined by the repeal of the Acts. Prices of low-classed ships built in Europe and Canada were often less than those built in the British Isles, but when the period of classification was equalised it was found that costs were roughly similar.

High import duties were levied on foreign timber imported into Great Britain, in order to encourage the British colonial lumber industry. Canada benefitted greatly from such duties, in spite of timber freights across the Atlantic largely offsetting the saving to be gained by the cheaper colonial timber. Some ships worked on a triangular route: outwards to the West Indies; then to American ports; and home with cotton from America or with timber and grain from Canada. Two large ships, *Columbus* and *Baron of Renfrew*, were launched at Quebec in the mid-twenties to take advantage of the booming Canadian timber trade. The former measured 3690 tons and the other 5294 tons, and after the shell of the hull was completed they were filled solid with timber, being designed to make only a single eastward passage before being dismantled. The masting, rigging and outfit was therefore of the simplest type.[14]

During the years of protection, British shipbuilders established the tradition of well-built, long-lasting hulls that received an A1 classification at Lloyd's of over ten years. Ships of 750 tons often took twelve months or more to construct but this leisurely attitude was unsuitable for a shipowner who wanted a vessel in a hurry because of a sudden rise in freights. A ship classed at 6 or 8 A1 could suit him and earn good money while a ship classing 12 or 13 A1 was still on the stocks.

6

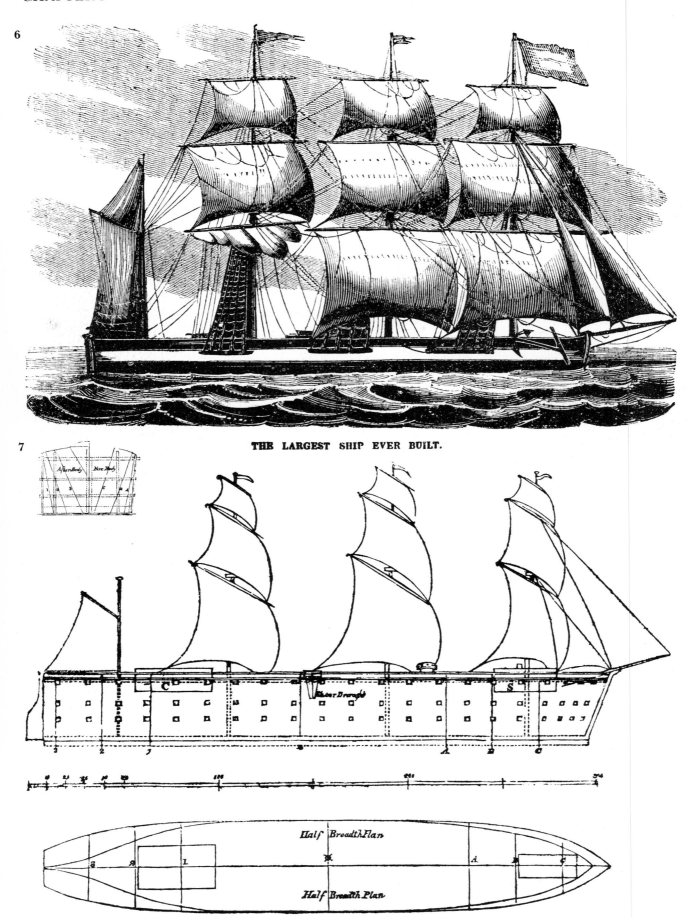

THE LARGEST SHIP EVER BUILT.

7

Half Breadth Plan

Half Breadth Plan

Fig 6. *From her rig, it may be that the* Columbus *was the first four-masted barque ever built.* Lloyd's List *of 2 November 1824 reported on her passage across the Atlantic as follows: 'The* Columbus, *M'Kellar, arrived in the Downs yesterday from Quebec, is a four-masted Ship; her length 310 feet — breadth 50 feet 6 inches — depth 30 feet — 3690 tons measurement — and has a cargo of 6300 tons of white and red Pine and Deals. She sailed from Quebec on the 5th September, and ran on shore on Bersiamitis Point, where she lost two anchors and cables, and sailed from thence 12 September. An anchor of 71 cwt and 70 Men were sent from Deal yesterday to assist her, she being very leaky.' Curiously enough another ship called* Columbus *was crossing from Quebec at much the same time. She reached Portsmouth on 8 November 1824 under Captain Jackson '26 days' from Quebec. The two ships should not be confused. (MacGregor Collection)*

Fig 7. Columbus. *Lines and sail plan reproduced from* Mechanics' Magazine *18 September 1824. Although a scale is drawn it is a pity the masts and yards were not drawn in the conventional way. 'She is built exactly on the plan of a Canadian bateau, being perfectly flat-bottomed and wall-sided, with the stem and sternpost nearly or altogether perpendicular, and both ends sharp, with very little of the fulness of bows and sterns of the ordinary construction'. Her passage of 50 days was probably occasioned by her small sail area in relation to her size, because her fine ends and long hull could have made her much faster. A hull with this length had a speed potential of about 20 knots.*

Fig 8. *Photographed in a dockyard in South Wales in the late 1840s, the Rev Calvert Jones has caught the atmosphere well. Baulks of timber lie in the foreground and over the roofs are the masts of a full-rigged ship with the topgallant masts housed.*

If the Lloyd's Register surveyor at Sunderland was correct in 1847 in stating that a ship could be built there with imported Danzig oak more cheaply than one built at Danzig with the same material,[15] then after the repeal of protective duties British shipbuilders had little to fear from European builders. The European view on iron shipbuilding is summed up in the following remarks, submitted in 1847 to the Select Committee on Navigation Laws as part of the evidence about Hanseatic (Bremen, Hamburg and Lubeck) shipping:

Supposing the abolition of all protection, England must always possess a superiority in shipbuilding, owing to the greater cheapness with which she can build iron vessels. At present, the cheaper rates of materials and labour enable foreign nations to build wooden vessels perhaps cheaper than the English; but if the iron system should be found on a fair trial to succeed (and to steamers the point has not been denied), Great Britain must ever possess the power of underselling the foreigner.[16]

With no outside competition, except from lower-classed colonial ships, there was no burning incentive to exploit the natural resources of coal and iron with which Scotland and the north of England were so liberally endowed. If Parliament had not intervened with laws of protection, British capital and enterprise might well have developed iron shipbuilding at a quicker rate. As it was it took time to convince shipowners and a

Fig 9. *A delightful engraving by Jean Baugean of Dutch vessels entering a port at high water. It was published in 1817 in* Recueil de Petites Marines *as plate 11.*

Fig 10. *This group of vessels, lithographed by John Ward of Hull, shows a brig, a sloop, a full-rigged ship and a schooner — in fact, all the principal types of rig that were currently afloat at that time. (MacGregor Collection)*

Fig 11. *The barque rig was fast becoming popular, and although some sported skysails on fore- and mastmast, many others were rigged like the* Anna Robertson *of Scarborough, pictured here leaving Malta in 1849. She carried sizeable trysails on all three masts, that on the main having its own trysail mast, and no staysails are drawn between the masts. She was built at Sunderland of 317 tons nm in 1842. The painting is by Nicolas Cammillieri.* (Private Collection)

cautious Lloyd's Register — which for years insisted on annual surveys of iron ships — of the great benefits to be obtained by the exclusive use of iron in ship construction.

LLOYD'S REGISTER OF SHIPPING

The criticism of Lloyd's Register lay in the classification system before 1834 in which ships were classed according to their age and where they were built. In this arbitrary system, ships built on the Thames invariably received a longer period of years at A1 than ships built elsewhere, and when this period terminated the ships automatically lapsed to a lower grade irrespective of whether they had been carefully repaired or not. Thus there was no incentive for ships built outside the Thames to improve their standards nor for ships to be properly repaired so as to continue in an A1 condition.[17]

In the 1798 register book, the Committee introduced a new classification system without consulting the subscribers, in which a Thames-built ship was to receive an A1 class for thirteen years but a ship from a northern port of equally good construction was to be granted only eight years A1.[18] Unable to obtain redress, a committee representing the shipowners began publishing their own red-bound register in 1799 which rivalled the underwriters' green-bound book. The 'green' and the 'red' books continued separately until they were merged in 1833 and the new joint book first appeared in 1834. During the period of the separate existence of the red book, a slight discrimination was still evident in favour of the London or, as they were always styled, 'River-built' ships, which were classed at A1 for twelve years, while 'country' or provincial-built ships were classed for only ten years. Other grievances were that the rules included no provision for survey while the ship was being built; that there was little supervision of the surveyors; and that standards of construction varied from port to port.

Although the name 'Lloyd's' was retained by the new registration society, it had been reconstituted as a self-governing body under the title of 'Lloyd's Register of

British and Foreign Shipping' and new classification rules were immediately adopted. These rules covered 23 pages in the 1835 book and for the first time listed standards of construction to be adhered to, and scantlings and descriptions of the various classes. For the first time an A1 ship could have the original period of classification extended by being 'kept in the highest state of repair and efficiency'. The new society proceeded to survey all British ships of over fifty tons, a task which occupied five years for some 15,000 vessels. Ships that did not seek classification were droppped from the 1838 register.[19]

At the inquiry into the Navigation Laws held in 1847 before a Select Committee, Charles Graham, Secretary of Lloyd's Register, explained how ships could have their A1 class continued beyond the original period of classification by undergoing a detailed survey. He showed that a 12 A1 ship could be extended for another four years and a 7 A1 ship extended for another two years; after that, and subject to a second detailed survey, the former could be extended another eight years making twenty-four years A1 altogether, while the latter could be extended five more years making fourteen years A1. Even then the final extension for each could result in the original 12 A1 ship remaining A1 for twenty-seven years and the original 7 A1 ship remaining A1 for sixteen years.[20]

A small ship built by an illiterate or ignorant builder often caused a Lloyd's Register surveyor far more trouble than a 1000-ton vessel — and the seas of those days were crowded with small ships as W S Lindsay recalls:

> Let anyone survey from the fort of Tynemouth and ancient churchyard adjoining — a favourite walk of mine when I represented that borough in Parliament — and see from 200 to 300 ships going out at one tide, or watch the passing of ships from Flamborough Head or from the cliffs of Dover, or let him steam through the endless crowd of herring boats off the Scotch coast, and he will have a stronger impression of the magnitude of the mercantile marine of Great Britain than can be derived from the most careful study of all our Blue Books on the subject.[21]

The second oldest classification society was the Bureau Veritas which was founded at Antwerp in 1828; two years

later an office was opened in Paris which became the headquarters in 1833. The first shipping register was issued in 1829 and the first set of rules for building wooden ships appeared in 1851. Rules for iron ships were issued in 1858, and for composite ships in 1865. The registers only listed classed vessels, but another volume entitled *Repertoire de la Marine Marchande* was first published in 1870–71 and listed all ships including non-classified ones. This publication continued until 1939.[22]

APPRAISAL OF EARLY IRON SHIPBUILDING

The early builders of iron ships obviously miscalculated the strength of the metal or they would not have replaced the massive framework in timber to which they were accustomed with small, widely-spaced angles for frames and beams, which proved to lack stiffness and strength. In making the plating unnecessarily thick, they fortunately preserved the structure of the hull from disintegrating under strain. This over-thickening of the plating was a primitive form of longitudinal structure, as later advocated by such men as I K Brunel and J Scott Russell. But by stiffening and thickening the frames, engineers such as John Grantham moved unconsciously away from the longitudinal structure and copied more the wood forms to which they were accustomed. Here lies the root of the trouble: shipbuilders unacquainted with the properties of iron or how best to employ the plates, angles and

tee-bars in the fabric of a ship, inevitably followed the practice adopted in wooden shipbuilding, and some time was to elapse before a code of practice was gradually perfected, following empirical tests with actual vessels. That the large iron steamer *Great Britain* withstood the gales of two winters when she remained ashore on the Irish coast and was refloated without having become strained, was a great moral victory for the protagonists of iron shipbuilding.

The ductile quality of iron was not yet fully comprehended and short lengths of the material were still scarphed together in the manner of wooden shipyard practice. The eventual formation of the frames by bending a single length of angle iron to the required shape greatly speeded up the process of construction. The engineers and boilermakers, who were among the first to employ iron in shipbuilding, had to ensure that the shell of the vessel was watertight and that it remained so under any strain to which it might be subjected. With so many varied problems demanding answers, it is hardly surprising that text books on shipbuilding and articles in magazines tended to concentrate on iron shipbuilding rather than on wooden construction. But improvement in mechanical skills was extending to every branch of engineering usage and the shipbuilder benefitted from the growing ease and reduction of costs that accompanied the construction of iron hulls. Shipowners, merchants, surveyors and governmental bodies, were gradually forsaking their prejudicial opinions as regards iron ships which had inevitably restricted the process of development.

Not all shipowners bothered to apply to Lloyd's Register of Shipping for Classification of iron ships, partly because Lloyd's regarded iron construction as of a somewhat experimental nature prior to 1850. One has only to study a few of the reports of those ships that were surveyed to realise the great variety of methods employed in the building, and of the wide range of scantlings used for similar parts of the hull. By inviting the co-operation of selected shipbuilders, a code of practice for building iron ships was eventually adopted, but much goodwill was required on all sides to permit its successful acceptance and it was not until 1855 that a set of rules was issued by Lloyd's Register for building in iron. The history of how these rules came to be compiled is described in detail in *Fast Sailing Ships*, Chapter Five.

ALTERATIONS IN TONNAGE MEASUREMENT

A review of tonnage measurement occurred in 1821 when a Commission was appointed by the Government to hold an enquiry, but no alteration in the law resulted from their deliberations. Suggestions were made to measure the hull internally by which the depth would have been measured for the first time, but the proposals were such an approximation and were greatly open to evasion and so were not adopted.

The subject again came up for review in 1833 when a second Commission was appointed. This was more successful and the proposals of Edward Riddle of Greenwich were recommended, in which three crude cross-sectional

Fig 12. The other rig not illustrated by Ward was the brigantine and in its more modern form the square sails on the main topmast had been dispensed with, and by the middle of the century the fore gaff sail had given way to staysails. Here the American Geo. W. Jones is pictured by Nicolas Cammillieri as sailing into Malta in 1853. This was three years after she was built. She was of 200 tons and constructed at Augusta, Maine. (Peabody Museum, Salem)

Fig 13. A watercolour that gives a good impression of the large numbers of sailing vessels that passed in constant procession along the coast. (Parker Gallery)

areas were employed to determine the tonnage. For the first time, dimensions were in feet and tenths of a foot. The recommendations became law on 1 January 1836.[23]

In my two books *Fast Sailing Ships* and *The Tea Clippers* (1983 edition) I have fully covered the subject of how tonnage was calculated under this 'New Measurement Rule', and readers are referred to these books for fuller details. It should be noted that there were two tonnage figures given for many ships between then and 1854, when the tonnage system changed again. In the annual volumes published by Lloyd's Register, the uppermost tonnage figure is that by the old measurement rule; the lower figure is according to the new measurement rule, and is printed in a slightly smaller type face. When only one figure is given, it should be the old measurement for ships built prior to 1836, but the new measurement for ships built subsequently. The new divisor in the calculations was 3500 which resulted in awkward fractions. Although the survey reports compiled by the Lloyd's Register surveyors do include the ship's dimensions, these were not printed in *Lloyd's Register* until 1863. Precision in the description of mechanical and technical matters was still in its infancy and most writers were virtually inarticulate when confronted with the need for definitions.

Fig 14. At Swansea in the mid-1840s: on the left against the quay is the Mary Dugdale *and on the right, some distance from the quay but sitting upright in the mud, is the* Countess of Bective. *The former ship was built at Hull in 1835 for John Dugdale and measured 109ft 0in × 27ft 9in × 20ft 0in and 375 tons om. The latter was built at Sunderland in 1843; the two posts sticking up by the knightheads must be whisker poles that have been hinged up whilst in port. Both are full-bodied ships. (National Maritime Museum, Greenwich)*

2

SQUARE RIG AND FORE·AND·AFT 1815·1835

PRESERVATION OF RECORDS

It is incredible that so few models and plans have survived for single- and two-masted vessels when one considers how many thousands of such craft were constructed around the coasts of Great Britain from the beginning of the last century. Throughout history the articles in most common use are the ones least recorded and those most difficult to reconstruct; yet at the same time these articles are for later generations the most interesting objects to study and repay such research with fascinating and intimate glimpses of how people used to live. So with the smaller craft. The barges that carried cargoes in the creeks; the smacks taking mails or passengers by water; the schooners carrying fish or fruit or perishable goods at speed; the brigs and snows filled with bulk cargoes of coal, sugar and corn, manufactured goods or deck-loads of timber – all were so commonplace that they were never given a second thought. That interest should have been taken in their construction, rig and handling a century and a half later would have been thought laughable. But pride in craftsmanship or affection for a favourite vessel occasionally resulted in retaining some evidence of these craft in a model or a painting. Perhaps even the haste of modernising an old shipyard resulted in some half-models being thrust into a forgotten corner, to be retrieved by later generations and lovingly dusted and repaired. Small square-rigged ships fall into the same categories, but the larger vessels were thought more deserving of preservation because of their design and appearance, and because of the greater capital investment involved.

The very manner of building these smaller vessels militated against preserving any records of construction, hull-form, rigging or costs. They were built, for the most part, in the smallest shipyards, frequently on an open beach above highwater-mark, and often by uneducated men. A successful foreman-shipwright would set up on his own with an order he had obtained. He had little capital and if he had agreed to build a ship for a low price when times were bad, and prices of timber and materials later advanced, he would close down his yard as soon as the vessel was launched, having possibly made a loss or no profit on the transaction. The only record of building this vessel would be that his family went hungry when timber prices rose. A shipwright who made a success out of his first sloop or brig would be anxious to secure another order and what had begun as a speculative venture might for a year or two be turned to good advantage. He would design his own hulls by carving a half-model and showing it to a prospective owner, but it would be most exceptional for him to know the rudiments of preparing plans of a ship. He would certainly arrange to have masts and spars cut to length by rule of thumb and the vessel would be rigged, as indeed she was built, according to the custom prevailing at the port. What records would have survived here? An unnamed rough model and a greasy notebook full of figures and calculations? And who would have bothered to keep either of them? Even a well-established shipyard could fail and the contents be sold and dispersed or a fire could destroy the accumulated records of many years' work.

Nevertheless, in spite of the paucity of plans and models, pictorial evidence and particularly the printed word show how vast was the number of these small vessels and the multiplicity of rigs put on them. The names of rigs used during the eighteenth century seem infinite and often strange to those only accustomed to nineteenth century names and, in addition, a certain rig could be represented by something quite different fifty years later. Two glaring examples are the brigantine and the ketch. By 1815 the brig and sloop were the commonest rigs in use for cargo work, other than the ship. In this year *Lloyd's Underwriters' Register* (green book) listed twelve rigs: ship, sloop, snow, smack, schooner, schoot, brig, galliot, hoy, dogger, cutter, ketch. The *Shipowners' Register* (red book) also listed these and added the barque, lugger and yacht. The *Underwriters' Register* added the name barque in 1819. Prior to amalgamation in 1834 neither book listed a brigantine in the key.

No better idea is provided of a shipbuilder's concept of

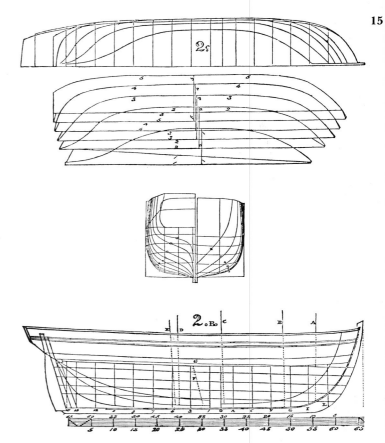

15

Fig 15. Combination of three separate diagrams to the same scale submitted by a contributor, who styled himself 'Noah', to the Mechanics' Magazine *of 29 September 1827. He used the following notation: A and D are centres of masts for a brig; B and C mast centres for a schooner; C is mast centre for a smack; F is centre of gravity when light and greatest transverse section; G is centre of gravity when loaded. Below the half-breadth plan at the top, the five areas within the waterlines have been drawn separately in order to work out the specific gravity according to 'Noah's' recommendations. He does not comment on the hull-form, sail areas, or why he adopted one plan for differing rigs.*

Fig 16. According to Lloyd's Register, *there is only one ship that could be the* Amazon *of Hull, and that is the one built by Robert Steele in 1811. No other ship or barque fitted this description in the years when William F Settle (1821—97), to whom this watercolour is attributed, was painting. The* Amazon *came to Hull in about 1830 and was still owned there in 1865. In this picture the yards are drawn end-on and no skysail yards are crossed; curiously enough, there is no main trysail gaff, although one is drawn on the foremast.* (Peabody Museum, Salem)

a typical vessel than through the plans he submits to a magazine for publication. For instance, a contributor to the *Mechanics Magazine* in 1827, who signed himself 'Noah', submitted plans of a yacht and of a merchant vessel.[1] The dimensions of the merchantman, scaled off the small drawing, are approximately 67ft 6in tonnage length × 22ft 0in × 13ft 0in which he calculated to give a tonnage of 110. 'Noah' estimated the weight of his vessel with her stores as 64 tons and that she would carry 160 tons of cargo. She is shown as a short, deep craft with a drag of 2ft 6in and bears a strong resemblance to Hedderwick's schooner *Glasgow* of 151 tons (figure 52) which had measurements of 71ft 9in tonnage length, 22ft 1in maximum breadth, and 13ft 6in depth of hold. Furthermore 'Noah' shows, by the mast centres given, that his design was equally suitable for a brig, a schooner or a smack. Due to the elastic quality of rig in relation to hull-form, cutters were converted into ketches, brigs became brigantines and finally schooners, three-masted schooners reverted to brigs, and so forth. Indeed the size of brigs often overlapped that of barques and sometimes also of full-rigged ships, so that exchanges of rig in all classes of vessels were common. This illustration emphasises the desirability of considering the brig, schooner and smack in the same chapter and the need to eliminate the separate categories into which differing rigs are frequently placed.

BOOKS ON NAVAL ARCHITECTURE BY HEDDERWICK AND RICHARDSON

Peter Hedderwick was a naval architect and shipbuilder of considerable experience when in 1819 he gave evidence before a Select Committee of the House of Commons about certain Leith smacks. Six years earlier he had received a silver medal and twenty guineas from the Society of Arts for a double-acting piston pump which he had invented.[2] But other than that he operated a shipyard at Leith, little else is known about him.

His chief claim to fame was the publication in 1830, at his own expense, of *A Treatise on Marine Architecture*.[3] This is an important work because it excludes men-of-war and concentrates on merchant ships, a fact which the author explains in his preface as being the reason for its publication. There are eight plates of geometric diagrams at the back of the book but the twenty-one plates of ship plans are bound in a separate atlas and several examples of his plans are used here. All his craft are heavy, burdensome vessels, but they are good examples of draughtsmanship and painstakingly show the external embellishments of the hull. Although the schooner *Charlotte* is the only vessel specifically referred to by name in the description of the

16

plates (pages 398-401), it is possible to identify other vessels with varying degrees of accuracy by consulting the tables he gives on pages 147 and 182-83. Identification of his brigs and schooners is dealt with later in this chapter, but of the full-rigged ships, Hedderwick gives plans for vessels measuring 347⁷⁸/₉₄, 400 and 500 tons. On page 183 he states that the ship of 400 tons is an enlarged version of the *Arcturus* of 370 tons, and that the ship of 500 tons is based on the design of the *Severn* of 567 tons. The *Arcturus* was built at Leith in 1826 and the *Severn* at Calcutta, but her date has not been discovered.

In a table on page 147 of his book, Hedderwick comments briefly on the proportions of twenty-five named vessels and several of his remarks are pertinent to the consideration of the hull-form then in vogue. One of those listed is the *Brilliant* of 322⁸²/₉₄ tons which measured 96ft 4in × 27ft 6in × 19ft 0in and she can be identified as being built in 1800 by Robert Steele. Hedderwick's comment is: 'Thought to be a broad vessel. Fast sailer'. The lines derived from her half-model show a hull-form influenced more largely by the 'cod's head and mackerel tail' theory of design and with greater deadrise than is generally to be seen in Hedderwick's plans.[4] Her design and hull-form were described in more detail in Chapter Three of *Merchant Sailing Ships 1775—1815*, pages 126-27, where her lines plan is also reproduced.

Other broad ships are the *Clyde* and *Severn*. The former was of 454⁴⁰/₉₄ tons and measured 105ft 0in × 31ft 6in × 21ft 3in; Hedderwick's comment: 'A very broad ship'.

Positive identification is not possible as the *Clyde*, which Steele built in 1813, was 50 tons smaller and two feet narrower. The *Severn* of 567³⁵/₉₄ tons is described as 'a broad ship; built in Calcutta by J Horsburgh'; and on page 183 he adds: 'Carried a great cargo; sailed fast.' Her dimensions are given as 116ft 0in × 33ft 4in × 22ft 2in. The L/B (length/breadth) ratio of *Severn* is 3.48 and of *Clyde* 3.32.

Peter Hedderwick thought the *Amazon* which Steele built in 1811 of 443 tons to be a 'good proportion'; her L/B ratio is 3.66. The *Mary* and *Albion* which are also listed were built by Steele in 1803 and 1818, and their L/B ratios are 3.61 and 3.86 respectively. Hedderwick's comment on the *Albion* is: 'Thought rather deep.' This great depth is confirmed here in the table on page 127 of *Merchant Sailing Ships 1775—1815* in which some of Robert Steele's deep ships are listed. The *Albion*'s building contract is given here in the section on Robert Steele & Co of Greenock.

An unnamed ship which Hedderwick labels 'narrow' and 'crank' has ratios of 3.94 L/B and 5.80 L/D on dimensions of 116ft 0in × 29ft 5in × 20ft 0in and 452 tons. With the same length as the *Severn* she is obviously shallower and narrower, but by his definition all the clippers and many of the bulk carriers appearing from 1845 onwards would have been 'narrow and crank', yet this was to be only fifteen years after his book appeared! By employing such broad, full-bodied forms for his ideal ships, he must bear some responsibility for prolonging the poor performance of many British vessels.

17

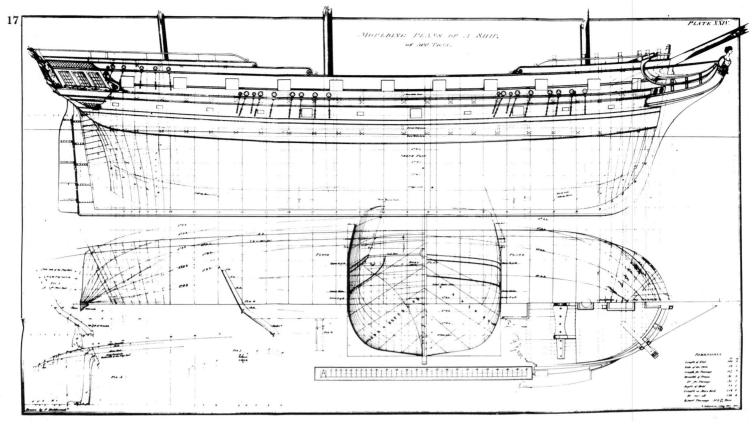

18

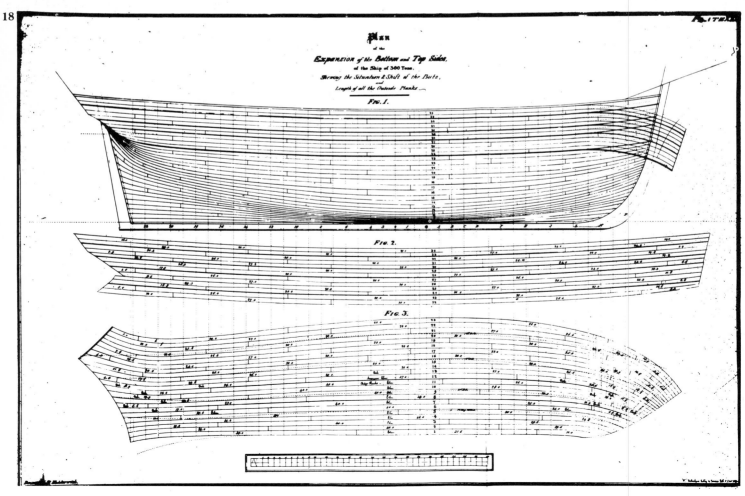

Fig 19.

It is worthy of note that out of the eight named ships listed by Hedderwick, four of them can definitely be ascribed to Robert Steele, which indicates the high regard in which he was held. It is interesting to conjecture whether Peter Hedderwick learnt the art of 'ship-draughting' from Robert Steele, which might explain why he gave examples of so many of his ships and why three are dated before 1812, by which time Hedderwick might have completed his training.

Although Hedderwick gives no clue as to where the design for his ship of 347⁷⁸/₉₄ tons is derived, it seems reasonable, because of his high estimation of Steele's designs to search amongst this shipbuilder's vessels for a possible candidate; after examining the yard list the ship closest in measurements is the *Mary*, launched 1803 of 364 tons. Hedderwick's draught (plate XXIII) is for a vessel of the tons stated with measurements of 102ft 6in length for tonnage and 27ft 7in extreme breadth. The *Mary*'s length is identical and only the breadth and tonnage are slightly higher.

The importance of Hedderwick's sail plans cannot be over-estimated, for the publication of such detailed scale plans was unique at this date. That of the 500-ton ship is reproduced in figure 20 and of the schooner *Glasgow* in figure 53, and both are accompanied by lines plans; a sail plan and lines plan of his smack were redrawn and appear here as figures 70 and 71.

As stated earlier, the design for the 500-ton ship is based on the *Severn* of 567 tons. The lines plan (figure 17) shows a full-bodied ship with slight deadrise, slack bilges, wall sides and some tumblehome. The excessive number of construction lines may make the hull-form difficult to

Fig 17. Ship of 500 Tons. Lines Plan reproduced from Peter Hedderwick's A Treatise on Marine Architecture *(1830) pl XXIV. Dimensions given on plan: 117ft 2in (tonnage length) × 31ft 0in (tonnage beam) × 22ft 0in; 119ft 6in length on main deck; exact tonnage 503⁷⁹/₉₄ om. The waterlines are dotted, but the diagonals are in solid lines.*

Fig 18. External planking for a ship of 300 tons. The middle diagram shows the planking of the topsides drawn out flat; the lower diagram is the planking below the wale. Now called a 'planking expansion' plan. (Peter Hedderwick, A Treatise on Marine Architecture, *1830, pl XXI)*

Fig 19. Lithograph by John Ward (1798—1849) of a ship running before the wind. The mizzen topsail yard has been lowered to bring wind on to the mainmast and all the upper stunsails on the foremast have been taken in. (MacGregor Collection)

follow. The diagonals are drawn solid, indicating the importance attatched to them in the design, but the water-lines are dotted as also are the superimposed constructional timbers in the longitudinal section. The stern and quarter galleries are most elaborate and a heavy head-work supports the figurehead. Small ports are shown along the line of the 'tween decks together with three larger openings which would permit such a ship to carry passengers. Although the design shows a broad ship, it is not a deep one compared with the general tendencies of the period. The ratio of depth to length is 5.3 to 1, and of breadth to length 3.77 to 1, based on the following dimensions: 117ft 2in length for tonnage, 31ft 0in extreme breadth and 22ft 0in depth of hold. Her exact tonnage measures 503⁷⁹/₉₄. Although the lines show a hull primarily intended for carrying the maximum amount of cargo, they give a finer entrance than the *Baffin*, and apparently no deadflats amidships.

The sail plan is described in more detail in the next section, but its chief characteristic is the shortness of the yards, resulting in a tall, narrow plan, which is very typical of ships of this date. Because of the comparative shortness of the hull the yards could often not be longer if undue overlapping was to be avoided; but stunsails could be set each side and these almost doubled the area of canvas on a single mast. John Ward's lithograph of a ship running before the wind (figure 19) is a very lifelike representation of Hedderwick's 500-ton ship.

Three years after Hedderwick's book was published, Thomas Richardson issued six plans of merchant ships accompanied by a slim volume of text which gave brief instructions on drawing the plans.[5] Richardson described himself as a shipbuilder at Hull, but referred to only one ship he had built, the whaler *Andrew Marvel*, launched in 1812 and based on the lines of the whaler *Isabella*, which was built much earlier, in 1786. Plate V of his book gives the latter's lines and a tonnage of 370. No other plate is connected with a named ship. The hull-form is a little finer in the waterlines than Peter Hedderwick's hulls, although the midship section and rise of floor are similar. It would appear that Richardson's book spanned a period of twenty or thirty years and that the form of hull he advocated consisted of a series of enlarged or reduced versions of a favourite type, just as in Hedderwick's case. Richardson was probably influenced in his designs by the requirements of the whaling trade and there are unmistakable traces of *Isabella*'s proportions throughout the plans he published. He divided merchant shipping into three classes:

1. Coasting trade: vessels of 88 to 140 tons, 56 to 66 feet long on the keel. Plates I and II illustrate these.
2. Trade to Europe: vessels of 200 to 300 tons, 75 to 85 feet long on the keel. Plates III (2 masts) and IV (3 masts) illustrate these.
3. Trade to Asia, Africa, and America, and whaling: vessels of 370 to 410 or 420 tons, 90 to 95 feet long on the keel. Plates V (*Isabella*) and VI illustrate these.

His actual remarks on classes 1 and 2 are quoted in the section on Colliers and Other Brigs in this chapter.

In the preface to his work on marine architecture, Thomas Richardson complained in 1833 that draughtsmen in His Majesty's dockyards had ample facilities to describe their own systems of naval architecture but that the reverse was the case for the builders of merchant ships, with the result that 'there is scarcely a draught of a merchant vessel published that is complete'. Any student of naval architecture would endorse his opinion but it is a pity that he did not practice what he preached and publish some really comprehensive sets of merchant ship plans. He implied that some published plans differed little in certain features from those published a century before. Nor does it take much skill to follow, in the period of 1775 to 1845, the identical plates and sketches which are repeated from one encyclopaedia and book to another, with the quality of the engraving gradually deteriorating.

SAILS AND RIGGING

Peter Hedderwick's detailed sail plan of a 500-ton merchant ship forms a convenient central point on which to base some observations on masts, sails and rigging of the period.

The most prominent feature of this sail plan, reproduced in figure 20, is the great height of the masts in relation to the hull length; the height of the main skysail truck above the deck is approximately equal to the length from stem head to taffrail, a proportion which is also to be found in the *Baffin* and other ships. By contrast, the height of the tea clipper *Maitland*'s main truck above the deck is equal to the length from her stem head to mizzenmast. (See *Fast Sailing Ships*, figure 248.) To obtain sufficient sail area by which to propel the vessel, the short and deep ships of Hedderwick's day had to resort to height rather than breadth or an excessive amount of overlap would have occurred with shorter masts and longer yards, thus reducing the effectiveness of the canvas. In any case, Hedderwick preferred tall, narrow sails rather than the 'long and unhandy yards' which shorter masts produced. He recommended that the length of masts and yards be calculated in proportion to both breadth and length of hull rather than by breadth alone, and he gives rules in his book to achieve this. In a full-rigged ship, the lengths of all masts are based on that of the main lower mast and all yards on the mainyard.[6]

It will be noticed that in this plan the royal masts are fidded abaft the topgallant masts which was a fairly common practice at this date, although it results in a number of quite short masts, with extra caps and trestletrees adding to the weight aloft. In severe weather, the separately fidded masts could easily be sent down to reduce the windage aloft and the large crews were regularly accustomed to do this.

The fore course in Hedderwick's sail plan is cut with vertical leeches and as the foremast is stepped so far forward, the fore tack has to be hauled down to a bumkin rather than the cathead. The main course is cut with gored leeches so that the foot is three to six feet longer than the head. No crossjack is carried and ships did not normally bend one until the middle of the century when the spacing between masts had increased. Although a sailmaker might occasionally fancy that his square sails would stand better with curved leeches, it was normal practice to cut all square sails with straight leeches, the only recognised exceptions being topsails. The lowest reef cringle on the topsail had to be vertically under the yardarm in order to close-reef the sail, and sometimes this could only be achieved by curving the leech, if the foot of the sail was long and the head short. The head earing is kept some distance in from the shoulder or cleat where the yardarm joins the yard to allow sufficient room to take up the stretch of sail when the earing is hauled taut. This is

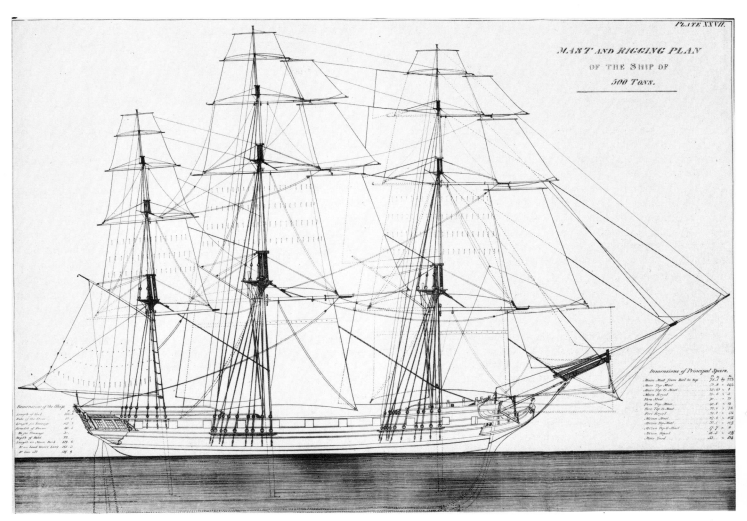

Fig 20. Ship of 500 Tons. Sail plan reproduced from Peter Hedderwick's A Treatise on Marine Architecture *(1830) pl XXVII. The sail plan of a full-rigged merchant ship drawn in such detail was rarely published and so no attempt has been made to re-draw it. See text for full description of rig.*

the reason why, when correctly drawn, the leeches do not present an unbroken line from skysail yard to bulwark rail. In the Navy there was generally no roach to the foot of the square sails but in merchant ships the practice was to allow some, particularly in topgallants, so that the foot might clear the topmast stay if the sail was set above a single-reefed topsail. For topgallants the roach was three feet in small ships and four feet in large ones.

Due to the elasticity of the hemp rigging there was considerable stretch and shrinkage, and with new rigging the crew was kept busy setting up the lanyards at frequent intervals. When under sail, the masts, hull and rigging all moved, and when heeled over, the lee rigging usually became slack. Hedderwick calculated his rigging sizes in terms of the ship's register tonnage. For a ship of 400 tons he estimated the fore and main shrouds – the heaviest rigging in the ship – to be $8\frac{1}{4}$in ropes; the fore stay $6\frac{3}{4}$in; the main stay $6\frac{1}{8}$in; the fore and main topmast backstays 6in; the mizzen shrouds $5\frac{1}{2}$in; the fore and main topmast shrouds 4 1/16in; and the mizzen topmast shrouds $3\frac{3}{4}$in.[7] The sizes are of course circumference not diameter. Although chain was in use for some running rigging, galvanised wire standing rigging did not appear in practical form until the 1840s, as related in the next chapter.

Peter Hedderwick's sail plan of a 500-ton ship gives the rigging in considerable detail and it will be noticed that it

is only the main brace which leads to the deck; it was not until the late 1840s that the fore brace and topsail braces also began to be led direct to the deck. Skysail yards often had no braces but Hedderwick does not even draw any for the royal yards, which was unusual at this date for a ship of 500 tons. In 1794, David Steel drew his twenty-gun frigate with the royals set flying and without lifts or braces. Some small square-rigged vessels of under 150 tons never had braces to the royals, but being sheeted home to the yard below they pivotted naturally on their parrals as the lower yards were swung.

Apart from the main staysail, staysails on the main and mizzen were usually four-sided with a deep nock and the leech was often vertical, making a right angle with the foot. They are not often shown set by artists. By the time Hedderwick's book appeared in 1830, the use of the main middle staysail had died out. It used to set halfway up the main topmast, between the topmast and topgallant staysails, and it appears on the sail plan of the *Baffin* (figure 83). When Darcy Lever was writing in 1808, the middle staysail stay sometimes terminated in a thimble running on a jackstay set up between the foretop and the topmast crosstrees, with a tricing line to the thimble. The *Baffin* also had a middle staysail on her topgallant mast. Darcy Lever himself observed that 'some ships in the East Country trade carry no middle staysail, but have [the main topgallant staysail] considerably larger, coming low down the fore topmast rigging.' By 'East Country' he means the north-east coast of England and refers to ships in the Baltic and coal trades in particular.[8]

Captain Heathcote published a book in 1824 advocating the replacement of four-sided staysails by triangular ones, an inner and outer jib to replace the big single jib, and a spencer or main trysail instead of the mizzen staysail.[9]

The *Baffin*'s main topmast staysail is cut with a sloping nock to miss the fore top, but usually this staysail set up on a spring stay below the fore top as in the *Medina* (figure 82 in *Merchant Sailing Ships 1775—1815*). The latter's main

topgallant staysail also sets up on a spring stay to avoid the fore crosstrees.

The standing jib was the largest headsail and was not usually divided into inner and outer jibs until the 1850s. The dolphin striker was often double, as Hedderwick shows it, its introduction coming late in the eighteenth century. Although Baugean's ships in figure 52 of his *Collection de Toutes les Espèces de Bâtiments de Guerre et de Bâtiments Marchards* (1814) has a spritsail set when running before the wind, nineteenth century merchant ships must rarely have carried this sail. The yard was, however, retained to spread the jibboom rigging; as the century advanced the yard was moved along the bowsprit until it finished on the hull itself, split into two as whisker booms by the catheads.

By 1815 the spanker had been almost completely adopted in the merchant service, superseding the smaller, boom-less mizzen that set from a gaff and was termed the 'mizzen course'. Simultaneously the word 'spanker' superseded that of 'driver' although some books on sea-

21 The following sketch exhibits the sails already treated upon expanded in their proper places :—it also shows the leading of the various ropes attached to the sails, as buntlines, clue-garnets, bowline - bridles, leech - lines, slab - lines, reef - points, cringles, &c. ; as also the shrouds, lifts, &c.

The sketch on this page represents the *studding-sails* spread **22** out beyond the leeches of the principal sails, attached to the foremast, where they appear as wings to the yard-arms ; as also the gear attached to the sails, &c.

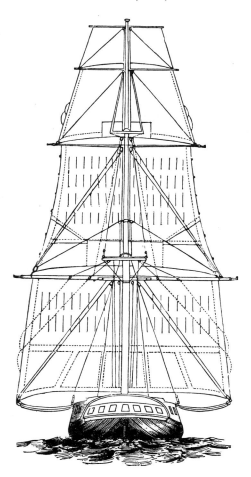

STERN VIEW OF THE SAILS ON MAIN-MAST.

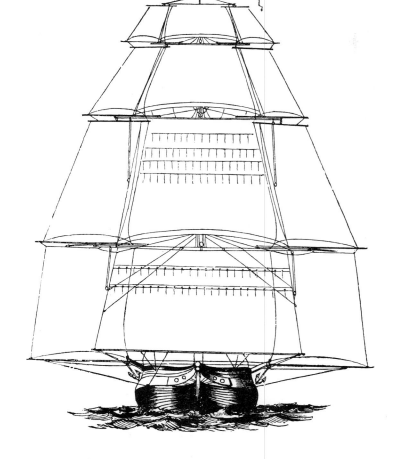

HEAD VIEW OF THE SAILS ON FORE-MAST.

manship continued to use the old term for many years.

Hedderwick's sail plan of the 500-ton ship shows trysails on fore- and mainmasts, hoisting on raking trysail masts which are stepped on deck abaft the lower masts and whose heads project about two feet above the tops. Darcy Lever wrote in 1808 that many ships were rigged with 'fore and aft mainsails'.[10] They soon became very popular and lasted on all three masts until the fifties when, with the increasing length of ships and the consequently greater spacing between the masts, the main topmast stay was set up on the deck and not to the lower masthead, thus making the use of the fore trysail difficult. However, many ships continued to set one on the mainmast only, as had also been the case in earlier years. The main trysail was also called 'spencer'. Paintings occasionally portray a trysail mast close abaft the mizzen lower mast as in a snow. The West Indiaman *Thetis*, built at Hull in 1827 of 460 tons, of which Cooke gives an

Fig 21. This elevation of the sails on the mainmast is reproduced from Robert Kipping's Elementary Treatise on Sails and Sailmaking *(1858) p72. This was probably the first edition in this form. His earlier work on sailmaking appeared in 1847 and 1851 with different plates.*

Fig 22. Elevation of sails on the foremast from Kipping's Treatise on Sails and Sailmaking *p73. The foot of the fore course seems to be extended on a bentinck boom which is probably a mistake of the engraver's, unless it is meant to show every combination available. In the text he refers to the advantages of parallel leeches in the fore course and of having bumpkins suitably placed to bring the tack right down, but I saw no mention of bentinck booms. Kipping had been foreman sailmaker to T & W Smith at North Shields, builders of the Blackwall frigate* Blenheim.

Fig 23. Danish West Indiaman Prinz Carl *painted by v H v Minden in 1827 with Kiel beyond. Her rig resembles Hedderwick's sail plan. (Peabody Museum, Salem)*

etching in his *Shipping and Craft*, disports trysail gaffs on both fore and main.[11] She is another example of Hedderwick's 500-ton ship in action. In the Navy, experiments had been conducted regarding the general adoption of trysails and a letter from the Store Office of the Navy Board in 1816 directed that main trysails should replace mizzen staysails, but that the main storm staysail was to be continued as the use of a fore trysail was not a unanimous choice by the captains engaged in the experiment.[12]

To avoid the trysail gaffs fouling the topmast stays, the latter were often led through an eye on the afterside of the lower mast cap as shown by Hedderwick. This resulted in what Copley Fielding called 'an irregular main topmast stay',[13] possibly because it did not form a continuous line with the lower stay.

In the eighteenth century the term 'bark' embraced hull-form as well as rig, and the definition was given in Chapter Two of *Merchant Sailing Ships 1775—1815*. By tradition, the 'bark' was confined to the east coast trades and was accordingly much used by colliers, like the one drawn by Edward Gwyn in about 1780.[14] Coal and timber cargoes were transported in such craft in the Baltic and North Sea, but it was not until the 1830s that the 'barque' rig suddenly achieved popularity. By this date the mizzen was purely fore-and-aft rigged without any square sails, although a survivor of the eighteenth century mode of having a square mizzen topsail was the *Foster* which was built at Whitby in 1826 (figure 24).

One reason for the sudden popularity of the barque rig may lie in the increasing length of vessels. Before the new method of tonnage measurement in 1836, short, deep vessels could be rigged adequately as brigs but when, following the advent of the new law, depth was reduced

24

and length increased, a third mast became necessary. The brig rig was uneconomical in manpower for the size of vessel but a third fore-and-aft rigged mast could be managed without increasing the size of the crew. The sail plan of the *Arab* (figure 94), which was built in 1839, shows the curious manner in which a third mast was added close to the mainmast. An earlier example, dated 1795, may be found in the Swedish *Fortuna* of Umea.[15]

An alternative reason may be that the redistribution of a brig's area of canvas on a barque's three masts had the same effect as when a sloop was converted into a schooner – namely that of making the sails individually smaller in size and thus manageable by a smaller crew. Economies were achieved in wages and in wear and tear of sails and rigging.

The increasing popularity of the barque rig after the 1820s can be judged from early photographs taken in Swansea harbour in 1845 in which most of the vessels are so rigged. An east coast barque can be seen in John Ward's pen-and-ink drawing (figure 25). She is shown carrying two sliding gunter masts, a long heavy bowsprit, bentinck boom, and three trysails which can be brailed in to the mast.

All these ships and barques could increase their 'plain' square canvas by setting studding sails (usually corrupted to 'stunsails') on each side of the sails on the fore- and mainmasts, as depicted on Hedderwick's sail plan. Square lower stunsails on the foremast were regularly carried but corresponding stunsails on the main lower

mast were unusual: David Steel gives lower stunsails on the fore- and mainmasts to the twenty-gun frigate in his *Rigging and Seamanship*; the *Encyclopédie Méthodique* (1783–87) has a frigate with lower stunsails set on all three masts;[16] and some other ships are illustrated here. Stunsails on the mizzen are definitely rare and authentic cases are cited here when known. Several warships which carried them in the nineteenth century did so for the purpose of training the midshipmen.[17]

The sail and rigging details outlined here remained generally unchanged until the 1850s and later, when the wider use of iron and the increasing size of ships brought about many new developments.

TOPSAILS ON THE DOUBLINGS

Countries in northern Europe often adopted a different method of setting the topsails in many one-, two- and three-masted vessels in the first half of the nineteenth century. Instead of the topsail yard parral sliding on the topmast from the hounds down to the cap of the lower mast, it slid on that part of the topmast that doubled the lower masthead below the lower mast cap. The sheave for the topsail halliard was sometimes in the topmast and the mast was set further away from the lower masthead to let the parral move freely. The doubling was also longer than was customary to give sufficient depth to the topsail. The result was a longer, lower mast and a shallower topsail, but also a very snug rig in bad weather. The topgallant

Fig 24. This photograph of the Foster *probably dates from the period 1854—59 when Captain Benjamin Orchard was master. It was copied from a glass collodion positive mounted on purple velvet when in the possession of Mrs Walker, one of Captain Orchard's descendents. Built in 1826 at Whitby, the* Foster *was lengthened in 1851 which raised her tonnage from 342 om to 445 om. Yards on the mizzen mast were rarely captured in a photograph. Spars have been erected aboard for working the cargo, some of which is probably being transferred to the smack alongside. Orchard was later master of the tea clipper* Lothair.

Fig 25. A pen-and-ink drawing of an unnamed barque, presumably done by John Ward as his signature is in the bottom left. There are sliding gunter masts fidded abaft the fore and main topgallant masts. (Mac-Gregor Collection)

Fig 26. In this stirring watercolour by D A Teupken, dated Amsterdam 1837, the ship Coliseum *is portrayed with a main moonsail and other flying kites. The bulwarks were coloured light blue, as were also the longboat, deckhouse, deck fittings, base of masts and inside of boats. The hull was black except for the wale which was in light raw sienna; all the spars were white. The ship was built at Medford, Mass, in 1828 and was of 296 tons.* (Peabody Museum, Salem)

25

26

was often as deep as the topsail, and sometimes much deeper. This form of rig gives the appearance of double topsails – indeed this rig may have been the precursor of them.

Artists recorded this form of rig most faithfully but it had really gone out of favour before the days of photography, although an early photograph taken near Swansea in about 1845 shows a schooner with a topsail yard rigged in this manner; this was reproduced as figure 78 in *Fast Sailing Ships*. A rig of this sort was especially popular in

Fig 27. An engraving of Christopher's new two-masted rig — there are also versions for one and three masts — 'with the topmast sliding up and down on the aft side of the lower mast', and the yards being labelled as lower, topsail and topgallant. I do not know if the rig was ever used in practice. (John Christopher, Shipwreck and Collisions at Sea Greatly Prevented by . . . Improvements in Naval Architecture, *London 1850, fig 8R)*

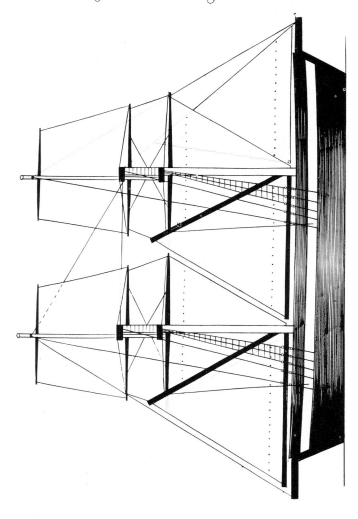

sloops, galliots or galeases with square sails, schooners and some brigantines. Comparatively few brigs, barques or ships were so equipped and these vessels usually possessed a galliot or kof form of hull. It is interesting to note that of Hedderwick's three published sail plans, that of the schooner *Glasgow* has this form of topsail, which must indicate that this was a common form of rig at Leith when she was built in 1826. Most books illustrating north European vessels of this date carry some pictures of the rig, although little acknowledgement of its existence has appeared. Hans Szymanski reproduces several one and two-masted vessels with these topsails in the years 1800–50, and also a barque of 1840. The schooner *Ferdinand* (*c*1820) of Stettin has such topsails and topgallants on both masts.[18]

In *Improvements in Naval Architecture* (1850), which is based on patents taken out the previous year by John Christopher, he refers on page 60 to this form of rig which he also advocates, although in a different style: 'That described reduced topsail has of old been used in small vessels – but it is objectionable in vessels with topmast shrouds, when the topmast slides up and down on the foreside of the lower mast, because the shrouds then prevent the topsail yard being braced up sharp'.

The plan in figure 28 illustrates a three-masted galliot so rigged, with square canvas on each mast. It was drawn in 1878 for *Souvenirs de Marine* by Admiral Paris and the accompanying test is translated for the caption.[19] In this it is stated that it was traced by Mr Roux, the marine artist, from drawings made by his father in 1805 and 1815, and that although galliots of this kind were still in existence in 1848, they had altogether disappeared thirty years later. Dimensions from the text, converted from metric figures, give 86.92ft length of keel, 23.22ft extreme breadth, 13.77ft depth of hold, and 9.84ft to 13.12ft draft of water. No tonnage is given, but Mackrow's tables indicate a figure of 210 tons om.[20]

Admiral Paris calls this ship a Dutch galliot but likens the hull-form to that of a flute. Both Chapman's flutes in plates XXVII and LIII have pink sterns with a square transom above the rudderhead; but his three-masted Dutch galliot or hoy in plate LIV is similar to the Paris plan.[21] In the latter, the stern is rounded right up to the bulwarks with the tiller coming over the top of them; the entrance is incredibly bluff but there is some fineness in the run; the floors are flat and the sides round all the way from bilge to tumblehome. One can understand why in the nineteenth century, with a gradually increasing desire for speedier forms of transport, the slow but sure flute that had safely carried cargoes for two centuries had to give way to newer hull-forms.

By the standards of the 1820s, this galliot would have had a very low rig and the two-piece masts were certainly short with narrow square sails, although stunsails would have increased the spread. The mizzen topsail and topgallant are very small, and if this ship survived until 1830 they would probably have been discarded in favour of a barque's rig. Hans Szymanski illustrates an unnamed barque rigged in this fashion, dated 1840, which shows many similarities with Paris' galliot. Szymanski calls her a

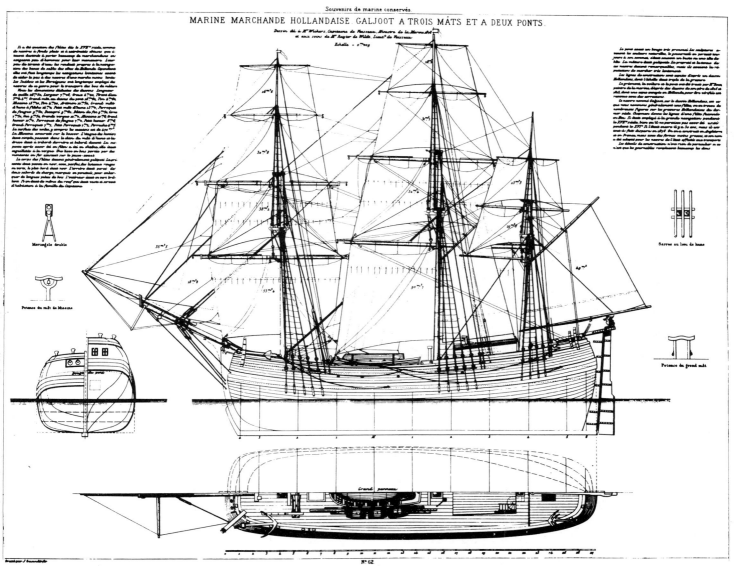

Fig 28. Plans of a Dutch three-masted galliot from the period 1805—15; measurements of the ship appear in the translation of the long caption in French.

Translation of caption to above figure:

We must now consider the 18th century flutes as flat-bottomed ships with bluff ends which were designed to carry large quantities of merchandise and yet were manned by a few hands. Their shallow draft made them very suitable for negotiating the sand bars off the Dutch coast. However they also undertook longer voyages for many years until they were displaced by less slow vessels. The Swedes and Norwegians have long employed this type of vessel for masting timber. The principal measurements may by taken from the plan as:

Length of keel 26.5m; Beam 7.08m; Depth of hold 4.2m; Draft 3m to 4m; Mainmast (above deck) 16.8m; Trestletrees to cap 4.6m; Foremast (above deck) 15.1m; Trestletrees to cap 4.2m; Mizzenmast (above deck) 12.3m; Maintopmast to pole 14.0m; Foretopmast 13.0m; Mizzentopmast 9.3m; Bowsprit 9.8m; Jibboom 9.5m; Gaff 7.5m; Boom 9.5m; Mainyard 12.0m; Foreyard 10.8m; Maintopsail yard 10.0m; Foretopsail yard 8.8m; Mizzentopsail yard 7.0m; Maintopgallant yard 7.7m; Foretopgallant yard 7.2m; Mizzen topgallant yard 4.5m

Sail area including royals 470 sq m*.

The tack of the foresail was secured to the catheads. The topsail ties were simple and passed through a sheave in the topmast. The starboard halliards were taken aft and the port ones forward†. The slings, formerly of rope, were now of chain and were lashed to the yard. A wooden rail on iron supports ran fore and aft.

Flutes' hulls were generally coated with tar, the wales painted black, sometimes with red or green mouldings, and the gunwales were black. The stern was pierced by two loading ports for long timbers, shown on the plan with dotted lines. The interior was painted in bright green as was the large deckhouse which provided living quarters for the captain and his family.

The deck had a pronounced camber. The carvings were in natural colours and the tiller head was always carved, often with a bust or with an animal's head. The masts were tarred. The cleanliness and maintenance of these craft was excellent, but they were reputed to be slow sailers. The lines were taken from a Dutch plan whose scale is three times that of the present engraving.

The rigging, sails and deck plan have been taken by Mr Roux, the marine painter, from plans drawn by his father in 1805 and 1815, a copy of which was sent to Holland and returned with corrections.

This vessel, described as a galjoot on the Dutch plans, is what we would normally call a flute and such vessels are frequently shown on Dutch engravings of the last (18th) century. Chapman shows the lines of a Heu-built flute and which was used in deep-water trade in the 17th century; such usage does not appear to have been usual in the 16th century.

Flutes existed until about 30 years ago but had vanished by 1878. They were also built in England and France on finer lines and the name was used to denote Government transport vessels. The constructional details are not remarkable except for the extent to which trenails took the place of nails.

Author's note:
* The lengths of the following spars are not listed:
   crossjack yard, fore royal yard, main royal yard, main trysail gaff.
† The meaning is not clear. The sail plan shows that the fore and mizzen topsail halliards are both led to port and the main topsail halliards to starboard.
   From the terminology it appears that there was no thought that the topsail had been split into lower and upper sails because the four yards are named as lower, topsail, topgallant and royal.

29

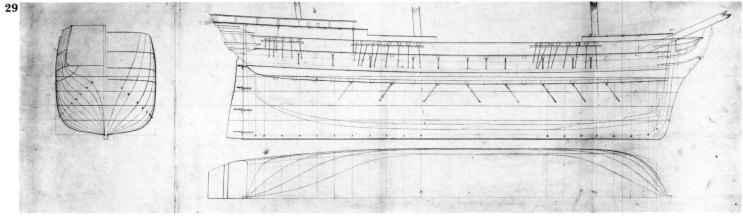

30

Fig 29. Princess Royal. *Lines plan. Built in 1841 (LR) or 1842 (Farr) by Hilhouse, Hill & Co at Bristol. Plan reproduced from original and examined when in the possession of Charles Hill & Sons. Tonnages 462 om and 543 nm; ship, later barque.*

Fig 30. The William Miles *was built at Bristol in 1816 by Hilhouse, Hill & Co as a ship for the West Indies trade; her tonnage was 323¾ with a length of 105ft 1in and beam of 26ft 6in; she was cut down to a barque in 1846. Eight years later she was lengthened to 137.4ft and 28.4ft beam and a new tonnage of 572 and although re-rigged as a ship was later made a barque again. The photograph must date from the second phase as a barque, when owned in Littlehampton from 1866 until wrecked in 1883. The photograph I have is stamped 'F W Spry, Photo'r, Littlehampton'. (MacGregor Collection)*

kof (*barkkuff*). She had masts fidded abaft the topmasts on fore and main with very long trucks above the royal yards so that flags could be flown without the need to lower the yards. Lower, topmast and topgallant stunsails are set on the foremast. From the style of the picture it was probably painted by D A Teupken.[22]

Examples of this rig in schooners and other craft are described later in this chapter. See sail plans of *Glasgow* (figure 53), *Magnus Troil* (figure 37) and *Harmony* (figure 72).

HILHOUSE, HILL & CO OF BRISTOL

The plans from this yard are now in the possession of the National Maritime Museum at Greenwich, but I was able to examine and copy them through the courtesy of John C G Hill, when they were still in the offices of Charles Hill and Sons, who were the successors to Hilhouse, Hill & Co.

Examples of ships designed by this firm have been given in *Merchant Sailing Ships 1775—1815*, and the surviving plans indicate that ships and barques continued to be built with full-bodied hulls throughout the twenties and thirties. The *Princess Royal*, built 1841 of 543 tons new and 462 tons old measurement, has been selected as typical, particularly as the drawing is one of the clearest for reproduction purposes. Her great depth of hull is immediately apparent; also the long parallel middle body, the full entrance and run, and the box-like form of the midship section, all of which closely resemble the form of other ships built by this yard in the previous twenty-five years. In the twenties and early thirties the Hilhouse ships were mostly built with long poops or raised quarterdecks but without any forecastle on deck, as may be seen in the longitudinal section of the *Renown* (*Fast Sailing Ships*, figure 12). Here the floor timbers, fore and after deadwood and other structural members are clearly depicted; also the deck structures on the poop and the after companionway. Diagonal iron trussing of the hull is also shown, which was one of the recommendations made by Sir Robert Seppings, one of the joint Surveyors of the Navy. The *Renown* was built in 1824 of 316 tons for the West Indies trade, and a note on the plan reads: 'Captain Gardiner made a passage to Barbadoes in 18 days – Captain Wilson'.

Captain Wilson is referred to again in connection with the ship *Victoria*, built in 1831 of 358 tons, whose proportions, general arrangements and deck layout are similar to those of *Renown*. There is an interesting letter attached to the *Victoria*'s plan, referring to a conversation with Captain Wilson in 1837 about ship design for various trades. He recommended that ships trading to Calcutta should have 'poops not too long'; and that the *Victoria*'s stowage capacities would have been improved if she had been built with a beam of 28ft instead of 26ft 2in, so that she could 'breast seven hogsheads in Jamaica trade with ease'. He was also in favour of omitting the deck planking amidships in the 'tween decks, apart from a narrow strip along the sides, thus increasing the stowage capacity; simultaneously the deck could be lowered which would make the ship stiffer. He considered the height of the 'tween decks should be not less than 6ft 6in from 'skin to skin', which was suitable for transport ships, but that a height of 7ft was better.

Plans of later Hilhouse ships certainly show much shorter poops, so perhaps his remarks did not pass unnoticed. The *Victoria*'s voyages took her to Mauritius, Barbadoes, Australia, New Zealand and Calcutta. In 1840 she took 105 days between Madras and Bristol.

The *Victoria*'s surviving plan is a longitudinal section and cabin plan, not a lines plan, but on a plan of the *Reliance* (yard No 77), it states that it was also 'used for No 78 *Victoria*'. A further reference to the *Victoria*'s design occurs on the plan of *Ajax* (yard No 85) on which is a list of four ships all built to a set of moulds numbered 243. These four ships were the *Victoria* (1831), *Ajax* (1836), *Caroline* (1836) and *Ruby* (1838). The extreme breadth of these four ships is fairly constant, varying only between 26ft 2in and 26ft 9½in, but the length differs between 99ft 0in and 109ft 11in. This difference in length was probably obtained by varying the length of the parallel middle body, which was such a prominent feature in the Hilhouse ships or, alternatively, the spacing between the frames could have been increased when the floor timbers were set up on the keel. The employment of similar moulds for several ships reduced time and labour and so cut costs. The *Victoria* was the largest of these four ships and her dimensions were 109ft 11in × 26ft 9½in (extreme) × 19ft 1in ('skin to skin' *ie* underside of main deck to bottom of floors); there was also a deadflat amidships 24ft 0in long, if the lines of the *Reliance* were followed exactly. It is probable that her design resembled that of *Princess Royal*. The *Victoria* had a poop which ran to the mainmast, no topgallant forecastle, and a number of iron hanging knees.

Between 1821 and 1850, Hilhouse, Hill & Co built fifty-five vessels, of which two were steamers.[23] Of the remainder there were a few schooners, cutters and brigs. The only plan of a brig to survive is the *John Cabot*, measuring 158 tons and built in 1826. Of the schooners, the majority appear to have been built on fine lines with large deadrise, and plans of six were listed in *Fast Sailing Ships* (page 74); the lines plan of one, the *Sappho*, appeared in figure 60 of that book. Of other vessels constructed by the firm, plans have survived for the *Steadfast* of 1839 which was a small barque of 178 tons; and the *Lord William Bentinck* (1828 of 564 tons) which was built for the East India trade and fitted with a double-tiered stern.

ADAMS OF BUCKLER'S HARD

There is another interesting and valuable collection of draughts of merchant ships, housed at the National Maritime Museum, Greenwich, which spans much the same years as the Hilhouse collection. Apart from the *Hydra*, all these represent ships built at Buckler's Hard by Henry Adams (1713–1805) and his sons Balthazar (1766–1821) and Edward (1768–1849). The plans were

CHAPTER 2

donated by Major F V Longstaff but are now scattered throughout the merchant ship collection. Like so many of these collections spanning forty or fifty years, it is fascinating to study the draughtsmanship and to follow the same style through one ship after another.

Henry Adams had been born at Deptford and went to Beaulieu in 1744 as overseer for a Navy Board contract, but two years later he married a local girl and in 1749 took over Darley's yard at Buckler's Hard where he continued for the rest of his life. However there was an interlude between 1763 and 1792 when he went into partnership with William Barnard and William Dudman to build ships at Deptford; he ran this simultaneously with the Hampshire business. The *Hydra* was built by Barnard and Adams. Barnard managed the yard after Dudman's death in 1772. When the partnership was dissolved in 1792, Adams retired, and his sons Balthazar and Edward took over. Their father had been responsible for building forty-three warships and numerous merchantmen; he died in 1805 aged 92. The two sons eventually ran into financial difficulties caused by late delivery of warships

for which they were heavily fined by the Admiralty under the terms of the contracts. Finally, the construction of some 74-gun ships proved too much of a strain for the yard's resources and they went bankrupt in 1811. Each brother rented part of the old shipyard where a few naval vessels and some merchantmen continued to be built, but farming became the chief family business.[24]

Balthazar Adams, who may have built both the ship *Thalia* and the brig *Mary* in 1818, died in 1821 which is the year that William Good, a shipbuilder from Hythe, situated on the western shore of Southampton Water, leased part of the Buckler's Hard shipyard. Good went bankrupt in 1824 to the tune of £19,000, but Edward Adams continued building and repairing ships until 1847, when he gave up the lease of the yard. His daughter married Richard Pinney, a shipbuilder at Poole, and his son Henry (1800–63) worked as a draughtsman in his brother-in-law's yard. In 1845, Henry was appointed Lloyd's Register surveyor at Aberdeen where he signed the reports on many clippers. Pinney was later a Lloyd's Register surveyor at Whitehaven.[25]

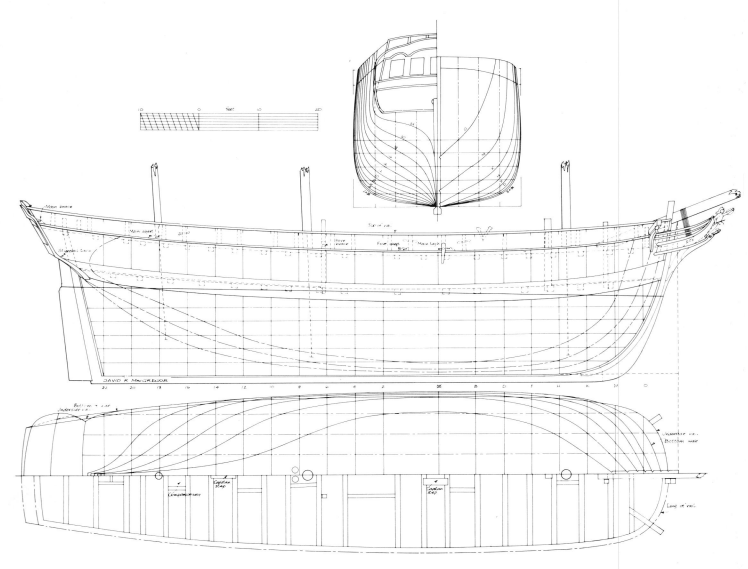

PLANS AT NATIONAL MARITIME MUSEUM OF MERCHANT SHIPS BUILT BY THE ADAMS FAMILY

Date	Name	Rig	Tons	Remarks
		Built by Barnard & Adams at Deptford		
1778	Hydra	ship	446	West Indiaman, bought into Navy 1778; plan 2930, box 44
		Built by B & E Adams at Buckler's Hard		
1790	Friendship	ship	307	round-headed rudder; 2 decks; plan T.5009
1796	Princess Mary	ship	465	round-headed rudder; 3 decks; cost £13 10s per ton; length on lower deck 112ft 6in; East Indiaman; plan T.3017
		?Built by Balthazar Adams at Buckler's Hard		
1818	Thalia	ship	357	lines plan reproduced here as figure 31
1818	Mary	brig	137	plan of brig *Chilmark* (1838) superimposed; plan T.1013
		Built by Edward Adams at Buckler's Hard		
1824	Neilson	brig	232	plans reproduced here as figures 32 and 33
1824	Friendship	sch	118	single deck; plan T.4009
1826	Australia	ship	373	two decks; plan T.3001
1827	Arab	ship	299	two decks; plan T.4001
1829	Alexander Robertson	bk	226	raised quarterdeck; name on plan *Alexander Robinson*; plan T.12001

There is a strong design similarity in all the ships built at Buckler's Hard but as the plans of *Thalia* and *Mary* are much cruder in execution and with many pencilled notes, it is possible they were built by Balthazar Adams, especially as they do not appear in a list of ships built by his brother Edward.[26]

It is interesting that many of the plans contain two sets of dimensions, the second of which is headed 'as built'. The figures in the latter case are usually larger than the others. On the body plan of the *Friendship* (1824) is a dotted line below the bilge against which is written 'Midship bend as built'. The result is a fairly full-bodied midship section like the other plans; as designed it would have resembled the *Neilson*. *Alexander Robertson* and *Arab* have a fairly full convex entrance with a finer run that has some hollow in the lower waterlines; both have a topgallant forecastle; *Arab* has a full height poop but the other has a raised quarterdeck. All the ships had quarter galleries and stern windows, and in the *Arab* are two ports resting on the lower transom, presumably to give light as she carried convicts to Hobart in 1836, taking 117 days on

the passage from London.[27] There are an additional six small rectangular ports along the side in the 'tween decks, and so she probably carried emigrants on her other voyages to Australia. Dimensions on the *Arab*'s plan give 99ft 8in length, 25ft 10½in breadth 'to a 3in plank', 17ft 6in depth of hold and 6ft 4in height between decks.

The *Australia* would have looked more handsome without such a high poop. In the half-breadth plan, her ends are more balanced than those of *Thalia* and she has the finest lines of any of these surviving plans. Compared with Steel's West Indiaman of 330 tons (figure 80, *Merchant Sailing Ships 1775—1815*), *Australia*'s measurements of breadth and depth are practically the same and it is only the length which has increased by 7ft. This confirms the general tendency of ships to grow longer in relation to depth and breadth. The *Thalia* and *Neilson* were the only two hulls to have such a marked concavity in the run; they are described fully in my book *Fast Sailing Ships*.

The schooner *Friendship*, built in 1824, is full in the ends and has a raised quarterdeck; the foremast is right up in the bows and the mainmast is stepped a long way aft, which must have resulted in the main boom overhanging the stern to a considerable extent. Two pencilled figures beside her mainmast state '56' and '60 feet'. The brig *Mary*, built in 1818, was of similar hull-form, but a little deeper; the 1822 *Lloyd's Register* calls her a snow. Even if Balthazar Adams did build her, the plan must have been acquired by his brother Edward after his death in 1821, because it was later utilised for another brig in Richard Pinney's yard at Poole. Henry Adams, Edward's son who worked in the yard, must have taken the plan with him, or else Edward advised on ship design there.

The plan of the *Mary*, mostly drawn in ink, has the stern of another vessel drawn on the sheer elevation abaft her own stern and beginning to overlap the body plan. A pencil note reads: 'New brig 1838 *Chilmark*'. An insight into design trends is afforded by this interesting example of employing the same draught twenty years later for another brig and yet retaining the same midship section and general appearance, the principal difference being an increase of seven feet in length. The comparative measurements are taken from the plan:[28]

	Mary 'as designed'	Mary 'as built'	Chilmark
Length for tonnage (plan scales 69ft 8in)	70ft 9in	70ft 11in	78ft 4in
Length 'aloft'		73ft 6in	
Breadth	21ft 1in	21ft 0¾in	21ft 9in
Depth of hold	12ft 3in	13ft 1½in	14ft 9in
Tons	137¹⁸⁄₉₄	137⁴⁸⁄₉₄	184²⁵⁄₉₄

Some plans distinguish between 'length for tonnage' and 'length aloft', and Peter Hedderwick, whose work appeared in 1830, quotes the rule for tonnage length as follows:

The length shall be taken in a straight line along the rabbet of the keel of the ship, from back of the main stern-post to a perpendicular line from the fore part of the main stem under the bowsprit.[29]

Fig 31. Thalia. Lines plan redrawn by author from builder's plan in National Maritime Museum, Greenwich. Built in 1818 at Buckler's Hard, possibly by Balthazar Adams. Dimensions: 99ft 0in (tonnage length) × 28ft 8in (extreme breadth) × 19ft 9in (approx depth of hold); 357 tons. No reconstruction; but a raised quarterdeck, drawn in pencil on original, is not included.

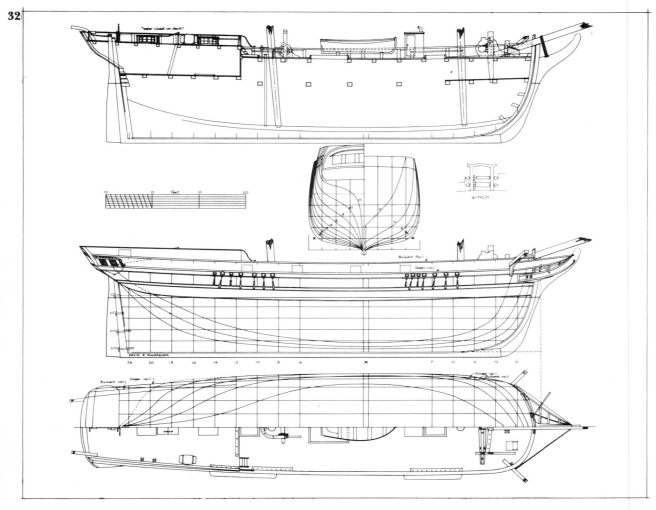

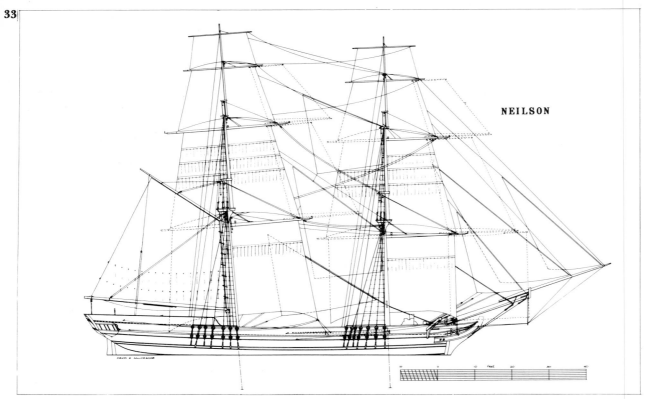

NEILSON

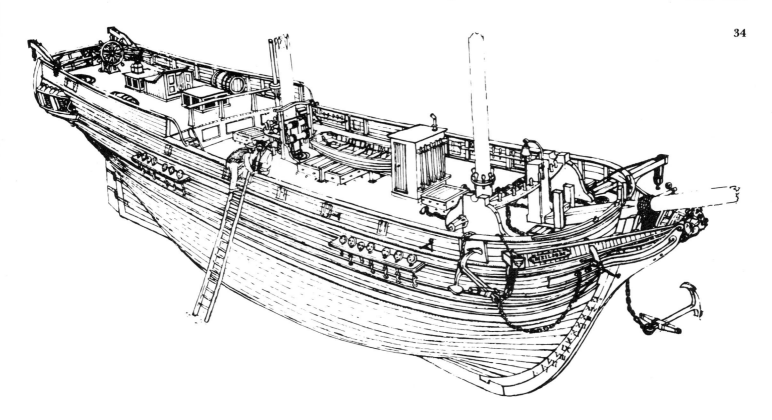

Fig 32. Neilson. *Lines, section and deck layout redrawn by the author from builder's plan in the National Maritime Museum, Greenwich. Built in 1824 by Edward Adams at Buckler's Hard. Dimensions (given on plan): 91ft 4in (length aloft), 89ft 4in (length of keel [and fore rake]), 24ft 1¾in (breadth), 16ft 2in (depth of hold); 231 tons. Reconstruction: the following had to be drawn in plan as they were only drawn in elevation: wheel and tiller, companionway and 2 skylights on poop, mooring bitts, windlass, cathead; all other fittings had to be reconstructed in plan and elevation. Sizes of hatchways given. She was in West Indies trade, but out of* Lloyd's Register *after 1830.*

Fig 33. Neilson. *Sail plan reconstructed by the author from lines plan and from spar dimensions feintly written in pencil on builder's plan. Items reconstructed from contemporary sources: lengths of topgallant masts, main trysail mast, stunsail booms and stunsail yards; also rigging and sail outlines.*

Fig 34. Neilson *drawn by T W Ward. Some additional deck fittings of contemporary vessels have been added over and above those drawn on the deck layout.*

Plans of four ships built by Richard Pinney in the years 1836–43 are discussed in the next chapter, but the style of draughtsmanship closely resembles that of the Adams plans.

One of the etchings by E W Cooke in *Fifty Plates of Shipping and Craft*, published in 1829 when Cooke was eighteen years old, shows a barque which the inscription labels 'Free-trader'. No name is given, but the letters 'HENR' are clearly visible on the stern of the longboat hoisted between the main and mizzen masts. The main-mast blocks out the termination of the letters on the longboat, but it surely stands for 'Henry'. As barques were comparatively rare at the end of the twenties, it was easy to determine that the only candidate for this etching amongst the vessels of this name listed in *Lloyd's Register* was the barque *Henry* which was built by Edward Adams at Buckler's Hard in 1825. The entry in the register books gives further particulars: her tonnage was 259; she had a 'single deck with beams' and was trading to Mauritius; her port of survey was London and she had iron knees, chain cables and had been coppered. Her hull must have closely resembled the brig *Neilson* or the ship *Alexander Robertson*.

This etching is reproduced here as figure 35 and it yields considerable information in the hull and rigging. At the starboard quarter the davits are still made of solid timber and stern davits are also fitted; the windlass is abaft the foremast with the belfry mounted above the pawl post and two handspikes are fitted in the barrel; the men on board make the barque look quite small. Aloft, there are gunter poles fidded abaft the topgallant masts with their heels stepped on the topmast caps, and there are crosstrees at the topgallant mastheads; no trysail gaffs

Fig 35. Etching by E W Cooke published in 1829 in Fifty Plates of Shipping *and* Craft *and entitled 'BARQUE Free-Trader London Docks'. The possibility that she might be the* Henry *of 1825 is discussed in the text.*

BAYLEY OF IPSWICH

The vicissitudes besetting the shipbuilder are well illustrated in John Leather's account of Jabez Bayley's shipyard at Ipswich and that of his nephew George. Between 1804 and 1814 Jabez had built thirty-one warships averaging 300 tons and, no doubt, merchant ships as well, and this success resulted in profits totalling £12,000 to £18,000. But only four years later, a profligate wife, overambitious investment in four Ipswich shipyards and heavy launching expenses for the Indiaman *Orwell*, forced him to suspend payment. The creditors were paid off three years later but Jabez was left penniless. While working for him, his nephew George had been reading works on naval architecture and avidly studying ship construction. He began business on his own in 1821 with a capital of £1500. Six months later he estimated his stock had depreciated by half, due to falling prices. No sooner had he contracted to build three ships of 500 tons each at £14 per ton, hull only, than the price of timber rose steeply. A serious illness temporarily incapacitated George, and his partner was obliged to obtain release from these contracts by a payment of £1100, and it was not until 1824 that his first vessel was launched. A number of ships were built

are fitted; the mizzen is stepped fairly close to the mainmast; the only stay from the mizzen lower mast leads from the cap to the main lower mast cap. The rigging on the mizzen shows clearly; the gaff is here employed as a standing gaff and the yard of the square-headed topsail has jaws that slide on the topmast. The main braces lead forward to the fore hounds but otherwise the leads are normal. It is interesting to note that the topsail sheets are of chain as are the bowsprit shrouds and the bobstay. The gear would have been considered heavy by later standards, nearly all the rigging being made of hemp and the sails of flax. Barques were sometimes as small as 100 tons, and at 259 tons the *Henry* is therefore a fair size. She is ten tons less than the barque *Arab* which James Geddie built at Garmouth in 1839, and it is worth comparing her with the *Arab*'s sail plan in figure 94 as there is a certain degree of similarity.

during the next few years, but although a patent slip was installed in 1826 the business produced only enough profit to pay expenses and interest on the capital, and the yard was accordingly closed in 1831.[30]

ANNESLEY'S LAMINATED CONSTRUCTION

The progress of shipbuilding and some of the innovations introduced were covered in Chapters One and Five of *Fast Sailing Ships*, but when mentioning William Annesley's laminated system no names of ships were given. The list below attempts to rectify this.

Annesley's patent was dated April 1818. The process was to set up temporary frames or formers around which the planking was laid athwartships and longitudinally in anything up to seven layers; in the latter case the total thickness was of 5⅝in. The planking was held together with treenails, and tarred paper was inserted between each skin. Finally the formers were removed. Up to the middle of 1822 the following vessels had been built on this plan:[31]

Date	Name	Remarks
1813	*Nonsuch*	10 tons, cutter, built at New York
1815	*Nautilus*	half-decked boat, possibly built at New York
1817 (Oct)	*Annesley*	45 tons, schooner, built at Belfast
1818 (Mar)	*New System*	60 tons, schooner, built at Belfast by William Ritchie & Co
1818	*Safety*	sailing barge built at Frindsbury, River Medway, by J and T Brindley
1819	*Annesley*	256 tons, brig, built at Deptford
1820	?	82ft × 17ft × 9ft, built at Vauxhall, had a round stern
1821	PS *Aire*	125 tons, built at Selby by Robert Myers
1822	PS *Hope*	56 tons, built at Deptford
1822 (May)	?	schooner barge, 80ft × 14ft × 7ft, built Frindsbury, River Medway, by J and T Brindley
1822	?	brig, 96ft × 24ft × 13ft to be launched fortnight after last by same builder

Lloyd's Register (red book 1821) lists the schooner and brig both called *Annesley* as having 'no timbers'. The schooner *New System* is reported to have been launched with ballast, crew and provisions aboard and to have set sail immediately after she took to the water.[32]

ALEXANDER HALL OF ABERDEEN

The type of ship under construction in Scotland was fairly similar to that produced in southern England. At Aberdeen, Alexander Hall (1760-1849) commenced building on his own account in 1811 after twenty-one years in partnership with others. He was then fifty-one. Alexander's two sons, James (1805-69) and William (1806-87), were taken into the business which became known as Alexander Hall & Sons. About 1830 they succeeded their father in the management of the firm but the same name

Fig 36. Broadsheet (size 18in × 14¾in) advertising William Annesley's new system of building hulls, dated London 23 October 1819. The text below the drawings is omitted. As the broadsheet is signed 'Annesley and Sowerby' the inventor must have been the Earl of Annesley. (MacGregor Collection)

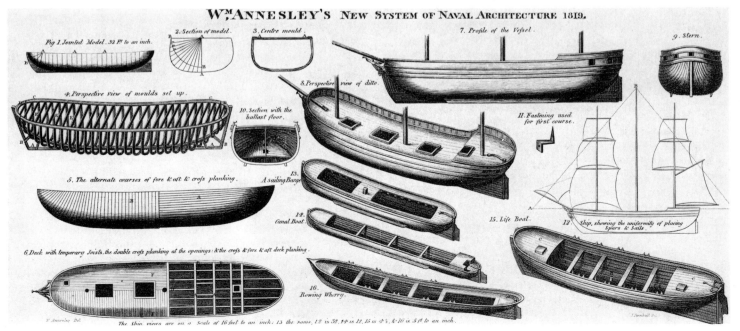

was retained throughout the nineteenth century.[33] By the end of 1835 the firm had constructed seventy-one vessels which consisted mostly of brigs, schooners and smacks, the exceptions being five full-rigged ships, one barque and two small paddle steamers. No plans or models appear to have survived for these years, and their earliest known model represents the schooners *Scottish Maid* and *Non-Such* and is dated 1839. But even in the absence of such plans, it would be highly unlikely that their designs differed from examples of other shipyards included here or from plans published by Peter Hedderwick.[34]

A transcription of Hall's yard books provides valuable data and includes spar dimensions of most vessels, together with offsets of a few built after 1868. This has been the painstaking work of James Henderson who has generously placed all his records at my disposal. A list of all vessels built by the firm in the years 1811-75 is given in Appendix 2 of *Fast Sailing Ships*. The particulars consist of yard number, date, name, rig, tonnage and cost.

The largest ship which Alexander Hall constructed prior to 1836 was the *Asia*, built to order and launched in 1818 for Aberdeen owners and which was, as her name suggests, intended for trade with the East. As she slid down the ways, the military band aboard played appropriate music. At the time of her launch she was the largest ship ever built at Aberdeen. Her dimensions in the builder's records are 118ft 6in × 32ft 5in × 15ft 2in and 532 tons, but no spar dimensions are given; her contract price was £6925 or £13 per ton and her finished price worked out at £8186 on which Hall made a profit of £290. Between 1820 and 1840 the *Asia* made seven passages to New South Wales with convicts, and two to Tasmania; her fastest run was one of 101 days to Tasmania made in 1840. She embarked 190 convicts on her first passage. Nine passages as a transport was exceptional: only the *Mangles* equalled it, while the *Surrey* was the only ship to exceed this number with eleven passages.[35]

Alexander Hall's four other full-rigged ships were far smaller in tonnage, their average being 328½ tons; but the barque *Europa* (1834) measured only 224 tons. The barque rig became popular during the thirties although few were built before then. Towards the end of the French wars, the contract price for two whalers built in 1814, the *Don* and the *Brilliant* of 332 tons each, was £15 10s per ton, and a year later the ship *Prince of Waterloo* of 287 tons cost £14 14s per ton. By the time the *Asia* was launched in 1818 the price had fallen again, but was still on its way down, as in 1824 the ship *Sir Charles Forbes* of 363 tons was contracted for at £11 per ton. None of these prices include the outfit or internal joinery work, but are for the hull, spars and external fittings. The spar dimensions of the *Sir Charles Forbes* show that her fore topsail yard and her spritsail yard were of the same length, namely 37ft 0in.[36] She has been described as a 'sharp-built ship', presumably because she had moderately fine lines for a merchant ship of that date.[37] This ship carried convicts on four occasions between 1825 and 1837, her average for three passages to Tasmania being 112 days.[38]

Shipowners tendered their ships to the Government if they wanted to carry convicts and the rates varied from year to year, an average rate paid during the 1820s being about £5 per register ton. At first, return cargoes from the colonies were difficult, if not impossible, to obtain and the East India Company was often induced to charter a ship for the return passage, thereby making the proposition more attractive to the owner and encouraging him to accept a lower rate for the outward passage.

Alexander Hall's first schooner was the *Plough* of 1812, whose particulars and sail plan are given in *Merchant Sailing Ships 1775—1815*, Chapter Three. His next schooner, the *James* of Portsoy, was built in 1821 and like the *Plough* had topsails and topgallants on each mast, the costs referring to a crossjack yard. She was Hall's last schooner to be built with yards on each mast, a rig often defined in Great Britain as a 'two topsail' schooner and in America as a 'main topsail' schooner; this arrangement was seen only infrequently after the first quarter of the century. Hall's schooners were usually rigged with topsail and topgallant yards on the foremast and it may be that their rig at this date was similar to that carried by the *Magnus Troil* (figure 37).

No lines plans have survived for these schooners and brigs, but it is probable that they conformed to the general style of coasting vessels then prevalent, which remained fairly static for the first thirty or forty years of the nineteenth century. The beautifully executed drawing by a member of the Geddie family of an unnamed brig or a schooner (watermark dated 1818), reproduced as figure 38, typifies the kind of small vessel then currently under construction in Scotland. The Geddies built schooners and brigs at Kingston on the mouth of the River Spey for much of the nineteenth century, as described in later chapters. There is a very attractive quality about this drawing suggestive of the final plan made by a pupil to demonstrate his mastery of ship draughting. It was common practice for aspiring shipbuilders to take lessons in naval architecture from an older, established shipbuilder, as for instance in 1790 when Alexander Hall taught Alexander Stephen 'the art of ship draughting as he now practices it for the sum of three guineas.'[39] It is not inconceivable that one or more of the Geddies might themselves have been taught by Hall. Later they must have been influenced by Peter Hedderwick's published plans, as the style of drawing changes in the thirties, after the publication of Hedderwick's book.

Fig 37. Magnus Troil. Sail plan reconstructed by James Henderson from list of builder's spar dimensions and from a contemporary painting in the Lerwick Museum. Hull conjectural. Schooner built in 1830 by A Hall & Sons, Aberdeen, with dimensions of 69ft 6in × 20ft 8in × 11ft 8in and 124 tons om.

Fig 38. Unidentified two-masted vessel. Plans of hull drawn by one of the Geddie family c1820—30. Photographed from original plan in Science Museum, London.

37

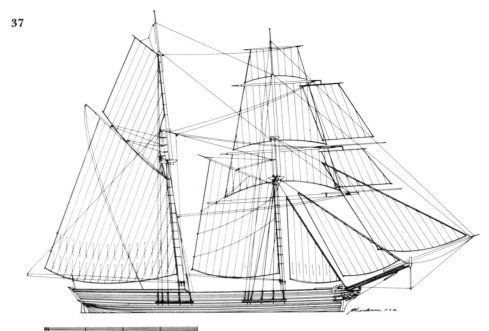

38

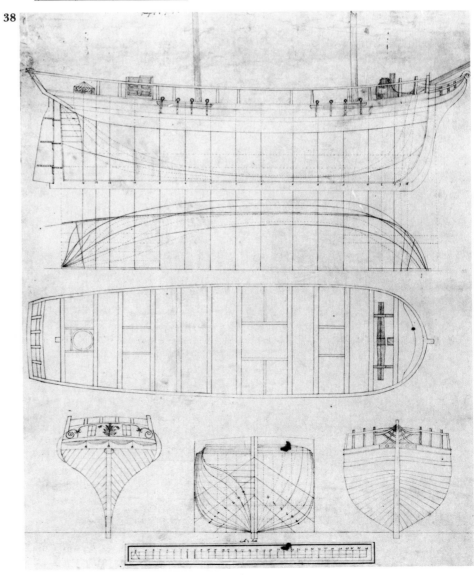

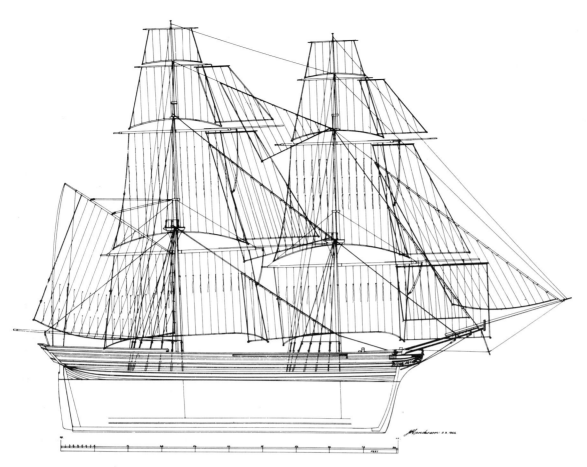

As the diagonals in the Geddie plan are firm lines, they obviously formed an important part of the design method, whereas the waterlines and buttock lines are drawn dotted. Dimensions scaled off the plan give length for tonnage of 55ft 8in, a moulded beam of 17ft 4in and an approximate depth of hold of 10ft 6in, resulting in a tonnage of 72. Hall's schooner *James*, built 1821, measured 52ft 8in × 17ft 5in × 8ft 8in and 66 tons.

Some of Alexander Hall's schooners are listed as having booms for the foresail although schooners are popularly supposed to have carried a boom-less foresail at this time. The schooner *John Pirie* (1827) had a royal yard, four stunsail booms, three stunsail yards and one swinging boom. The last vessel Hall measured by the old measurement tonnage rule was the *Buchan* in 1835, the second brigantine he built. His first brigantine was the *Matilda* in 1829 and her contract price was £8 12s 6d per ton to include the construction of the hull complete, including spars, internal and external joinery work, fitting the figurehead and stern carving, two new boats, and painting inside and out. She was fitted with a trysail mast on the foremast, and described by Hall as a 'schooner or hermaphrodite'.[40]

In common with other shipbuilders at Aberdeen, Alexander Hall launched a large number of brigs and snows during these years. Costs and several sets of spar dimensions exist, although the latter are spasmodic before 1830. For hull-form, reference should be made to the Geddie plan referred to above or to one of Hedderwick's plans. The *Expedition* has been selected as typical of Alexander

Fig 39. Expedition. *Sail plan reconstructed by James Henderson from builder's spar dimensions and contemporary illustrations. Mast spacings given. Built in 1817 at Aberdeen.*

Hall's brigs and her sail plan, reconstructed and drawn by James Henderson, appears in figure 39. The hull itself, as also the rigging and sails, is conjectural, but the spacing of the masts and the lengths of the spars are given.[41] The topsails have been drawn with hollow leeches although this was unnecessary except when the close-reef tackle lay outside the yardarm, measured vertically. The shape of the staysails on the mainmast is poorly defined at this date, but it is probable that the main topmast staysail was a four-sided sail with the nock extending below the fore top. It is worth noticing how narrow the sail plan is without the stunsails, which are all reconstructed. All the corresponding masts and yards are of identical lengths on the two masts, with the exception of the main lower mast which is 3ft 0in longer than the fore. Hall's yard book calls her a 'brig' but also lists a trysail mast and main boom. As already explained, terminology became hopelessly confused for rigs during the nineteenth century and many of the vessels labelled 'brigantine' by Hall have the spars of brigs or snows.

The *Expedition* was launched in 1817 and measured 80ft 4in tonnage length, 23ft 3in maximum beam, 3ft 9in rake of sternpost, 14ft 6in depth of hold, and 180 tons. Like the *Hannah More*, launched two years later, she was built for the Earl of Aboyne who provided the timber for the hull.

It was agreed that the cost of building the hull should be 17s 6d per ton which was for labour only; in the case of the *Hannah More* it was 20s per ton, and 4s extra was charged because the timber was not laid down before the winter, when wages advanced.

The estimate of expenses and income for *Expedition* may be summarised thus:[42]

	ESTIMATE	COST
Building hull at 17s 6d per ton on Custom House register 180¹⁰/₉₄ tons	£157 10s 0d	£120 5s 3d
Sheathing hull, finding labour and oakum only	28 0 0	23 9 10
Labour only for making spars; labour and timber for making tops, caps, crosstrees, anchor stocks, ballast stanchions complete	32 0 0	44 1 1
Stock of inventory and cash	–	39 17 8
Loss sustained on building	10 3 10	
	£227 13s 10d	£227 13s 10d

In the case of the *Hannah More*, the labour for making the spars was agreed at 1s per ton. An item for this vessel reads: 'For making and fitting figurehead, same style as *Louisa's*, finding all wood and carving as per agreement £38'. (This *Louisa* was probably the snow of 213 tons built at Aberdeen in 1815.)

Certain items of other Hall-built brigs are interesting: the *Corsican* (1827 of 87 tons) was the only brig he built which had a tonnage of less than 100; the *Childe Harold* (1828 of 115 tons) had a spritsail yard 24ft 0in long, and the fore and main trysail masts were approximately half the diameters of the lower masts which they fitted against; the *Walter Hamilton* (1831 of 127 tons) was fitted with Straker's patent windlass for £8, the ironwork for it costing another £4; the *Adventure* (1833 of 149 tons) was built on speculation and it cost £1 10s to advertise her for sale, but the purchaser required more work done in the cabin, on the skylights, and the making of additional spars.

Other Aberdeen shipbuilders of this period were: William Duthie, who had once been Hall's foreman; John Vernon & Sons, whose yard was later occupied by Walter Hood & Co; and William Rennie. Examples of Rennie's work include the barque *Rapid* (1834 of 165 tons) and the schooner *Florence* (1831 of 162 tons). William Rennie moved to Bathurst, New Brunswick, where he operated a shipyard from the late thirties for about ten years and some of his ships were owned in Aberdeen. Perhaps some of them were built to order, such as the brig *Mayflower* (1841) which George Thompson owned. In 1848 William Rennie took up residence in Liverpool where he built and designed many celebrated clippers.[43] He was referred to at some length in *Fast Sailing Ships*.

ROBERT STEELE & CO OF GREENOCK

The partnership of Robert Steele and John Carswell was dissolved in 1816 and Steele took his sons Robert (1791–1879) and James into the firm changing the name to Robert Steele & Co. James died some years before 1830 and in due course Robert took his own two sons, Robert and William, into the firm. The shipyard closed down in 1883.

The new firm established a high reputation at Greenock and by the end of 1835 had completed sixty-three ships. Whereas Alexander Hall had built only five full-rigged ships by this date, they had built thirteen of an average tonnage of 368. Of the nine steamers they had constructed, the largest was the *Eagle* of 495 tons, built in 1835. They had also built several yachts as well as the usual proportion of brigs, schooners and sloops.

The sixth ship built by Robert Steele & Co was the *Albion*. The yard list states that her measurements were 119ft 0in × 30ft 9in × 23ft 6in, with a height between decks of 6ft 6in, and that her tonnage was 505⁶⁸/₉₄. She was launched on 2 October 1818 and was built for Cropper, Benson & Co of Liverpool. No doubt she looked very much like their other ship, the *Bengal*, launched by Steele and Carswell in 1815. Both ships were employed in the India trade.

There is a copy of the building contract for the *Albion* at the back of William Simon's 'Spar Book', in the possession of the Glasgow Museum and Art Galleries.[44] Such documents are rare, particularly when so many vessels were built on speculation, and so it is given in full, through the courtesy of A S E Browning, Curator of Technology at the museum.

SPECIFICATION OF THE *ALBION*

Messrs Cropper Benson & Co
Gentlemen
The ship we have agreed upon to build for you is of the following dimensions viz:

Keel and fore rake	118 feet	To admeasure 480 tons or thereabouts
Extreme breadth	30 feet	
Depth below the hold beams	11 feet	
Depth between that and main deck	5½ feet	
Depth between upper and main deck	6½ feet	
Making in all 23 feet hold		

The keel to be either elm or American oak 13½ ins sided by 15 ins deep. The keelson in midships 14½ ins by 16 ins deep of three lengths of best American oak, having the mainmast to step on the scarf thereof. Stem 12 ins sided by 14 ins moulded. Sternpost at wing transom 12 ins sided. Floors in midships 13 ins sided by 15¼ ins deep on the keel and to average in midships 18 to 19 feet long; first futtocks in midships 12 ins sided at lower and averaging 12 to 13 feet long; second futtocks in midship to average 10 ins sided and 9 to 10 feet long; third futtocks in midships 9½ to 10 ins sided to run above the main deck binding top timbers 8½ ins sided at lower end, diminishing a little toward the top. Breadth and space 28 ins [presumably the equivalent of 'room and space']. The scantling on the bilge to be 11 ins, at the wales 8 ins and at the gunwale 5 ins.

Hold beams 13 ins sided and 12 ins moulded, with knees 7 ins sided. The main deck beams in midships to be 10½ ins sided and moulded with knees 6 ins sided. To be all of good British oak and to have American oak stringers both above and below the hold beams of $5\frac{1}{2}$ ins thick and 14 ins broad in midships, having the out and in bolts through them, as well as those in the knees, of copper. With oak stringers below the main deck beams of 5 ins thick, and a waterway above of 5 ins red pine. The upper deck beams to be of red pine 9 ins in midships sided and moulded. With British oak knees of 5 ins thick and a stringer under them of 5 ins red pine. The running plank on the floor to be of $3\frac{1}{2}$ ins elm, with four strakes of $4\frac{1}{2}$ ins on each bilge; from that to the light water-mark to be 3 ins and to be planked from that to the girth line strake with 3 ins British oak, and the girth line strakes which are to be of 4 ins, to be so low down as to have in the lower binding. The wales 5 ins, two black strakes, one of 4 ins and the other of $3\frac{1}{2}$ ins to be all of British oak. The topsides to be either British oak or pitch pine 3 ins thick. The paint strake and the covering boards to be of $3\frac{1}{2}$ ins British oak. The covering boards to be fastened with copper and also the upper deck planks which are to be of 3 ins Quebec yellow pine.

The main deck to be laid fore and aft with $2\frac{1}{2}$ ins pine. The ceiling below the main and lower decks to be of 3 ins American oak, well seasoned, and $2\frac{1}{2}$ ins red pine between the upper and main decks. The timber above to be well squared.

To be completely copper fastened as high up as the wales, and finished in all Plumber, Painter, Joiner and Glazier work, pertaining to the hull and cabin, with the Block-maker's work attached to the hull. To find one complete set of masts and spars, figurehead, stern carving and quarter galleries, with three suitable boats and oars, we finding paper, sheathing and put on the copper, when laid to hand. To find iron stanchions for rails, as also the binnacle and quarter davits.

The building of the vessel to be superintended by Mr Alexander Laird of Greenock, with leave to call in Mr Quentin Leitch or any other competent person if required. And to have her ready for launching in all September 1818 for the sum of thirteen pounds, eighteen shillings sterling per ton register, to be paid for by cash upon delivery of our certificate for the vessel.

We are,
Gent[n]
Your most obedt. Serv[ts]
(signed) Robert Steele & Co

Greenock
18 Nov[r] 1817

DECK ARRANGEMENTS

There is very little information that comes readily to hand regarding deck fittings. In the published plans of David Steel's West Indiaman of 330 tons, dated 1805, only a few fittings are shown: the windlass (plan and side elevation); the pumps (plan and side elevation of pipe only, without handles); two capstans (plan and side elevation); steering wheel (side elevation only); and tiller (side elevation). This amount of data can be considered very generous. Twenty-five years later, Peter Hedderwick's *Marine Architecture* gave much less information on deck fittings but, as an innovation, three detailed sail and rigging plans were included. Shipbuilders' plans vary in their information and the compilation of a drawing based on such sources usually requires the combination of details taken from several plans. Some of the best detail available comes from contemporary models, and warship models must be employed to supplement that found on merchant ships. Prior to 1815 the differences between fittings in merchantmen and men-of-war grows less distinct as one goes backwards in time.

After the cessation of war in 1815 and the gradual suppression of piracy, the necessity disappeared for having a speedily manned armament of carriage guns that were in a constant – or supposedly constant – state of readiness, with the result that additonal deck erections gradually appeared.

Basically, there are four kinds of deck layouts: flush decks; decks with an after structure but nothing forward; those with a forward structure but nothing aft; and decks which combine structures at each end. Generalisations in respect of deck layouts are so frequently proved incorrect that the following remarks are intended merely to offer comment on some of the arrangements most commonly found aboard ships.

Providing the deckhouses do not touch the bulwarks, a vessel may be described as flush-decked if she is fitted with one or more large houses, nor is the term invalidated if there is a low structure aft for the helmsman to stand on. Further, common usage generally allows a flush-decked vessel to have a tiny deck forward at half the height of the bulwarks, for ease in working the anchors. There are many examples of flush-decked vessels to be found prior to the 1860s, but their use gradually dropped out except in schooners and smaller vessels. The lack of protection from heavy seas sweeping over the rail of a large, deeply-laden ship must have made flush decks unpopular, and fine-lined ships would lose valuable cargo space by having the crew and passenger accommodation occupying part of the 'tween decks.

Examples of vessels with structures at each end – forecastle, poop or raised quarterdeck – are better known and many are shown in this book. When the windlass barrel was turned with handspikes, good headroom was needed to operate them if the windlass was to be under a fore deck; but as the windlass was usually stepped abaft the foremast and the latter was placed well up into the bows, a forecastle was not a practical proposition. The widespread introduction of the patent windlass in the 1840s enabled it to be placed inside the forecastle or under a low fore deck, but operated from the deck above. There are endless variations on this, as the plans show. Deck layouts with no forecastle, but with a full poop, are not seen much after 1850.

Although pinrails were fitted to the main rail abreast of the rigging on each mast, the fiferail which partially encircled the fore- and mainmasts had hardly begun to develop in 1815. At that date, most running rigging was led to the side of the ship through fairleads in the lower rigging, although there were jeer and topsail sheet bitts at the foot of the fore- and mainmasts. Several sheaves were fitted in the base of each bitt with a cheek block on the outside; the fall was belayed to the crosspiece, although few contemporary models have any belaying pins fitted here. The builder's plan of *Neilson* is unique in showing a semi-circular pinrail around the mainmast. Some models have two large cleats at the foot of the masts; others have large cleats fixed horizontally on the uprights supporting

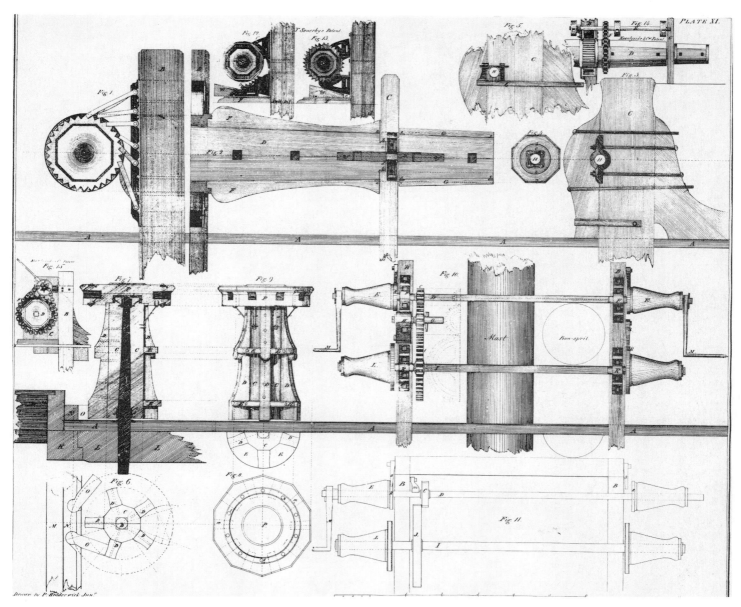

Fig 40. Drawings to scale by Hedderwick for a windlass operated by handspike levers before the days of pump handles, with various patent systems of pawls and chain drives inset; below, on the left, is a capstan, its spindle shown in black in the section at left; at bottom right is a 'double winch calculated for a smack of about 200 tons'. He adds that in smacks the winch is placed between the main hatch and the mast, ie abaft the mast, but before the mainmast on brigs and schooners. (Peter Hedderwick, A Treatise on Marine Architecture, 1830, pl XI)

the crosspiece on the bits. It is usually assumed that running rigging was belayed around any handy horizontal member, whether it was an open rail or the gallows for spare spars.

The builder's plan of *Thalia* indicates the position of sheaves in the bulwarks for the sheets and tacks of the courses, and these are plotted on the plan in figure 31. It will be noticed that there are three large cleats placed conveniently on bulwark stanchions to which these ropes could be belayed, and the chesstree for the main tack is marked; so is a V-shaped kevel at the after end of the fore rigging.

The mooring bits placed in the bulwarks were either covered by a hinged port or else the bulwark was left open, but models frequently make the bulwarks solid in way of these bits.

When the windlass was abaft the foremast, the single or double pawl post was frequently extended upwards to form a curved gallows frame for the spare booms. The after ends of the booms or spare spars rested on another

gallows forward of the mainmast, and the uprights for these gallows usually incorporated a cargo winch. When the galley was placed on deck, the gallows straddled it as in the sketch by W M Grundy (figure 41). The practice was, however, being adopted of lashing the spare spars on deck, although a vestigial form of gallows remained at the top of the cargo winch for some time. Iron davits were beginning to supersede solid timber ones, but they were still mounted in a fixed position with the boat slung outboard. Because the boats were not at first swung

41

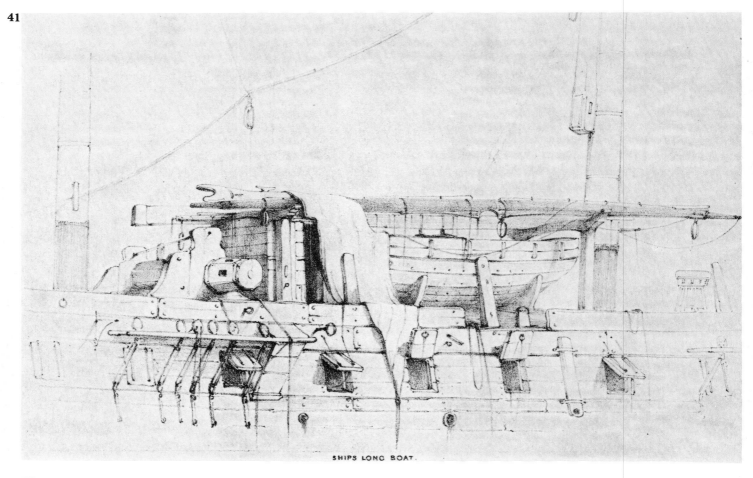

SHIPS LONG BOAT.

Fig 41. A drawing on stone by W M Grundy of the port side of a ship amidships, with fittings described in the text. (Parker Gallery)

Fig 42. Yetts' apparatus for securing a windlass by means of a 'safety pawl' which prevented the windlass from revolving when taking the strain of the anchor cable. A note says that it met with general approval. (Mechanics' Magazine 16 October 1824)

Fig 43. The Lamburn of Rye unloading coal into horse-drawn carts on Hastings beach about 1865. A derrick has been rigged between the masts for discharging into a sort of chute strapped to hull. (Printed from copy negative made by Cmdr H O Hill)

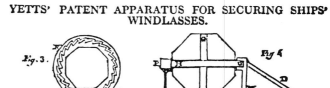

YETTS' PATENT APPARATUS FOR SECURING SHIPS' WINDLASSES. 42

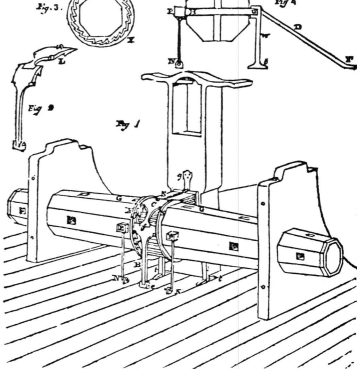

inboard, the heads of the iron davits are deceptively low and the keel of the boat may be below the rail. This is not incorrect in contemporary paintings and models.

The National Maritime Museum at Greenwich has the lines of an unnamed merchant ship of 221 tons which comes from the Longstaff Collection, although it does not follow that there was necessarily any connection with Edward Adams of Buckler's Hard. The watermark of 1826 infers a plan drawn at the end of the twenties and the high quality of the drawing suggests it was the work of an apprentice shipwright, such as Edward Adam's son, Henry. This plan possesses several useful details, such as the iron strap across the knee of the head to take the strain of the bobstay; the gallows and crutch for the fore lower swinging stunsail boom; the capstan abaft the mainmast; and the gallows above the windlass, seen slightly in perspective. Great care has been taken in showing the external works, the run of the planking down to the bottom of the wale, and the iron fittings; also of iron are the staple and hanging knees to the upper and lower deck beams as shown in the mid-section. The full-bodied hull is virtually the same as twenty years earlier, but she is a good example of a vessel with a raised quarterdeck and no forecastle.[45]

Handspike windlasses sometimes required six men to raise an anchor weighing 13 cwt and the process was long and back-breaking, so that any improvements were eagerly accepted by the otherwise ultra-conservative seaman. When the *Isabella* was launched in 1829 from George Straker's building yard at South Shields, it was noted that she was fitted with a patent windlass which Straker had newly invented by which one man and a boy replaced six men.[46] As noted above Alexander Hall first used Straker's windlass aboard a brig in 1831 at a cost of £8, the metal fittings costing a further £4. In the twenties and thirties other inventors were making improvements to the power of the windlass, and names such as J Keenlyside of Newcastle, Yetts, Sowerby, Nicholson and Young are associated with such work. However, considerable research is still required to elucidate and classify the various improvements to hulls and rigging at this date.

COLLIERS AND OTHER BRIGS

The coal trade was for a long period regarded as an excellent school for practical seamanship although this art was doubtless to be found along many other parts of the coastline. About 500 ships were employed in the coal trade by the end of the eighteenth century and could make on average eight or nine round trips per year,[47] although many individual vessels obviously exceeded this average considerably, to judge by the stories told. In 1795, the colliers reaching London numbered 4395 ships and sometimes there were as many as 300 of them in the Pool of London at one time. 'Coal was the basis of the country's economy and a domestic necessity', writes Raymond Smith in *Sea-coal for London*, adding that 'dislocation of the trade on any scale became a national concern and excited public comment.'[48] By 1824 the number of colliers entering the Thames annually had risen to about 7000. This represents between 775 and 875 individual vessels, allowing eight to nine round trips per year. Fifteen years later the number of colliers reaching the Pool had increased to over 9000 and congestion in the river was critical. In ten days during February 1837, no less than 721 ships arrived in London with coal, probably owing to a favourable shift of wind after several weeks of southerly gales.[49]

Of course there was a large trade from the coal-loading ports of north-east England, Cumberland and South Wales to other importing centres besides London so that colliers were trading around the entire coastline of the British Isles. Fleets of colliers and other coasters were counted in hundreds lying windbound or passing by some headland. Many colliers had to unload their cargoes on the beach if there was no quay available, as distribution overland from some ports was often slow and expensive. A photograph (figure 43) taken in the mid-sixties, shows the *Lamburn* unloading her coal on the beach at Hastings into horse-drawn carts. This small brig of 80 tons was built at Hastings in 1833 by Thwaites & Winter and was at first owned by George Thwaites. She would have been launched into the sea on ways laid across the beach. Of necessity she was heavily built and stoutly planked to withstand rough work on the shingle beach. This picture shows that she carried two trysail masts with a standing gaff on the fore, and a bentinck boom. Nothing is carried above the topgallants but she did set topmast stunsails and undoubtedly lower stunsails also.

Before the coming of the railway, 12,000–13,000 tons of coal were unloaded annually onto Hastings beaches and

43

44

45

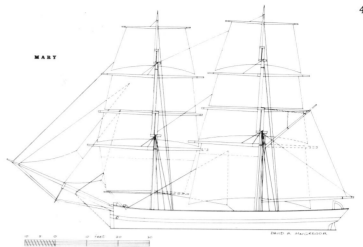

Fig 44. Lying on her side in the breakers during a gale at Hastings, the Lamburn *succumbed to the storm whilst unloading. (Printed from copy negative made by Cmdr H O Hill)*

Fig 45. An unidentified snow photographed by Samuel Smith at Wisbech on 25 June 1857. The foremast is stepped so far forward that the windlass stands abaft it. The two planks of her wale are painted a light colour. She looks an old vessel. (Wisbech Museum)

Fig 46. Mary. *Sail plan drawn by the author from tracing made in Whitehaven Library of plan dated 27 May 1872 and signed 'W.K.', ie Wm Kennaugh, sailmaker at Whitehaven. Built in 1831 at New Brunswick with dimensions in 1875 of 71.7ft × 22.1ft × 13.9ft and 109 tons net. She is a little smaller all round than Hedderwick's* Mary. *On this plan, double topsails have replaced single ones, and she probably was built with a longer main topgallant mast to carry a royal, even if none was carried on the fore. The jib would originally have been a larger sail with the foot cut low. This sail plan shows a cut-down rig in old age that was being perpetrated in the 1860s and 1870s.*

nineteen vessels were named in 1852 as regularly unloading coal and other cargoes there. Only two of these craft were of over 100 tons.[50] Michael Bouquet records how a storm arose at low water, one day in 1850, when the *Lamburn* and two other colliers were discharging on Hastings beach, and how the *Lamburn* only just managed to haul off to her anchor at high water against a south-westerly gale.[51] Sixteen years later she was wrecked on the same beach and another photograph shows her lying on her side amidst the breakers (figure 44). These rare pictures, from the collection of the late H Oliver Hill, illustrate episodes that were repeated times without number along the beaches and narrow creeks of the British Isles.

Another excellent example of the small, heavily-built brig is afforded by a photograph taken at Wisbech on 25 June 1857 of an unnamed vessel moored alongside the river bank. She has a plain bow without a head knee and was probably fitted when first built with a handspike windlass, although the rocker arms for a patent purchase are visible in the photograph. The windlass is located close abaft the foremast. The old style cargo winch with gallows on top, the bentinck boom, and the standing gaff with spanker brailed into the trysail mast can also be seen. Theoretically she should be without a main boom in order to class as a snow. The decoration on the inside of the washboards along the quarterdeck is the same as the diamond and rectangular panels in the plan of the brigantine *Violet* (figure 134). It is debatable whether she carried a fore royal, but the topgallant pole on the mainmast looks long enough for this purpose.

Ships that could be deeply laden and safely take the ground in harbours at low water formed the majority of vessels built in Great Britain and Northern Europe, and Thomas Richardson's remarks on the subject are very applicable. He was a shipbuilder at Hull and under 'Preliminary Observations' in his book on *Marine Architecture* published in 1833, he wrote:

There are three descriptions of trade to which commercial shipping is applied: the first is the coasting and Irish trade, which requires vessels from 88 to 140 tons register admeasurement, and from 56 to 66 feet keel. These vessels having frequently to load and deliver in dry harbours, should have several floors of the same rise in the centre of them, that they may more effectually sustain themselves when loaded, sit easy on the ground and draw little water. They likewise should have more sheer in proportion to their length than larger vessels, to keep them dry and lively in the sea, as they are mostly put well down in the water; and they are much better when they have a good height of bulwark. The sweep of the lower part of the stem should always be of greater radius than beauty would seem to require, in order to give them more flair in the stem-head, which supports them when pitching, and throws off the spray; not forgetting to give them the best entrance and run that such a construction permits.

The second description is foreign trade to the European ports, for which the most suitable vessels are those measuring from 200 to 300 tons, having 75 to 85 feet keel, carrying and sailing well, but not drawing too much water.[52]

The third class was for deep-sea trade and was referred to in detail earlier in this chapter. Plate 1 in Richardson's book has no masts shown, but was probably a smack. Plates II and III are two-masted vessels of 140 and 205 tons respectively and are generally very similar in hull-form and proportions to Hedderwick's ships. Richardson's dimensions for the brig in plate III are the same (to within one inch) as those which Hedderwick gives for the brig *Mary*, (built at Leith in 1826 of 205 tons), which suggests either that they each employed the same source material or that many vessels were similar in size and form.

Hedderwick gives dimensions on plate XVIII of 75ft 0in keel, 8ft 6in fore rake, 23ft 6in tonnage breadth and 15ft 5in depth of hold; from these it seems reasonable to identify this plan as representing the brig *Mary*, as they are virtually the same as those for the brig given in one of his tables.[53]

On the east coast of Great Britain the two staple trades were the coal and Baltic trades, which were closely integrated. Many of the colliers voyaged to the Baltic during the summer months and regular Baltic traders betook themselves to the Mediterranean or the West Indies during the winter. Others were laid up between December and March because insurance premiums were so high in consequence of the bad weather. Any enforced idleness was used as an opportunity to repair and overhaul the vessel, and local shipyards were busily employed as a result.

From London and the south and west coasts of Great Britain the majority of vessels sailed to the Mediterranean, West Indies and British North America. A brig in the Jamaica trade was the *Christiana* which William Simons and Co launched on the Clyde in 1818 of 276 tons, on dimensions of 94ft 0in × 25ft 8in × 17ft 6in. Her draft of water was 12ft 0in. Her builder commented: 'This vessel sailed very fast but carried a great quantity of ballast having a round floor and was too high built upon. Was lost in the Channel a few years since 1831'.[54] Her round floor probably made her take the ground at an awkward angle which could have serious consequences.

A large brig engaged in foreign trade was the *William Young*, built at Leith in 1824 from designs by Peter Hedderwick, and plate XX of his *Marine Architecture* has the lines of an unnamed brig but with dimensions exactly similar to those of the *William Young*. These consist of 94ft 7in length for tonnage, 27ft 0in breadth for tonnage (*ie* extreme breadth above or below the wales), 18ft 10in depth of hold, and 303$\frac{88}{94}$ tons, which is large for a two-masted vessel. Hedderwick calls her 'a very fast vessel'. She traded to India at first and by 1830 was going to Australia. In describing her as a 'brig', *Lloyd's Register* (green book) agreed with Hedderwick, but Lloyd's red

47

48

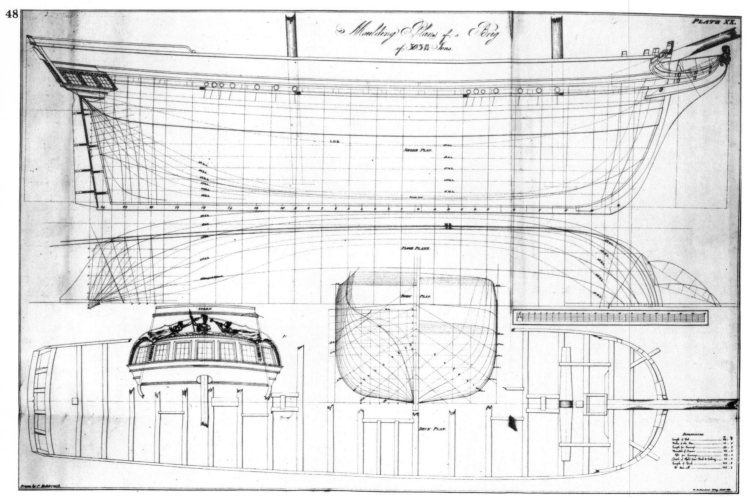

Fig 47. Photographed when in her 70th year in 1897 off Christianiaf-jord, the Gratitude *displays her bentinck boom in use. No doubt in a cut-down rig the hull suggests a slight hog. She was built in 1827 of 193 tons at Tönsberg, Norway, with a length of 82ft. (*Nautical Photo Agency*)*

Fig 48. William Young [*identified*]. *Lines and stern elevation reproduced from Peter Hedderwick's* A Treatise on Marine Architecture *(1830) pl XX. Identified as described in text. This brig built at Leith in 1824 with measurements of 94ft 7in × 27ft 0in (max) × 18ft 10in and 303 tons. The waterlines are dotted but the diagonals have solid lines; there are also some cant frames projected in the fore and after bodies.*

Fig 49. Betty *entering Palermo close-hauled on the starboard tack with her courses clewed up, her fore trysail brailed in, and the tack of her spanker hauled up the trysail mast; away to port, she is shown leaving the harbour under full sail. (*Parker Gallery*)*

book or shipowners' register called her a 'snow'. This contradictory rig nomenclature is cited to show the frequent unreliability of contemporary descriptions without supporting evidence.

The *William Young* has more rake fore and aft than Brocklebank's large brig *Balfour* mentioned in Chapter Three of *Merchant Sailing Ships 1775–1815*, but a very similar midship section. She has a bust figurehead, perhaps of William Young himself, and an elaborate stern carving. There is a deck-beams plan which shows a fore scuttle 2ft 6in × 2ft 9in leading to the crew's quarters and placed between the heel of the bowsprit and the pawl post; also a step for a capstan 10ft 0in abaft the mainmast. She has a full entrance but a finer run and represents a reasonably

average hull-form for cargo carrying combined with sailing qualities. There is no hollow in the entrance, the lower waterlines being quite straight as they run into the stem. Like most of Hedderwick's designs, she is a short deep ship, and looks to be a scaled-down version of his 500-ton ship (figure 17). Although there is no sail and rigging plan of *William Young*, his spar proportions for brigs, and the sail and rigging plan of the full-rigged ship would yield sufficient data to reconstruct one.

Peter Hedderwick stated that the area of canvas on a brig should equal that on a three-masted ship of the same tonnage and that to achieve this the yards on the fore- and mainmasts would have to be longer than the equivalent ones on a three-masted ship. Rules, some of which are very curious, are given by him for finding the lengths of the masts; they are based on the length of the load line and maximum breadth. The lengths of the yards on the foremast were sometimes made slightly shorter than those on the mainmast but 'are now commonly the same length' for ease of shifting the sails from one mast to the other. Brigs in the coasting and coal trades were to have shorter yards than those in foreign trade, although the diameters were not to be reduced; in the foreign trade 'a brig may be rigged so square that the length of the main- and fore-yards added together is equal to the length of the load-water line'.[55]

Most text books on shipbuilding gave rules for calculating the spar lengths, but whereas David Steel and Peter Hedderwick obtained the length of the mainmast by employing both the ship's length and breadth, John Fincham and later writers proportioned the length of the mainmast to the breadth only, and the lengths of the yards to the ship's length.

Although Hedderwick listed no actual brig of less than 150 tons, many of under 100 tons were built and even a few of less than 50 tons, particularly before 1830 when the sizes of all craft were proportionately smaller. For example, out of six brigs built in the port of Bideford in 1828, four were of less than 100 tons, their relative tonnages being 59, 84, 97 and 99. The brig *Rosa* of 54 tons, built at Bideford in 1821, is probably the smallest brig built there after 1815.[56]

In light favourable winds, many captains would rig gunter poles abaft the topgallant masts to set skysails, as can be seen in the picture of the *Betty* entering Palermo in 1830. The heel of the gunter pole would be secured to the mast above the topgallant yard, at the level of the topgallant backstays, and there would be an iron band known as a 'cranse iron' which was fixed to the head of the topgallant mast, and through which the gunter pole passed. The *Betty* is shown setting both royals and skysails on these masts, because her topgallant masts are not tall enough to carry royals; in her case, the gunter poles are stepped on the topmast cap. This practice was sometimes adopted by ships sailing in winter from northern latitudes, by which they were able to reduce the weight aloft in bad weather, yet gain full advantage of light winds in calmer seas through use of these gunter poles.

The fore trysail, also with its own trysail mast, was a regular feature in many snows, and in the *Betty*'s case the head of the trysail mast continues up to the level of the lower mast cap with its own tiny truck or cap; it shows less clearly on the mainmast. The *Betty* was built at Workington in 1817 of 187 tons.

By studying contemporary illustrations to clarify rig and masting peculiarities, it is also possible to derive great enjoyment at the same time from observing the different techniques employed by various artists who had evolved their own styles and to which they rigidly adhered. Several of the paintings reproduced in this work will confirm these observations and illustrations have been chosen to show the work of as many artists as possible. Today their work is often labelled by the art world as 'primitive', and yet whatever the style may be it was painted for a most discerning eye – the master, mate or owner who would require the detail to be perfect. As such, these paintings are accepted as reliable portraits before the days of the camera, and the work of certain artists always ensures that this was the case: Robert Salmon, D A Teupken, Jacob Petersen, Nicolas Cammillieri were leading international names at this time. The painting of the *Betty* is signed 'W C D'. Two other paintings in identical style have been found which show brigs in similar positions to the *Betty*. One is of the *Amazon* of Baltimore, shown simultaneously entering and leaving Palermo in July 1836, in the collection of the Maryland Historical Society, Balti-

50

more. The other shows the *Pilgrim* and forms an illustration in a new two-volume edition of R H Dana's *Two Years Before the Mast*. In each case, the port quarter view shows the brig with skysails and stunsails set, while the starboard broadside has the fore trysail brailed in, the courses clewed up and the two American vessels have their skysails and royals furled. Although at first glance, each picture looks almost identical, close inspection reveals many differences in hulls and rigging.

Another painting of a vessel entering Palermo depicts the brigantine *George Canning* of Stettin in 1834. The foremast is a four-piece mast with the royal set on a gunter pole stepped on the topmast cap, abaft the topgallant mast; the fore lower mast is little shorter than the main lower mast, and a foresail is set from a gaff as well as a square sail from the lower yard.[57] This was a popular rig combination at this date. The *Hero* of Dundee was painted by Charles Shlei in 1831 with the town of Riga in the background. She is masted and rigged like the *George Canning*, but in addition the foresail is sheeted to a bentinck boom, and the fore gaff sail hoists on a trysail mast placed close abaft the fore lower mast. She carries stern davits. An interesting point is that a scale in English feet (extending to 84ft) is drawn at the foot of the painting below the massively-lettered title.[58]

HEDDERWICK'S SCHOONER *GLASGOW* AND HER RIG

While there are a number of unrelated plans of schooners of the twenties, all pointing to experiments in rig and masting, we do not get on to firm ground until the appearance of Peter Hedderwick's published plans to accompany his *Treatise of Marine Architecture*. He contributes three lines plans of schooners, two of which are designed to the maximum size that will pass through the locks of the Forth and Clyde Canal and one of these two was named *Charlotte*, having been built to his own designs. Both of these schooners measure 104 tons and from the text it

Fig 50. The trysail mast of the German snow Daniel & Emilie *is stepped on the boom, not on the deck, but the mast hoops and gaff can still slide up and down it. There are three headsails here from the fore topmast. She was built in 1817. The artist is J J Pfeiffer. (Altonaer Museum, Hamburg)*

Fig 51. The artist, Charles Shlei, painted the brigantine Hero *at Riga in 1831, and a scale of feet is carefully drawn below the lettered title. This makes the register length about 76ft and the main boom 36ft. The scale is divided every 12ft. The* Hero *was built at Montrose in 1828 with a tonnage of 145. Lloyd's Register gives her rig as a schooner as brigantine was not recognised at that time. (Altonaer Museum, Hamburg)*

51

GLASGOW

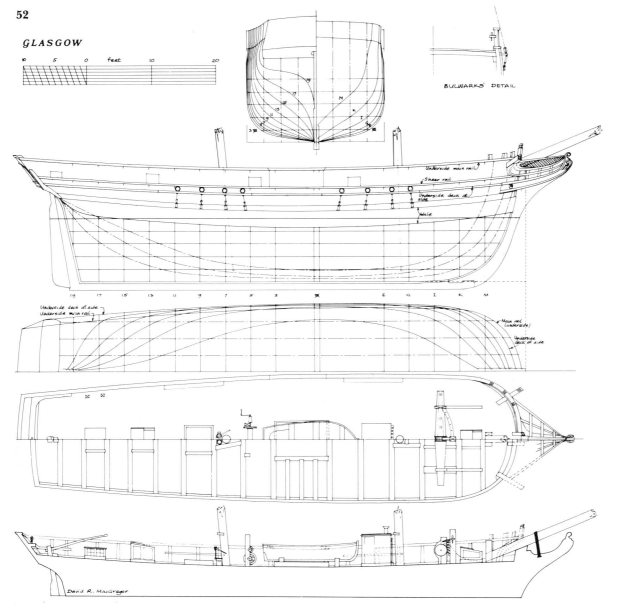

BULWARKS DETAIL

David R. MacGregor

appears that both were fitted with sliding keels as invented by Captain Schank and improved by Hedderwick, although the keels and their fittings are only shown on one of the plans.[59] The *Charlotte* was to Hedderwick's normal design with a square stern; but the other schooner, designed for fishing, was double-ended and of shallow draft with an outside rudder, and bore a close resemblance to the English herring buss style of fishing boat, with her long parallel sides and round stern. On the Continent, this form of hull was called a galliot.

The third schooner design submitted by Peter Hedderwick probably represents the *Glasgow*, for the following reasons: firstly, it is apparent from previous investigations that the majority of plans reproduced in his book are of actual vessels; secondly, the *Glasgow* was actually built to his design which is a good reason for reproducing her; thirdly, no other schooner in his book approximates so closely to the dimensions on the plans as does the *Glasgow*, which is evident from the table below:

Dimensions scaled off Hedderwick's plates XVI and XXVI	*Glasgow*[60]
Length for tonnage	71ft 9in	72ft 0in
Breadth for tonnage	22ft 1in	22ft 4in
Depth of hold	13ft 6in	13ft 6in
Tonnage	151	155⁴⁴⁄₉₄

The *Glasgow* was built at Leith in 1826 by T Morton & Co and sailed in the Leith to Hamburg trade; Hedderwick wrote that she 'sails fast and carries a great cargo'.[61] *Lloyd's Register* gave her tonnage as 161. The plan indicates that she was very similar in shape and proportion to Hedderwick's brig *William Young*, which was referred to in the last section. Indeed all Hedderwick's designs have a family likeness: a deep, short hull with small deadrise, rounded bilges, a full entrance and a hollow run, which gave good cargo capacity and fine weatherly qualities. There was little change in these designs from those of twenty-five years earlier, and his book contri-

Fig 52. Glasgow. *Identified as described in text. Lines and deck layout redrawn and reconstructed by the author from Peter Hedderwick's* A Treatise on Marine Architecture *(1830) pl XVI. Schooner built in 1826 at Leith by T Morton & Co with dimensions of 72ft 0in × 22ft 4in × 13ft 6in and 155½ tons. Reconstruction: deck fittings in plan and elevation from plan of deck beams and contemporary illustrations.*

Fig 53. Glasgow. *Sail plan reproduced from Peter Hedderwick's* A Treatise on Marine Architecture *(1830) pl XXVI. Sail plan of a merchant schooner drawn in such detail and to scale was rarely published.*

buted to the continuation of the same ideas for another quarter of a century. Figure 52 shows the *Glasgow's* lines plan, which has been redrawn from plate XVI in Hedderwick's book and is now easier to read with waterlines and buttocks plotted at regular intervals. A deck plan has been reconstructed from the deck beams plan given on the original and from other Hedderwick plans and contemporary sources. The perspective view of the *Neilson* which appears here as figure 34 shows many similarities. In the *Glasgow*, the fore scuttle for the crew has been placed between the bowsprit bitts and the pawl post; no fore hatch is shown in Hedderwick's plan; the galley, longboat, cargo winch, stern davits, tiller and pinrails are conjectural but based on reliable evidence.

Many of these features are corroborated by other deck plans in this book.

What makes the plans of the *Glasgow* especially valuable is the correlated sail and rigging plan, and it is fairly safe to state that there is no other such plan of a merchant schooner in existence for this period which is so detailed, apart from drawings made from models or reconstructed from other sources. Hedderwick's own drawing of the sail plan is so satisfactory that it has not been redrawn, but appears here as figure 53.

The *Glasgow's* bowsprit is still a massive stick, so that the length of the jibboom beyond the cap is somewhat shorter than the bowsprit outside the knightheads. The double forked dolphin striker is mounted on the foreside of the cap and the rigging here is of the simplest: a single martingale stay either side, set up to each cathead. In addition there would probably have been a bowsprit guy each side and possibly a jibboom guy as well. The presence of a fore boom is to be noted, but its topping lift to the main trestletrees is almost hidden behind the foremost main shroud. Prior to 1840, most vessels took the topping lifts on each mast to the hounds of the same mast and the *Glasgow* is thus an exception. Channels are

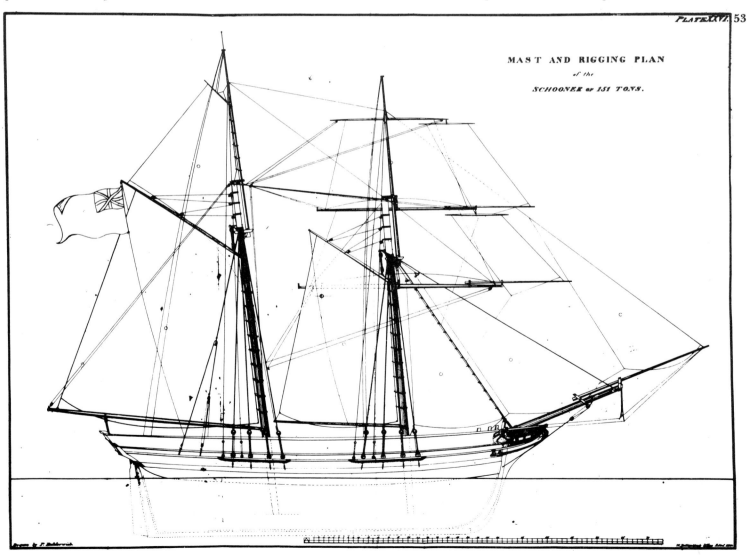

Fig 54. The Frankfort Packet *greatly resembled the* Glasgow *as pointed out in the text. She was still afloat in 1847 with tonnages then of 127 om and 121 nm. Painted by F Albinus of Hamburg. (Parker Gallery)*

Fig 55. The billy-boy Lively *and the schooner* Mulgrave *at Whitby. The* Lively *has a long head for the mainmast and the topgallant yard has been freed from its parral and lowered down on top of the topsail yard. She was built as a sloop in 1786 of 49 tons; she was wrecked in 1886 when 100 years old. The schooner* Mulgrave *has double topsails. Photograph taken by Frank M Sutcliffe.*

shown here but some schooners set the lower deadeyes on the main rail. Although not drawn, there would have been ratlines on the shrouds arranged in the usual manner. As is common in many fore-and-aft rigged vessels, there are running backstays on the mainmast – one to port and another to starboard – the falls of which lead from a long-tackle block.

A remarkably close likeness to the *Glasgow* may be seen in the picture of the *Frankfort Packet*, reproduced in figure 54, and painted by F Albinus of Hamburg. This schooner was built at Leith in 1818 of 127 tons and she and the *Glasgow* were both owned by the Leith, Hamburg and Rotterdam Shipping Co of Leith. It is even possible that Peter Hedderwick designed the earlier schooner although he does not mention her in his book. The rigging of the two ships is very similar and the only two differences worth pointing out are that the *Frankfort Packet* has a jib on a stay from the fore lower masthead, instead of from higher up the topmast, and her foresail is apparently boomless. Otherwise she supplies very valuable additional evidence as to how the *Glasgow* was rigged. One naturally imagined that the latter could set a square sail from her lower yard but now a small royal without braces is obviously possible. The stern davits in *Glasgow* are also confirmed, but no galley on deck is visible and the longboat occupies most of the space between the masts; the fitting of low washboards abaft the

mainmast is a feature that would not be shown on a plan although they were frequently carried. Hedderwick's manner of drawing the foot of the stunsails is not illustrated, although the sails are cut with a convex foot; their booms are not run out to their fullest extent perhaps because the smaller suit of stunsails is set.

An interesting point about the sail plans of the two schooners is the method of rigging the topsail yard which, as the *Glasgow*'s plan shows, hoists on a parral on the topmast *below* the cap, and halliard blocks can be seen close below the cap. The head of the lower mast has been specially lengthened for this reason and now measures 13ft 0in above the cheeks while the comparable dimension on the mainmast is only 11ft 0in. In topsail schooners, the head of the lower mast is usually about the same length on each mast and 13ft 0in would be excessive. The topgallant sail thus becomes deeper than the topsail.

This method of slinging the topsail yard below the cap was described earlier in this chapter and an illustration given on how it was fitted to a three-masted ship-rigged Dutch galliot (figure 28). Its merit was to concentrate the principal strain on the massive lower mast, allowing the topmast to be a lighter and shorter spar. This arrangement worked particularly well when the topmast was fidded abaft the mainmast. Investigation shows that this manner of fitting the topsail yard continued during the first half of the nineteenth century, particularly in the North Sea area, but that it was gradually superseded by the alternative method of slinging the topsail yard from its own masthead.

Some of the illustrations in this chapter show this older method of fitting the topsail yard, such as figure 55 which depicts the billy-boy *Lively* lying beside the schooner *Mulgrave* at Whitby. (The former was built in 1786 as a sloop of 49 tons and the other was built as a lugger in 1818 of 28 tons.) The topsail yard on the *Lively* is shown lowered and the halliard can be seen below the cap, while the yard is held by the standing lifts. The lift blocks for the lower yard are secured halfway up the masthead rather than to the cap and there is a big hoist for the topgallant yard. The topsail and topgallant braces lead through a pair of double blocks lashed to the head of the mizzen and the topgallant braces are obliged to ride over the topsail lifts when the yard is lowered. A photograph of the schooner *Alert*, built at Whitby in 1802 as a sloop of 43 tons, shows an identical arrangement. These photographs are some of those taken by F M Sutcliffe. In neither case are there any topgallant lifts nor are there any footropes to the topgallant yard, which meant that it was necessary to lower this yard close to the topsail yard to get it furled by men standing on the topsail yard footropes. This was in effect a disguised form of polacre rig and the topgallant yard was held to the mast by its halliard passing inside a traveller.

The schooner drying her sails at Swansea, reproduced as figure 78 in *Fast Sailing Ships*, resembles the way the *Glasgow* was rigged, especially the topsail yard hoisting on the cap, as can be seen by the position of the lifts. The fore lower yard has been cock-billed so that it has assumed a vertical position; on the fore topmast there is sufficient height to set a topgallant and a royal. Altogether the photograph yields a great deal of valuable information: lead of running rigging; shape of crosstrees; setting of jackyard topsail and main topmast staysail; cut of the sails; bilge keel, suggesting a fair amount of deadrise coupled with the need to take the ground. Although the photograph was taken about 1845, there is no guarantee that the schooner was newly built, but merely that she was in existence. It is impossible also to tell if she was an east coast schooner or indigenous to the Bristol Channel, but the pen and ink drawing by Calvert Jones of the *Cambria* at Cardiff, dated 1828, shows the square topsail rigged in a similar way and the topgallant yard lowered to the cap, and confirms that this rig was also used in the south-west (figure 56).

Alexander Hall's schooner *Magnus Troil*, built in 1830 for Lerwick owners, was rigged like the *Glasgow* and *Frankfort Packet* and the head of her foremast was 12ft 0in long against 9ft 0in on the mainmast. Her name is said to be derived from a character in one of Sir Walter Scott's novels. The sail plan in figure 37 was drawn by James Henderson who has reconstructed it from the builder's

Fig 56. Pen-and-ink drawing dated 28 November 1828 done by the Rev Calvert Jones and entitled 'Entrance to the Cardiff Sea Lock'. Names written in pencil on the top, from left to right, read: 'Sivor. Scarbro. [gap for mast] Cambria. Cardiff'. Sivor is drawn as a brig and Lloyd's Register has her as built at Whitby in 1828 of 172 tons. The only schooner named Cambria listed in 1828 was built at Milford Haven in 1803 with a tonnage of 73. This schooner has her topsail yard slung from the lower mast cap, and the topgallant yard is resting on it. (MacGregor Collection)

Fig 57. A Swedish schooner lying bow-on to a quay as drawn by Jean Baugean. She has two long lower mastheads and the cranse iron fixed to the head of her main topmast clearly shows that a gunter pole could be fidded, as on the fore. (Jean Baugean, Recueil de Petites Marines, *Paris 1817, pl 114; plates loose in folder)*

Fig 58. A Dutch schooner in the foreground drying her sails. (Jean Baugean, Recueil de Petites Marines, *Paris 1817, pl 105)*

spar dimensions and a contemporary painting in the Lerwick Museum. This painting shows a single row of reef points on both the topsail and topgallant which do not appear on the plan. The foresail could be brailed into the mast by using the three brails shown, a common practice which saved having to lower the gaff in order to furl the sail. A main topmast staysail must have been available for setting and probably also a square sail from the lower yard. The *Magnus Troil* measured 124 tons on dimensions

Baugean del. et sculp.

ENTREE D'UN PORT.

Baugean del et sculp.

Galiotte Hollandaise et Goelette faisant sécher leurs voiles.

59

of 69ft 6in tonnage length, 20ft 8in extreme breadth, and 11ft 8in depth of hold from top of ceiling to underside of deck. The contract price was £9 per ton, which allowed a profit of £60 13s 4d; the set of spars cost £43 1s 2d.[62]

As described in Chapter Three of *Merchant Sailing Ships 1775—1815* the Salem schooner *Fame* which was built in 1795, carried topsails below the cap on both fore- and mainmasts. So also did a Swedish schooner drawn by J Baugean and reproduced in figure 57.

Captain W B Whall wrote that he had seen paintings by the English marine artist Thornly, dated 1806, in which the detail was correct but the colliers set double topsails on the foremast.[63] This sounds like a reference to the *Glasgow*'s rig. Billy-boys continued to set their fore topsails thus for as long as they retained square canvas, as may be seen in the *Blue Jacket* of Blakeney, and numerous Danish paintings show a similar rig.

ADOPTION OF SCHOONER RIG

In Europe, square rig remained popular throughout the nineteenth century, and brigs and brigantines continued to be built after 1875, nor was any schooner really complete without some square canvas. In America, the schooner rapidly ousted the brig after 1815 and was generally employed in coasting work and in the trade to the West Indies. But square canvas was retained on the foremast for short ocean passages with three yards and large stunsails in addition. Brigantines were also popular on longer voyages. After 1840 the popularity of the schooner was rapidly increasing and it was found that the fore-and-aft rig made her more efficient and more economical to run than a topsail schooner, although a single yard was sometimes retained. The hull was usually broad and of shallow draft for coasters, with almost flat floors and rounded bilges with fullish entrances but longer hollow runs. There was a raised quarterdeck aft enclosing a house on deck. In the West Indies and Gulf of Mexico

trades, hull-form was of a sharper model on the Baltimore clipper style with greater deadrise; speed as well as armament were important to escape from pirate craft. The schooner rig was commonplace in America by 1850 and two-masters of up to 400 tons were constructed. By contrast, the schooner rig only became popular in Europe after 1850, even though artists were fond of painting them in the earlier decades.

In Britain the cutter was for long preferred as the model for fast vessels which greatly retarded the development of the schooner. The small number of schooners produced is evidence of the unpopularity of the rig, but the table shows how the schooner rig gained in favour after the beginning of the 1820s.

NUMBERS OF SLOOPS, SCHOONERS AND BRIGS BUILT 1791–1850 IN THREE BRITISH PORTS

	1791–1800	1801–1810	1811–1820	1821–1830	1831–1840	1841–1850
A. HALL & SONS, ABERDEEN (shipyard opended 1811)[64]						
sloops smacks			11	6	4	0
schooners			1	6	11	29
brigs snows brigantines			15	10	24	5
PORT OF WHITBY[65]						
sloops smacks	4	21	6	12	3	0
schooners	1	6	0	10	18	14
brigs snows brigantines	55	67	64	73	51	51
PORT OF BIDEFORD[66]						
sloops smacks	25	32	28	27	20	15
schooners	2	18	11	14	47	47
brigs snows brigantines	21	19	28	38	9	5

The schooners built by Alexander Hall & Sons reflect the changing tastes of local shipowners who were their principal clients until their yard obtained nationwide fame in the late forties. The port of Bideford, which includes Appledore, is represented by a number of yards on the River Torridge, and being separated from an industrial hinterland provides a different outlook from Whitby, which built principally for the coal and Baltic trades.

A comment on the adoption of the schooner rig is provided by T & J Brocklebank's first schooner, constructed in 1802, which was appropriately named *Experiment*. It may be inferred that this experiment was not considered successful as twenty-one years were to elapse before the next schooner was built.[67]

Illustrations in this and other chapters show that the dividing line between brigantines and schooners in the matter of rig was fairly tenuous, for when the foremast

Fig 59. Unidentified American schooner entering Havana Harbour in 1860 with Morro Castle on the port bow. She has a square topsail and topgallant set and must date from the pre-1850 era. (Peabody Museum, Salem)

Fig 60. The round-sterned Rival *as painted by the Amsterdam artist D A Teupken in 1849. She was built at Hull in 1830 and owned in Wisbech. Tonnages were 70 om and 58 nm. Note the curved luff to the flying jib. Copied from original in the Wisbech Museum.*

became fully clothed with square canvas, in fair or following winds, it was difficult to tell the difference between a schooner and a brigantine.

ONE AND TWO-MASTED RIGS

The elastic quality of rig in relation to hull-form has already been observed and an alteration of the mast position was sufficient in many cases to convert the hull of a schooner or small brig to that of a smack or sloop. Such a conversion would broaden the range of examples presented here of single-masted craft, which are restricted partly from lack of space and partly from the small number of plans extant in relation to the number of vessels employed.

The rigs of the round-sterned galliot and the square-sterned galleas were described in Chapter Three of *Merchant Sailing Ships 1775—1815*, and paintings indicate that similar proportions of rig continued in the period 1815–35. In a picture of six such vessels owned in Rendsburg in 1835, the two galleases carry royals on the mainmast while the four galliots set nothing above topgallants.[68] Whereas vessels were becoming defined by rig rather than hull-form, the continuation of the terms 'galliot', 'galleas', 'kof' and 'hooker' did indicate something about the hull, while 'ketch' and 'sloop' did not. But the first four terms seem to be confined to the Continent although the word 'galliot' does appear in *Lloyd's Register*

60

RIVAL OF WISBEACH. THOMAS TEED COMMANDER.

61

Fig 61. A pencil drawing by E W Cooke entitled 'Billy-boy' clearly shows the leeboard, round stern and flying jib with curved luff. (Mac-Gregor Collection)

Fig 62. E W Cooke drew this galliot in five different positions as she sailed towards him and then sped away. The topsail and topgallant are both shallow sails. (Private Collection)

62

and other English shipping registers.

One English equivalent of the galliot could be the billy-boy which was herself a sea-going version of the keel. By 1815, the latter was confined to the Rivers Tyne and Humber, the inland waterways of Yorkshire, and to East Anglia. Whereas the keel was propelled by a square sail and square topsail set on a single mast stepped in a tabernacle, the billy-boy was sloop- or ketch-rigged. In either version, the billy-boy's mainmast carried two or three square sails in addition to fore-and-aft headsails and a big gaff sail, but in a ketch there was naturally a mizzen mast in addition. She was normally larger than a keel with higher sides, improved sea-keeping abilities and often without leeboards. She was suitable for coastal or short-sea trading, as portrayed by the painting of the *Rival* off the Dutch coast, reproduced in figure 60. D A Teupken of Amsterdam who painted this picture in 1849 is known for the accuracy of his work, and his method of placing his subject in two positions makes a pleasing change to the stereotyped style of a plain broadside and a far-off stern view.

The *Rival* was built at Hull in 1830 and when this picture was painted was owned in Wisbech and measured 70 tons om and 58 tons nm. The hull is undoubtedly that of a billy-boy with a round stern and outside rudder, the large sail area being essential to drive the full-ended hull along. The topsail hoisted to the lower mast cap, as in the schooner *Glasgow*, and a topgallant and square sail were also set on a fair wind. The braces to the topsail yard lead forward to the jibboom end; the lower yard has two sets of braces, one leading forward on to the bowsprit and the other leading aft. The flying jib with a curved luff has her halliards taken to the crosstrees rather than the topmast head, to save strain on the mast in a fresh breeze. Frank Carr described two methods of setting such a sail in the 'boomy barges'.[69] There are numerous other examples of craft with such a sail set.

After the middle of the century, economies in crews required the large mainsail of a sloop-rigged billy-boy to be split into two, and the ketch rig was generally adopted. A photograph taken at Wisbech about 1860 shows a billy-boy of the largest size rigged as a ketch with three yards on the mainmast and stunsail booms on the lower yard.[70] However, some Humber keels that were rigged as sloops remained in trade until the early 1930s without adopting the ketch rig.

It seems likely that the keel and billy-boy were developed from the same source as the English herring buss whose essential features were a long parallel and deep body; full ends; flat floors and little tumblehome; and wales taken round to the sternpost to give a pink stern. Chapman gives a plan of one such vessel.[71] She was rigged like the dogger which he illustrates in plate LXII, figure 7, which has a square-rigged pole mainmast and a fore-and-aft mizzen. Chapman also gives the plan of a Dutch dogger in plate LIX which is like a flute, with great tumblehome all round. From this evidence, it seems that the English and Dutch busses had developed along different lines. However, the pink stern of the English buss was not repeated in the keel or billy-boy, although the Hast-ings fishing lugger retained it.

A shipping register published in Glasgow in 1828 lists the names of 3965 vessels but enumerates only one classified as a 'ketch', with the exception of a prize.[72] This 'ketch' was called the *Experiment* and was built at Leith in 1820 of 63 tons and her very name suggests that there was something novel either about her rig or hull shape. This register also lists seven galliots of which one was built at Saltcoats in 1793, one at Greenock in 1806 and the remaining five – for the Edinburgh, Glasgow and Leith Shipping Company of Leith – at Topsham in 1817. These last five (*Active*, *Alert*, *Dove*, *Fly* and *Lark*) must have been built on very similar lines as their tonnages only range between 48 and 50. If the Continental definition of 'galliot' was followed, than all these vessels would have been round-sterned, built on full lines, and almost certainly ketch-rigged with up to four yards on the mainmast. The rig could have resembled that of the Blankenese galleas *Freund Georg* shown here as figure 157.

In the first edition of his *Nautical Dictionary*, published in 1846, Arthur Young's entry for a 'ketch' reads: 'A vessel with two masts, rigged somewhat like a galliot.' And for 'galliot' he says: 'A flat-bottomed vessel whose bow and stern are similar, being round and bluff. It is commonly fitted with lee-boards, and has two masts; the foremast, which is the tallest, is rigged like a sloop's mast, while the after mast carries a sail which, like the foresail, is also set upon a boom and gaff.'[73]

Employing Chapman's rig of a dogger with a pole mainmast carrying three square sails and a fore-and-aft rigged mizzen, Admiral Paris published the plans of the *Volonté de Dieu*, built in 1816 in Provence by Joseph Vence. Being somewhat similar to a bomb ketch in rig, she was referred to as a *bombarde*. Her plan in figure 63 shows that the mainmast is stepped a long way aft and the absence of top, crosstrees or trestletrees suggests it may have been a polacre mast; the topsail yard certainly has the downhauls common in the polacre rig. The hull has plenty of sheer, with rising floors and slack bilges, and she must have been a fast sailer. With her square stern, it only needs a gaff sail on the main to give her the appearance of a galleas from northern Europe.

Sloops varied considerably in size and a number were built of more than 100 tons. The larger vessels were really scaled-down versions of brigs, and a good example is the *Clio* which was built at Whitby in 1816 of 86 tons. A set of lines in the local museum has been redrawn as figure 64, and indicates a general similarity with the New England sloop, whose plan was given by Lauchlan McKay in his *Practical Shipbuilder* of 1839, although the *Clio* is deeper and has a finer run.[74] Dimensions scaled off the plan give a tonnage length of 55ft 8in, extreme breadth of 17ft 4in and depth of hold approximately 8ft 6in. The hull is comparatively broad and shallow with well-rounded bilges and flat floors. Although there are no spar dimensions, a sail plan has been reconstructed from Hedderwick's proportions. On *Clio*'s original plan, waterlines were only drawn in the afterbody between the light and load lines, and diagonals were projected to fair the body plan.

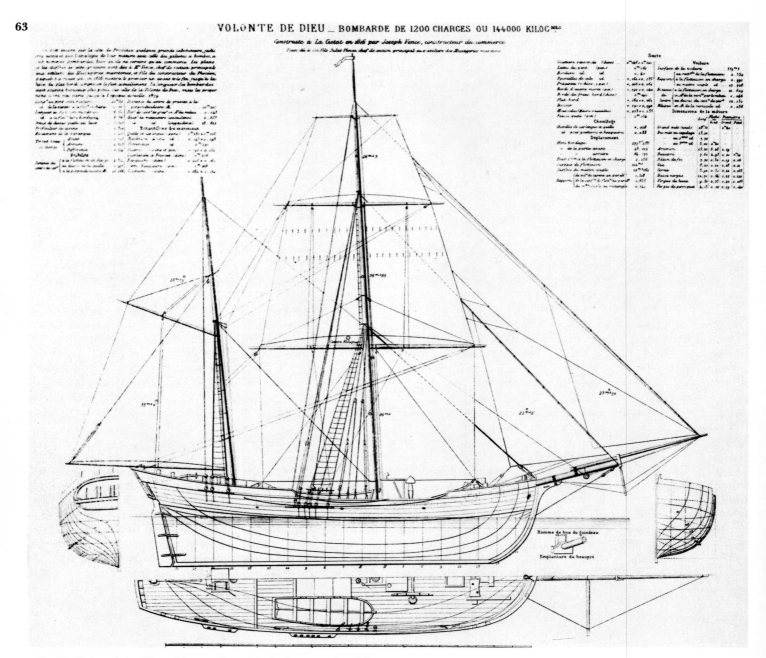

Fig 63. Volonté de Dieu. *Lines, sails and deck plans reproduced from* Adm Paris, Collection de Plans ou Dessins de Navires *from 1871 (usually called* Souvenirs de Marine*) pl 46.*

Fig 64. Clio. *Lines plan drawn by the author from plan found in museum run by Whitby Literary and Philosophical Society. Dimensions scaled off plan: 55ft 8in (tonnage length), 17ft 4in (max breadth), 8ft 6in (approx depth of hold). She was built at Whitby in 1816 and measured 86 tons.*

Fig 65. Clio. *Sail plan reconstructed by the author, based on Hedderwick's proportions.*

CLIO

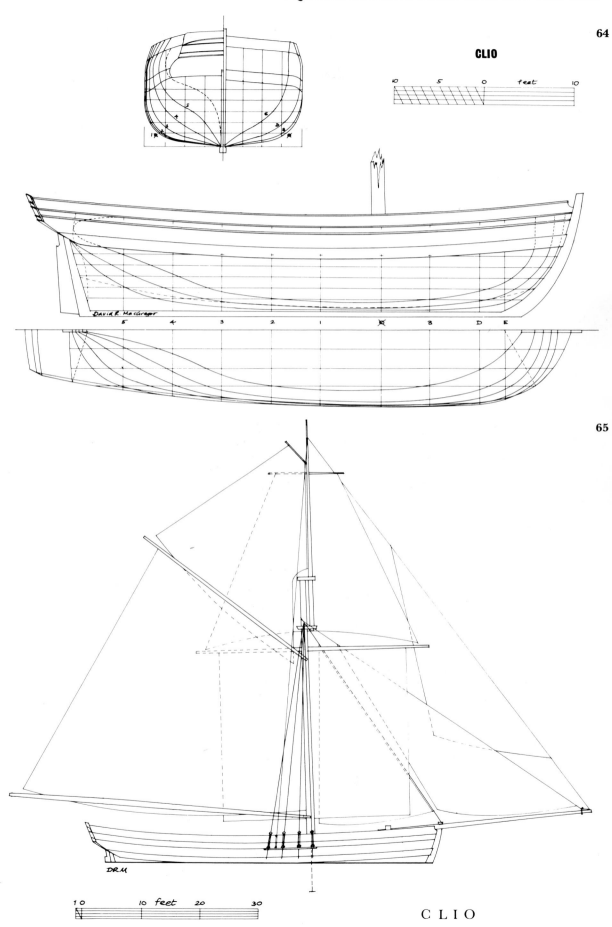

10   5   0   feet   10

DAVID R. MacGREGOR

5   4   3   2   1   ✕   B   D   E

DRM

10   10 feet   20   30

C L I O

Another important type of local trading vessel was the Severn trow which traded inland up the rivers, and also along both sides of the Bristol Channel; occasionally she went 'round the land' into the English Channel. The hull was round-bottomed with full ends, shallow draft and a large hatchway; for long she has been notable for the deep, square-tuck stern, but has carried a variety of rigs on one or two masts. These variations have already been described in Chapter Three of *Merchant Sailing Ships 1775—1815* which covers the evolution of the ketch rig in more detail. The chief feature of Atkinson's etching, dated 1808, entitled 'Dock at Bristol with a Trader' (figure 4 in *Merchant Sailing Ships 1775—1815*) is a ketch-rigged vessel. As already noted, the fore topsail yard is shown below the cap so that the rig is of the kind to be found on the Continent. Perhaps this is the type described as 'galliot' in English registers. It is uncertain whether the two stern ports are cabin windows or timber ports. During the 1840s and 1850s, almost all the trows were converted to normal ketch or sloop rig.[75]

A fore-and-aft rigged trow or barge appears on the left of the pen-and-ink sketch made by Calvert R Jones in South Wales on 30 August 1828 (figure 66). The sloop *Gannet* of Bideford is on the right of the drawing. Calvert Jones later took up photography and produced fine photographs around Swansea from about 1845.

In his book on shipbuilding, C F Partington listed eight different kinds of barges in 1826 which consisted of 'a company's barge, a row barge, a royal barge, a sand barge, a severn trow, a ware barge, a light horseman, a West Country barge'.[76]

Local types of cargo boats were generally described as 'barges' and there were considerable variations from one district to another. Many people today think only of a Thames spritsail barge when the word 'barge' is mentioned, but barges were both round and flat-bottomed vessels rigged with gaffs or sprits. The flat-bottomed barges working the Thames and adjacent rivers had short masts which carried a spritsail; but larger versions of this hull which worked the tidal estuary and into East Anglia were sloop-rigged, and often carried a bowsprit and square sail yard. The hull was still a swim-header. West Country barges were round-bilged craft and gaff-rigged,

Fig 66 Three distinct types on the shoreline in South Wales on 30 August 1828, as drawn by the Rev Calvert Jones in pen-and-ink. On the left a trow or local barge; in the centre, the brig Alexander *of Sunderland (which has not been identified); on the right of the cutter* Gannet *of Bideford. (MacGregor Collection)*

Fig 67. Broadside and bow view of a swim head barge 'Sloop-rigged', that is to say, with a gaff instead of a sprit and with no mizzen. Drawn in pencil by E W Cooke. (MacGregor Collection)

Fig 68. Horses and cart beside a swim head barge rigged with a spritsail, as drawn and etched by W H Pyne and published in 1802. (MacGregor Collection)

66

August 30. 1828.   Alexander of Sunderland

Sloop-Rigged Barge.

69

COWES BOAT &c. coming out of the Harbour.

70

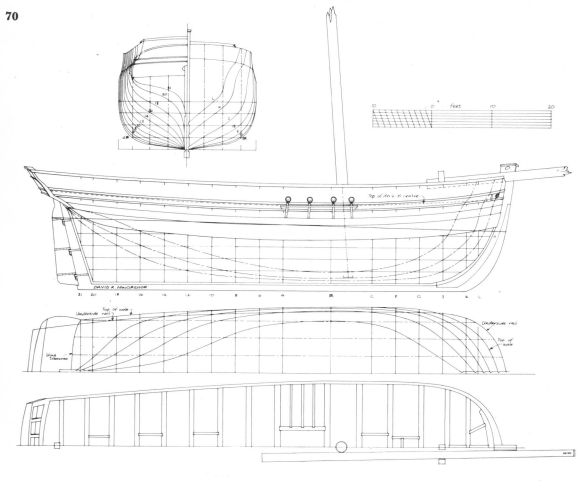

Fig 69. E W Cooke's engraving of a Cowes ketch, showing a double-ended craft with a short bowsprit and sporting a fore-and-aft ketch rig. Published in Fifty Plates of Shipping and Craft *(1829).*

Fig 70. Hedderwick's Leith Smack. Lines and beams plan reconstructed by the author from Hedderwick's A Treatise on Marine Architecture *(1830) pl XVII. Not identified and no name assigned. Dimensions on plan: 73ft 2in (keel and forerake) × 23ft 6in × 12ft 6in and 173 tons.*

Fig 71. Hedderwick's Leith smack. Sail plan redrawn by the author from Hedderwick's Treatise *pl XXV. Smack not identified.*

and the *Mary* of Truro, built in 1875, probably represented a type that worked the creeks and parts of the coastline for half a century. For vessels that had frequently to take the ground, sliding-keels or centreboards were not satisfactory because mud and shingle were forced up inside the case and jammed the plate. For this reason, leeboards were employed on flat-bottomed craft and occasionally on shallow-draft, round-bottomed hulls as well. Leeboards also had the advantage over centreboards of being cheaper to make and fit, and of not obstructing the hold.

E W Cooke has drawn a craft that was often fitted with leeboards, although his etching does not show them. Described as a 'Cowes boat' and published in 1829, his etching depicts a type nowadays referred to as a 'Cowes ketch'.[77] The hull was round-bottomed, with a round stern and outside rudder although later Cowes ketches usually had square sterns. No square sails or yards appear in Cooke's etching; the bowsprit is short; and she is a purely fore-and-aft rigged ketch of a type that was built around the Solent throughout the nineteenth century.

Examples of cutters and sloops appear in these pages

but the great age of the large cutter of over 100 tons with an enormous main boom projecting over the stern was fast drawing to a close. These beamy craft, with vast spreads of canvas incorporating two or three square sails in addition to an assortment of fore-and-aft ones, were being lengthened and converted into schooners in the late 1830s. Fast schooners and growing steamer competition gradually took away the business they had enjoyed in carrying passengers from Leith to London or across the Irish Sea, as well as to the Continent.

The plan of the Leith smack given by Peter Hedderwick in his book was of 173 tons with dimensions of 73ft 2in (keel and fore rake) × 23ft 6in × 12ft 6in, but the vessel has not been identified by name. The lines plan he gave has been redrawn here as figure 70 and his sail plan as figure 71. The main boom measures 66ft 0in and the bowsprit projects 38ft 0in outside the stem. Hedderwick gave evidence to a Parliamentary Select Committee in 1819 about designs for a Post Office packet from Dublin to Holyhead, so he was undoubtedly an expert on the design of these craft.

The distance from Leith to London is about 460 miles and the fastest smacks could travel the distance in 50 to 54 hours, although five to six days was the usual fast average. Captain Todd of the *Eagle*, built in 1814 of 196 tons, claimed a speed of 10½ knots when running free. Coaches were sometimes carried on deck, their owners sleeping in staterooms while steerage passengers got no bunk but had to sleep where best they could.

In northern Europe and the Baltic, single-masted craft remained popular as cargo carriers in coastal waters and short-sea routes. Many carried up to four yards on the mainmast. But schooners gained in popularity as in Great Britain and the cutters and sloops were given two masts or had their hulls lengthened.

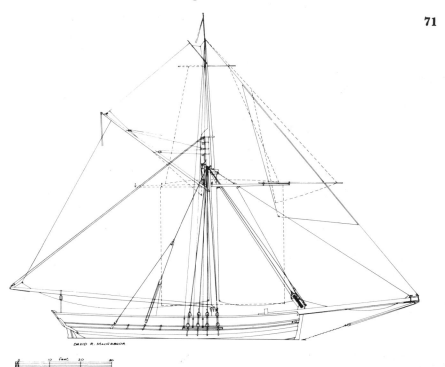

71

ALEXANDER HALL'S SLOOPS AND SMACKS

Between 1811 and the close of 1835, Alexander Hall & Sons built nineteen sloops and smacks at Aberdeen, varying in size from 36 to 112 tons, with an average tonnage of 59. By far the largest was the *Rotterdam Packet* of 112 tons, built in 1816 as a passenger and cargo smack. Many of these craft must have been built on speculation, such as the sloop *Reliance*, constructed in 1817 with measurements of 53ft 6in × 17ft 1in × 8ft 9in and 64½ tons. The cost account for the *Reliance* states:

> By value of vessel as she stands on stocks completely finished with masts, spars and cabin fitted out and painted, measuring 64⁶⁴⁄₉₄ tons per register as per inventory 31 July 1817

at £7 15s per ton	£501	16s	3d
deduct allowance to finish	16	16	3
	£485	0s	0d
per loss sustained by above valuation	179	4	10
	£664	4s	10d

17 Oct 1819 sold to Alexander Adam, shipowner, Aberdeen,

complete and painted as agreed	£490	0	0
2 stamps		10	0
loss sustained on this vessel	15	11	6
1/6th share of loss at £3 17s 10d shared by John Catto and Saunders and Mellis	7	15	8
	£513	17s	2d[78]

The *Reliance* must presumably have earned money for Hall and his partners in the two years before she was sold.

In 1823 he built the sloop *Harmony* under contract for John Pearson of Dysart:

To build new sloop – hull, masts, spars &c 74⁹³⁄₉₄ tons CH measure at £8 8s per agreement	£629	18	2
extra expense to nail deck with copper instead of iron nails	2	9	10
	£633	12s	11d[79]

Note that figures copied from yard book may not add up correctly.

She had a square stern, no gallery and no figurehead, as might be expected. The dimensions were 53ft 9in × 18ft 5½in × 10ft 3½in (depth of hold 'skin to skin'), making her a very beamy craft with only three beams to her length.

The following are the costs for the *Harmony*:

Memel mast 59½ft × 14½in 86-10-5 @ 3/-		£13	0s	7d
Bowsprit ex ship *Superior* cost		3	18	9
Crossjack [yard] ex ship *Superior* 42ft × 7in		1	5	0
Norway log topmast 36½ft × 6¼in			18	0
Tops'l yard 31½ft × 7¼in		1	10	9
Main boom		4	16	8
Gaff			15	0
Trysail gaff and swing booms			13	0
2 stuns'l booms and 2 stuns'l yards			13	0
Topgallant yard			6	6
		27	17	3
Timber and plank		379	9	3
Treenails		14	6	6
Iron bolts and nails		5	19	7
Copper nails &c		2	2	2
Pitch, tar and oakum		6	7	11
Carpenter's wages		149	11	10
Cash: carpenter's allowance 10/6; launch expense £3 16s; carver 15/-		5	1	6
Boat building			4	6
Composition bolts &c		8	17	3
James Abernethy & Co – one set of 14 ins windlass metal		3	10	0
George Black – ironwork		12	15	2
Profit arising on this vessel		17	10	0
		£633	12s	11d[80]

Note that: the weight of the Memel lower mast is given after its length; the trysail gaff was probably for use as a storm gaff.

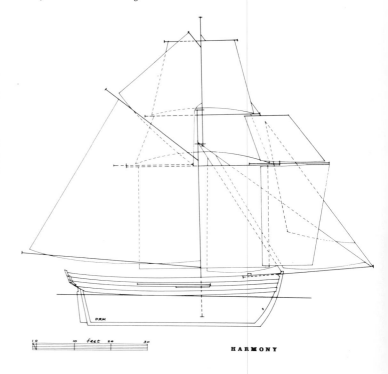

Fig 72. Harmony. *Outline sail plan reconstructed by the author from cost account and Hedderwick's proportions. Built in 1823 by A Hall & Sons, Aberdeen. See text for dimensions.*

HARMONY

Spar dimensions are not given for any sloop or smack before the *Cock of the North*, launched in 1835, although the rough sizes from the above cost account give approximate sizes, which have been utilised to reconstruct a spar and sail plan for the *Harmony* (figure 72). The lengths of the bowsprit, boom, gaff and masthead have been estimated according to Hedderwick's proportions. The resultant plan bears a strong resemblance to the *Rival*, built at Hull seven years later (figure 60). In view of the evidence presented here concerning the position of the fore topsail yard below the cap on the east coast in the twenties and thirties, it seems logical to give the *Harmony* a similar arrangement. In general appearance she would not have been dissimilar to the sloop drawn by Calvert Jones in 1828 (figure 73).

Fig 73. A pen-and-ink drawing by the Rev Calvert Jones of an unnamed sloop dried out on the shore, presumably in South Wales. The date is 30 October 1828. The lower yard has been cast loose from its gear and is lashed in the rigging. (MacGregor Collection)

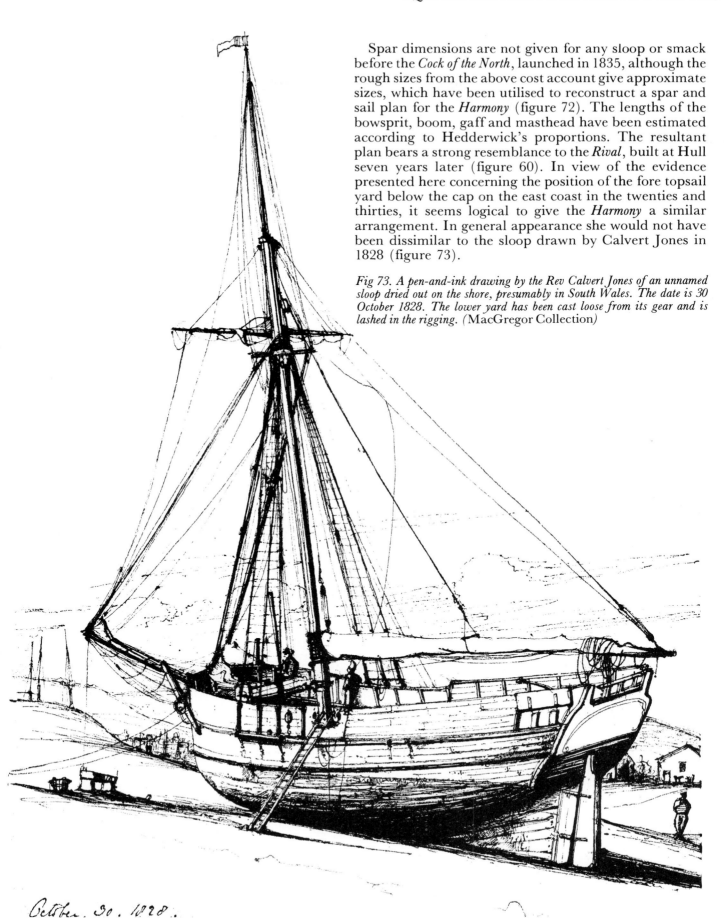

October. 30. 1828.

THREE-MASTED SCHOONERS

In William Anderson's painting of the *Royal George* at Greenwich in 1822, there are two unidentified three-masted fore-and-aft schooners at anchor with their sails brailed into the standing gaffs. Both the vessels appear to have funnels and the probability is that one was the steamer *James Watt* (1821) engaged on the Leith to London run.[81]

Other examples of English three-masted schooners are the yacht *Calypso*, in commission in 1826; the *Elbe* of 111 tons, built at Sheilds in 1827 of 111 tons; the naval packet *Seagull* designed by Seppings in 1829.[82] These are sufficient examples to prove that the rig was known and appreciated long before 1850. In masting the early steam vessels, many were rigged as three-masted schooners, some purely in a fore-and-aft rig and others with an almost fully square-rigged foremast. Several, such as the PS *Monarch* of 1833, must undoubtedly have been rigged as three-masted barquentines in all but name.[83] The absence of contemporary comment on the early three-masted schooner rig suggests that it was much more common than has often been thought today.

A number of three-masters were built in America, principally on Chesapeake Bay, and were usually built on clipper lines for specialised cargo work or as coastal packets where speed was important.

T & J BROCKLEBANK AND THE BARQUENTINE *BONANZA*

The Whitehaven shipbuilding firm clung to the brig throughout the period 1815–35 as being the rig most suited to their business as shipowners. During these years they built the following types, according to the rig; 4 ships, 8 barques, 24 brigs, 4 brigantines, 5 schooners, 1 barquentine, 3 sloops, 2 flats, and 2 paddle steamers. Compared with the vessels built in the years 1793–1815, barques made their appearance for the first time as did brigantines, and a barquentine was also a new experiment. Several of the brigantines are disguised in Thomas Brocklebank's notebook under the rig of 'schooner' but the spar dimensions give the lie to this. The *Mazeppa*, built in 1831, is called a 'brigantine' on one page of the book and the facing page calls her 'Brig forward Schooner aft'. She was

74

re-rigged as a brig in 1840. The rig attributions in the company history by John Gibson are not correct in all cases.[84] In the yard book, a table of offsets and spar dimensions is given for every vessel, except in rare cases, so that a lines plan and a spar plan could in theory be drawn for most vessels by which an accurate picture of a shipbuilder's entire production could be assembled.

In some cases, the types of wood used in the construction are listed. The brig *Rimac*, built 1834 of 214 tons, had a keel of Quebec oak, a false keel of elm, the frame timbers of English or African oak, the bottom planking of 3in elm, and the planking of the bilge up to the light waterline of Quebec oak.

A number of the vessels were built on the lines of others, and any differences were confined to a short list of amended offsets, without repeating the entire table again. The brig *Gazelle* (No 82) and the barque *Helvellyn* (No 83), both built in 1826, had the same offsets and the former was 4ins longer and 1 ton larger. The spar dimensions were compared side by side, the mast lengths for the two being identical with the exception of the barque's main lower mast which was 1ft longer; but the barque's yards are unfortunately not listed. A comparison of the spar dimensions of a brig and a barque, both built in 1840 by

Alexander Hall at Aberdeen, is given here in Chapter Three, page 116. Of the three brigantines, *Buoyant* (1828, No 92), *Tampico* (1830, No 99) and *Mazeppa* (1831, No 101), No 99 had thirteen different offsets to No 92, and No 101 was described as follows: 'Same as new ship No 92 with the following exceptions – has 4 flats forward and the keel dropped down 3 inches, with the following heights at their respective frames'. Then came a short list of changed offsets. Nos 92 and 99 had identical spars. The barquentine *Bonanza* had the same lines as the barque *Maypo*, with the exception of three offsets, as described later. On the page for No 97, the barque *Hindoo* of 1831, it states, 'as altered from No 96' which was the *Avoca* and 10 tons smaller.

Fig 74. The three-masted topgallant schooner May *was a coastal packet between Boston and Baltimore in 1834. She was built the previous year at Essex, Mass, and was of 126 tons. The foot of the big square sail is extended on a passaree boom. (Peabody Museum, Salem)*

Fig 75. Bearing the distinctive Brocklebank markings of the broad white stripe on her hull, the brig Rimac *has not crossed her royal and skysail yards. Beyond her is another Brocklebank vessel rigged as a brigantine. (Merseyside County Museums)*

76

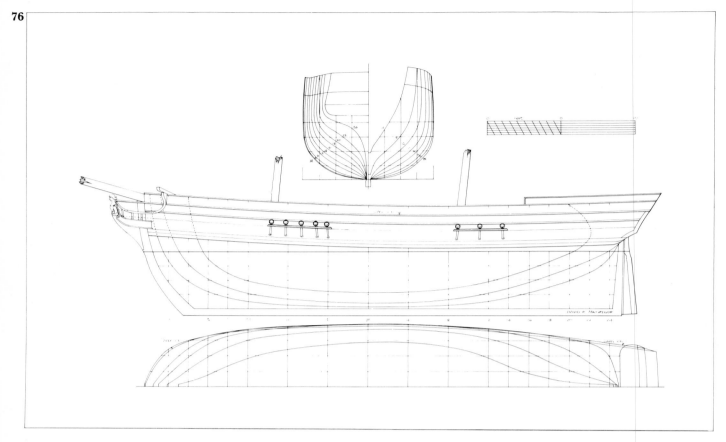

77

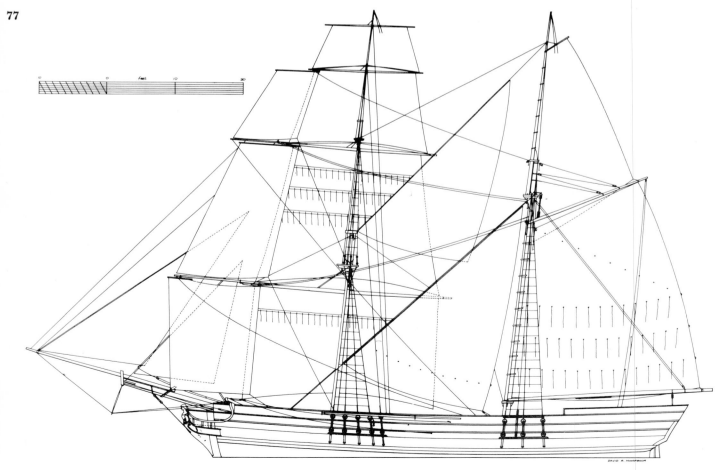

One of the four full-rigged ships built in these years was the *Jumna* which was the first ship to sail direct from Liverpool to China and return with tea. On the outward passage to Canton in 1834, she took 110 days to the time when she picked up her pilot on 1 September; on the return passage she was 102 days to Liverpool from Canton – 1 December 1834 to 13 March 1835 – both of which were quick passages. The *Jumna* was built in 1833 of 364 tons, with dimensions of 107ft 10in (aloft) × 27ft 9¼in × 18ft 11in. She was built on the model of the barque *Patriot King* of approximately similar length and depth but 12in broader. 'She is very roomy between decks and is constructed on the modern plan with partition for ventilation between the timbers which experience shows is the surest preventative of the dry rot.'[85] In 1856, Brocklebank's sold the *Jumna* to the Tay Whale Fishing Company of Dundee who converted her into a steamer in 1863. In the same year, she was crushed in the ice at Melville Bay.

Of plans surviving for the period 1815–35, there are few lines plans but there are sail plans of the brigantine *Oberon* (No 85) and the schooner *Courier* (No 81). The former plan was used in reconstructing a sail plan for the brigan-tine *Dash* which appears in figure 77, her lines are in figure 76. The notebook entry for *Oberon* bears this remark: 'Dimensions new ship No 85 same as No 81 in every particular, only has three flat frames.' The *Courier* was 3ft 5in shorter on the keel, being presumably without any deadflats. The *Oberon* was converted into a brig in 1833.

Fig 76. Dash. Lines plan reconstructed by the author from body plan, elevation of topsides and plans of other Brocklebank vessels. Built 1828 at Whitehaven by T & J Brocklebank for their own use. Dimensions: 66ft 3in × 17ft 3in × 10ft 2in; 86 tons.

Fig 77. Dash. Sail plan redrawn by the author from tracing made of builder's plan when in possession of T & J Brocklebank; other details reconstructed from painting done by Jacob Petersen off Elsinore.

Fig 78. Courier. Sail plan redrawn from tracing made of builder's sail plan. Built 1826 by T & J Brocklebank; dimensions 77ft 2in (deck) × 20ft 7in × 12ft 1in and 142 tons. Reconstruction: main topmast staysail, braces, mast trucks above rigging, mast hoops, ratlines, dolphin striker and all bowsprit rigging, mainsail topping lift, fore gaff halliards, all sheets, reef points and hull profile below load waterline. The shape of the three headsails is like the original.

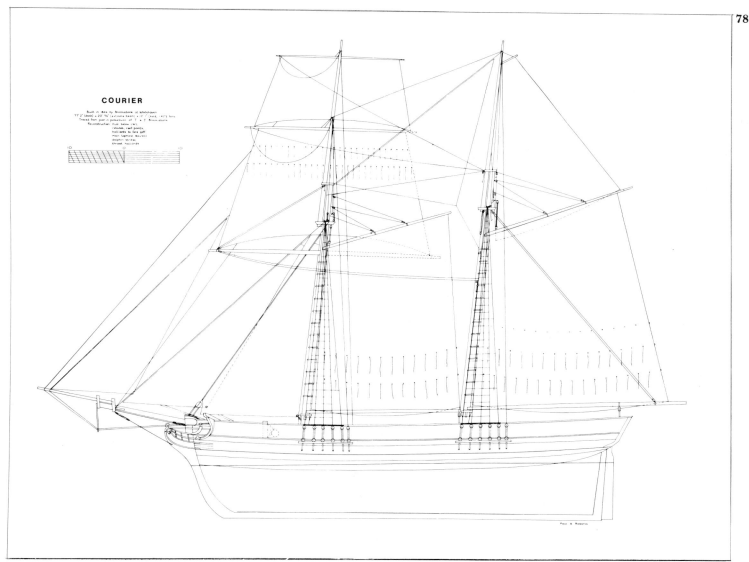

COURIER

Built in 1826 by Brocklebank at Whitehaven
77'2' (deck) x 20'7' (extreme beam) x 12'1' (hold), 142 tons
Traced from plan in possession of T & J Brocklebank
Reconstruction: hull below LWL,
ratlines, reef points,
halliards to fore gaff,
main topmast staysail,
dolphin striker,
throat halliards.

78

79

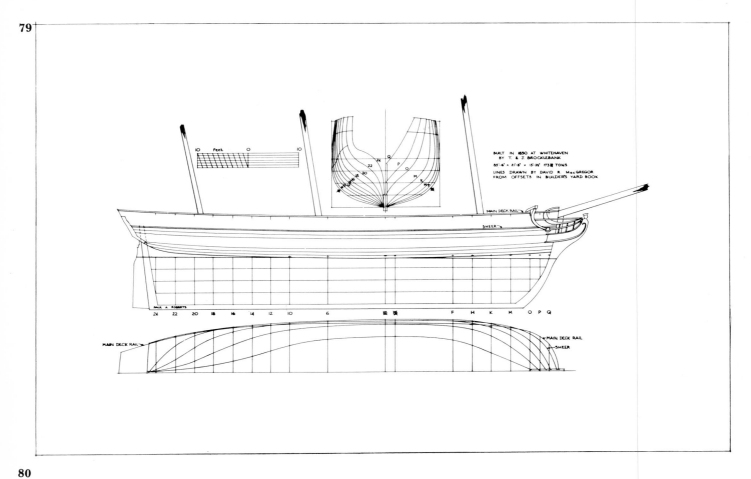

BUILT IN 1830 AT WHITEHAVEN
BY T. & J. BROCKLEBANK
85'-6" × 21'-8" × 13'-2½" 173½ TONS
LINES DRAWN BY DAVID R. MacGREGOR
FROM OFFSETS IN BUILDERS YARD BOOK

MAIN DECK RAIL
SHEER

PAUL A ROBERTS

24 22 20 18 16 14 12 10 6   F H K M O P Q

MAIN DECK RAIL
SHEER

80

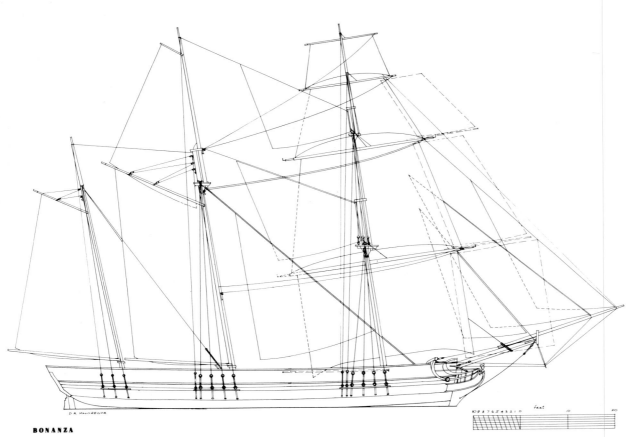

D R MacGREGOR

10 9 8 7 6 5 4 3 2 1 0   feet   10   20

BONANZA

Their dimensions are compared below:
No 81 *Courier*, built 1826, 142$\frac{1}{94}$ tons
   deck length 77ft 2in; keel 75ft 3in; ext beam 20ft 7$\frac{1}{4}$in;
depth of hold 12ft 1in.
No 85 *Oberon*, built 1827, 150$\frac{5}{94}$ tons
   length aloft 80ft 0$\frac{1}{2}$in; keel 78ft 8in; ext beam 20ft 7$\frac{1}{2}$in;
depth of hold 12ft 1in.

SPAR DIMENSIONS FROM BROCKLEBANK'S YARD BOOK COMPARED

	Courier (schooner)	*Oberon* (brigantine)
Fore lower mast (deck to hounds)	41ft	29ft
Fore topmast (heel to hounds)	20ft	23ft 6in
Fore topgallant mast (heel to hounds)	12ft	14ft
Main lower mast (deck to hounds)	43ft	43ft
Main topmast (heel to hounds)	32ft	32ft 10in
Fore yard (cleated)	38ft	34ft
Fore topsail yard (cleated)	29ft	25ft 6in
Fore topgallant yard (cleated)	20ft	18ft
Fore gaff	23ft 6in*	–
Fore boom	27ft†	–
Main gaff	25ft	25ft
Main boom	37ft	37ft
Bowsprit ('without') [outside knight-heads]	18ft	†
Jibboom (outside cap)	11ft†	†

* dimension written on plan
† dimension scaled off plan

From these spar lengths it can be seen that *Courier* had a larger sail area, especially when one takes into consideration the area of a square sail set from the lower yard. The head on the sail plan looks old fashioned and so does the short jibboom; another unusual feature is that there are five shrouds to each mast.

Offsets indicate that the shape of *Courier*'s midship section was similar to that of *Maypo* and *Bonanza* as drawn in figure 79, with sharply rising floors that round up the whole way, and so she was obviously intended to make fast passages. Her midship section is placed about 9ft forward of amidships.

The discovery that *Bonanza* was a barquentine and not the 'three-masted schooner' so described in the yard book is an astounding event and makes one wonder what other barquentines might have been afloat in these years, perhaps disguised under the pseudonym of 'three-masted schooner.' The so-called 'first' vessel of any rig is often proved to be a myth by later discoveries. Apart from the

Transits, rigged as five-, four-, and three-masted barquentines in the years 1800, 1809 and 1819, it had been assumed that the first 'orthodox' three-masted barquentine was the *Fanny* of Bremen, built in 1850. Plans of the *Transit* were given in *Fast Sailing Ships*, figures 40 and 41. The lines plan and sail plan of *Bonanza* given here prove that she was an 'orthodox' barquentine.

The lines plan in figure 79 has been drawn from offsets given in Thomas Brocklebank's notebook for the barque *Maypo*, ship No 93, laid down in May 1828 and launched on 17 June 1829. The reason for using these is because the entry for *Bonanza* in the notebook begins: 'Dimensions New Ship No 94 same as No 93 except about 1$\frac{1}{2}$ins fuller upon O, P & 2 at the Main Deck Rail Harpin'. The *Bonanza*, ship No 94, was launched the following year. The dimensions of the two vessels are compared here:

	Maypo	*Bonanza*
Length aloft [=from foreside stem to taffrail measured along sheer line]	84ft 8in	85ft 6in
Length of keel [=tonnage length of keel and fore rake]	82ft 6in	82ft 7$\frac{1}{2}$in
Breadth extreme	21ft 9in	21ft 8in
Depth of hold	13ft 4in	13ft 2$\frac{1}{2}$in
Tonnage	174$\frac{70}{94}$	173$\frac{79}{94}$

The offsets principally consist of measurements for the hull within the rabbet line of keel, stem and sternpost, and up to the 'sheer'. First a list is given to enable the diagonals in the body plan to be drawn and then a table gives dimensions for constructing the cross sections in it. There are six diagonals in this case. Although other columns give the 'main breadth' and the 'sheer height' above the keel rabbet, there are no further dimensions to extend the body plan sections between the top diagonal and the sheer. However, by using the same Dixon Kemp curve which had faired in the body plan, the sections were extended upwards. Additional data had given the bulwark height as 3ft, and the tumblehome at sheer and main deck rail, so that the midship section was certainly correct. The rake of the sternpost and the shape of the stem rabbet were given. The breadths at main deck rail from stations H to Q were also given, so that the flare at the bows was correct.

Fortunately, a copy had been made of a Brocklebank lines plan of an unnamed vessel of '175 tons' with the Whatman paper on which it was drawn bearing a watermark of 1821. The hull-form turned out to be very similar. At first it was thought that it might be the *Maypo* herself as she is the only vessel around this period of 175 tons, and the figures '84 22 & 13-4' appear under the stem – figures which are surely the three principal dimensions and which closely approximate those of the *Maypo*. This plan provided useful data for the shape of the stern and rudder, keel and stem thickness, and run of topsides. No head was shown, and this has been taken from the sail plan of the schooner *Courier* and adjusted to suit the scale. The plan was drawn at $\frac{1}{4}$in scale as it enables the sail plan to fit conveniently on the sheet, whereas the Brocklebank plans at this date were in proportional scales such as 1:30 for

Fig 79. Bonanza. *Lines plan reconstructed by the author from builder's offsets in yard book at Merseyside County Museums; ink tracing of this for reproduction made by Paul A Roberts. Built 1830 by T & J Brocklebank at Whitehaven; dimensions 85ft 6in × 21ft 8in × 13ft 2$\frac{1}{2}$in and 173 tons. Reconstruction: head rails &c from schooner* Courier.

Fig 80. Bonanza. *Sail plan. Reconstructed by the author from builder's spar dimensions. Reconstruction: bowsprit, jibboom, dolphin striker, yardarms, mizzen gaff, length of doubling on mainmast, all rigging, all stunsail booms and yards, all sail outlines.*

Oberon, 1:25 for *Dash* and probably 1:35 or 36 for *Courier*, which make the head of the masts disappear off the sheet.

The resultant plan is a fine-lined hull with considerable deadrise, floors that curve up into slack bilges and top-sides which tumble home to give an elegant body plan. The conventional waterlines have been plotted and these produce a short, sharp convex entrance, a long middle body which really curves all the way although there are two deadflats; and finally a long fine run with some hollow near the sternpost. It is certainly a hull-form designed for a fair turn of speed, and hulls of this kind indicate that Brocklebank ships were not intended to carry the maximum amount of cargo without regard to their sailing qualities. It is often said that shipbuilders who built for their own account did not require fast vessels but merely ones to carry the maximum amount of paying cargo, but it looks as if some reappraisal of the design of Brocklebank ships is now due.

The sail plan of *Bonanza* in figure 80 is full of interest, and the most notable feature is the great rake of the masts. Most entries in Brocklebank's notebook do not give either mast spacings or the rake, but both are given here, presumably because she departed from the customary sail plan. The foremast rakes 1½in to a foot, the mainmast 2in and the mizzen 2½in. In the mast spacings, dimensions are taken from the 'huddin' which is assumed to mean the 'hood ends' or where the planking fits into the stem rabbet. No dimensions are given for bowsprit or jibboom, for yardarms, mizzen gaff, doubling on mainmast, or dolphin striker. Nor are any stunsail booms listed; they hardly ever were by shipbuilders, but they always formed part of the inventory. The absence of a trysail gaff on the foremast makes the rig of an 'orthodox' pattern, but the stepping of the foremast so far forward results in having to provide a bumkin to bowse down the fore tack, even though the leeches of the fore course are cut without a gore. It seems unlikely that the foot would have been shorter than the head. The staysails from the mainmast follow the pattern of those in the sail plan of the brigantine *Oberon*, as do the headsails. The head yard of the main topsail is drawn on the evidence of the words 'Gaff Top Gaff' under the list of mainmast spars, although no figure is entered in the column. She was later converted into a brig between the years 1841–43, but no dimensions of the new rig have been found.

With this knowledge of *Bonanza*'s hull-form her fast passage from China falls into its correct perspective. She was mostly engaged in the South American trade. At the end of 1843 she sailed for Lima, which she reached in 102 days from Liverpool; then she crossed over to Hong Kong and went up to Shanghai, presumably to load a cargo of tea at the newly opened Treaty Port. Between Shanghai and Liverpool she took the very short time of only 91 days at the end of 1844.[86] This was an incredibly fast run at that date and equals the time taken by the *Hallowe'en* in 1874–75 between Shanghai and London.[87] Brocklebank's history unfortunately does not give any actual dates to substantiate the claim. It should be remembered that for this record run she was rigged as a brig, although she had spent at least eleven years on ocean voyages as a barquen-

tine. She was sold by Brocklebank's in 1856 and lost the same year.

Compared with the *Bonanza*, the sister ship *Maypo* – whose name *Lloyd's Register*'s red book of 1830 spelt '*Maypole*' – had fore- and mainmasts 2ft taller than the *Bonanza*'s foremast, and yards of approximately similar length, the chief difference being that her topsail yards were 2ft longer. *Maypo*'s mizzen lower mast was 29ft 6in long.

THE *BAFFIN* AND OTHER WHALERS

The same dedicated research has not been undertaken in the British whale fishery as has been the case in the United States and plans of British whalers are very scarce, so it was fortunate to find plans of the *Baffin* in the Whitby Museum. This ship was built at Liverpool in 1820 and her design undoubtedly owed a great deal to Captain William Scoresby (1789–1857). His father William Scoresby (1760–1829) had, for about thirty years, been master of whaling ships sailing out of Whitby to Arctic waters, during which time he brought in 533 whales. The son obtained his first command in 1810 in the ship *Resolution*, and after two voyages in her transferred into the *Esk* for five years. A great deal is known about these ships and their voyages through the journals kept by father and son. It is in one such journal that the construction of the *Baffin* is described, although the costs were entered in a separate account book.[88]

In November 1818, William Scoresby Jnr agreed to join the Liverpool shipowners Hurry & Gibson in fitting out a whaler for the Arctic. As a suitable second-hand ship

Fig 81. Whaling in Arctic waters, as painted by John Ward of Hull. The ship is not identified but she is British and is hove-to as her boats pursue a whale. (Richard Green Gallery)

could not be found they decided to build a new vessel, and after getting 'proposals' from different shipyards they signed a contract in June 1819 with Mottershead & Hayes of Trentham Street, Liverpool, for building a whaler 'in every respect complete for the fishery (hull & spars) and entirely to our plan and dimensions'. The contract price was £16 per ton on a measurement of 321½ tons which resulted in a total of £5144. In 1856 the term 'hull and spars' meant that the builder did not supply the sails, canvas, rigging, cordage, anchors, chain cables, water tanks or any outfit or furnishings.[89] These builders had in 1815 launched the first steamer to be built on the Mersey, the *Princess Charlotte*, and the *Baffin* was said to be the first ship built at Liverpool especially for whaling. The *Baffin*'s tonnage was 321 and dimensions scaled from the plan are: length for tonnage 103ft 3in, maximum beam (moulded) 25ft 10in, depth of hold 17ft 0in (approx).

The *Baffin*'s keel was laid on 25 June 1819 and the erection of the frame timbers took about eight weeks. She was very strongly built: the sternpost had 8 transoms below the wing transom and 3 fashion timbers on each side; the after body frames, including 3 cant frames, numbered 22 pairs and the fore body frames 10 pairs, and there were 8½ of the same mould for the deadflats amidships. The first plank was laid on 21 August and on 2 October the shipwrights began fastening the lower deck beams, which were spaced about 5ft 3in apart 'suited to the lengths of the casks'. The deck was laid in four days. Before the ship was doubled, the hull was filled with water to locate the leaks, which were then stopped. The doubling was then laid on diagonally outside the main skin, from stem to stern, between the bilges and the bends. The thickness varied from 3in forward to 2in aft. The hull was very strongly built in the bows: known as 'fortifications', the framing was solid from the stem for 17ft on each side and was strongly secured with heavy breasthooks.

The launch took place on 15 February 1820. Scoresby describes it in these words:

The ship was to be projected over a high quay and the *launch* was run several yards into the river ...

At 11.50 am the retarding shores were struck off and the ship instantly started and with a velocity that increased much beyond the usual rate, which was extremely fortunate, flew along the slides and cleared the quay, though the exterior part of the launch [presumably, meaning 'launching ways'] gave way the moment the weight came upon it. It was a beautiful sight ...

As soon as the ship was fairly afloat, she became our property and not till then; as such I immediately proceeded on board to take possession.[90]

The *Baffin* was taken into Salthouse Dock to be fitted out and the erection of masts and the stowing of casks began at once. One of William Scoresby Snr's innovations was filling the casks with water before the voyage began, to act as ballast. As whales were caught, the water would be replaced with blubber. This was undoubtedly a very early form of water ballast.

The outfit obviously occupied much room: 102 casks can be counted in Scoresby's journal and the cost account lists considerably more. Some were filled with water, twenty contained beer (weighing 10 tons), seven contained beef ('salted in Iceland under inspection'), five contained fresh water, and others contained provisions. In addition there were 22 tons of stone and shingle ballast arranged among thrity casks and placed near the keelson. Seven boats were carried of which one is referred to as a 'spare'. There were two capstans and a windlass.

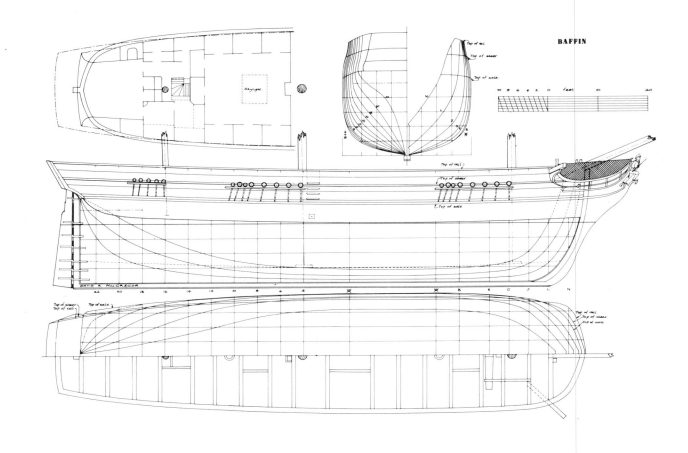

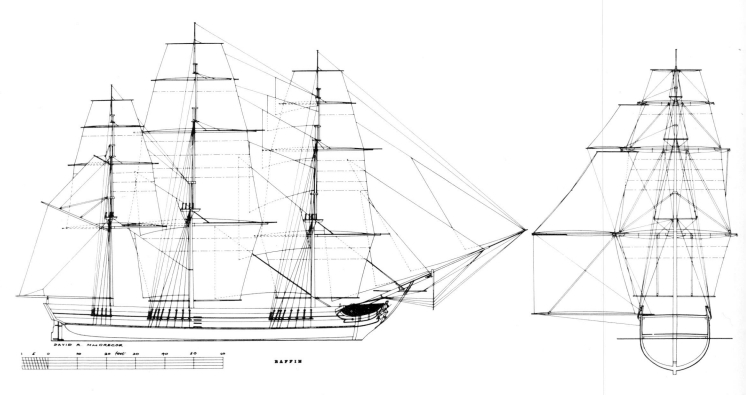

On 11 March 1820 the crew was mustered. The number 'required by law' was 42 men and boys. The first voyage lasted from 18 March to 23 August 1820 and was highly successful. The *Baffin* continued in the trade until lost in the Davis Straits in 1830 with about a dozen other vessels.[91]

A whaling ship had to combine many qualities in her design: she must be strongly built to resist the buffeting of ice and sea, yet easily manœuvrable to weather an icefield or a lee shore or to make a sudden escape through the closing pack ice. She also had to be capable of sailing fast and of cutting-in her whales easily.

As can be seen in her lines plan (figure 82) the *Baffin* has a full entrance, as one would expect, yet it is sharper than the *William Miles* (1808) and the same or a trifle sharper than David Steel's West Indiaman, while the run is undoubtedly finer than either of these and nicely formed, and there is a fair amount of deadrise with slack bilges. Amidships there is a length of 17ft 3in of deadflats but she has good deadrise and slack bilges. The rudder pintles are plotted at the heights given in Scoresby's journal. The figurehead is of a harpooner and is reconstructed from one of the sail plans which shows how the harpoon was held. The square plate on the hull below the gangway is perhaps a fixing for the cutting-in stage. Instead of a heavy, massive trailboard, which can be seen in the photograph of *William Miles* (1816) or other early vessels; the space is filled with a netting, probably of rope, although later ships had one of iron wire.

At first glance, the spacing of the stations seems odd. Scoresby wrote in his journal that from station B aft, room and space measured 2ft 4in but forward of that only 2ft 0in.[92] This agrees exactly with the lines plan as, omitting the deadflats, the positions of the stations abaft B are 4ft 8in apart (*ie* twice 2ft 4in), representing alternate frames, and forward of B they are multiples of 2ft 0in. Station C is omitted as the line was so close to B on the body-plan. The closer spacing of the forward frames would conform to the solid construction of the bows.

The *Baffin's* deck plan was much the same as in a normal merchant ship, being in this case flush-decked. The accommodation takes up all the space in the 'tween decks abaft the mainmast, and although the cabin plan shows no method of entry to the foremost cabin, a stairway was probably incorporated in the hatchway, shown dotted. There must also have been additional bunks in the forward 'tween decks with a scuttle possibly situated immediately abaft the bowsprit bitts, as in the barque *Arab* (figure 93). Whalers in the southern fisheries which were away from home for two or three years had to render-down the blubber on board and fill their casks with the oil, but in the Arctic regions the season was so short that the casks were merely filled with the blubber which was then rendered-down ashore on their return. The design of these southern whalers was somewhat different, as much of their work was done in warmer seas; but Greenland whalers were often converted into ordinary merchant ships and vice versa.

The plans of the *Baffin* which appear here, incorporate data from seven separate drawings in the Whitby Museum. The lines, cabin plan and deck beam plan have been redrawn and combined and so have the four sail plans. The latter presented many problems, being probably drawn by William Scoresby Jnr as his ideas crystallised. Two of his sail plans show only square sails: each contain three cross-sections of the ship on which are drawn the appropriate mast with its yards, sails and rigging, an example of which is shown here. For the purposes of easy reference here his plans are numbered 1, 2, 3 and 4. Nos 1 and 2 show the square sails with slight variations: no 1 shows loose-footed courses, including a crossjack; no 2 shows bentinck booms to the fore and main courses and no crossjack. Both show stunsails, although no 1 also shows a large square lower stunsail on the mainmast, set on a boom. The other two sail plans drawn by Scoresby give the fore-and-aft sails: no 3 shows the headsails, staysails, spanker and gaff topsail, with fore and main trysails superimposed in pencil; no 4 shows a novel idea of his own, in which trysail masts on fore and main extend five feet above the head of the *topmast*, and on these trysail masts, gaff sails and jackyard topsails are set. On no 4, a very foreshortened version of the square sails on the foremast is also given.

The sail plan shown in figure 83 is a combination of nos 2 and 3. No 2 was selected as it is known that Scoresby employed bentinck booms. For the sake of interest, the shape of the staysails has been copied from no 3 exactly as drawn by Scoresby, although the roach to the foot is unusual. All his sail plans were drawn to a scale of 1/10in to 1ft 0in. The fore lower stunsail boom projects no less than 37ft 0in outside the hull.

The sail plan given by Peter Hedderwick for his ship of 500 tons (figure 20) would be very similar to *Baffin* as regards the run of the braces and the fidding of the royal masts abaft the topgallant masts. Many ships had this arrangement, although some fidded the royal masts on the foreside. Scoresby has drawn the leeches of the courses, topsails and topgallants with a very slight hollow.

The whalers were perhaps the earliest vessels to use bentinck booms to spread the foot of their courses. When anchored to an icefloe they had to be capable of getting underway in an instant, and with most of the crew away in the boats they had to rig their sails differently. With a light boom bent to the foot of the courses and with no tacks or sheets but merely a tackle at the centre, the sails could be furled with the boom hauled up or dropped in a minute.[93] Bentinck booms to both fore and main courses, as in the *Baffin*, were rarely seen, although a model of the eighteenth century whaler *Harpooner* displays them.[94] This

Fig 82. Baffin. Lines, deck and cabin plans redrawn from plans found in the Whitby Museum, courtesy of the Whitby Literary and Philosophical Society. Built 1820 by Mottershead & Hayes at Liverpool; measurements (scaled from the plans): 103ft 3in (for tonnage) × 25ft 10in (moulded) × 17ft 0in (approx) and 321 tons. Reconstruction: figurehead from a sail plan; rudder pintles from Scoresby's journal; lines, cabins, and deck beam plan combined on one sheet.

Fig 83. Baffin. Sail plan reconstructed by the author from two different plans, as described in the text. By courtesy of Whitby Literary and Philosophical Society who administer the museum.

model was probably made in the nineteenth century to judge from the rigging of the bowsprit, and although the proportions of the model may be questioned, there is the evidence of these two bentinck booms to corroborate Scoresby's plan. There are paintings of two Hamburg whalers which had bentinck booms fitted to their fore and main courses: one was the Danish-built ship *Der Junge Gustaf* (1826);[95] the other was the brig *Hoffnung* ex-*De Junge Janus* (1780) which became the *Hoffnung* in 1800, and in addition to the bentinck booms she had trysail masts to each lower mast while at the main there was a trysail mast abaft the topmast to set a jackyard topsail. See figure 119 in *Merchant Sailing Ships 1775—1815* for illustration.

Other vessels that economised in crews and that worked in narrow waters also used these booms, although the fitting of the boom was usually restricted to the fore course. There are several illustrations here of vessels so rigged and it is incorrect to assume that any vessel with one was automatically in the coal trade, as is commonly believed.

William Scoresby Jnr was very keen on Arctic discovery and scientific research; he made his last whaling voyage in 1823, was elected a Fellow of the Royal Society in 1824, and the following year took up Holy Orders. Later he conducted research into the behaviour of the compass in iron ships.

A boom in Arctic whaling began in 1816 and continued for a decade, but as whales became scarcer, ships had to venture further northwards in the search for them, and as a result got nipped in the ice more frequently. Ships sailing from London and King's Lynn were down to a handful by the early 1820s, whereas Hull sent out 60 ships in 1820. Meanwhile, the ports of Dundee, Aberdeen and Peterhead were fitting out more ships. In 1816 the whaling fleet numbered 146 ships but by 1830 this had decreased to 91; in the latter year disaster struck, as 19 ships were lost in the ice and 21 returned 'clean'. There were further heavy losses of ships in the mid-thirties as the ice fields moved further south in the late summer. The crews endured great hardships and in the winter of 1836–37, the *Swan* and the *Advice* were trapped in the ice for the whole winter before being freed. In the 1840s, Peterhead supplanted Hull as the principal whaling port, and sealing off Newfoundland helped to prolong the sea-son and add to the profits. The trade continued thus until the introduction of the auxiliary engine in the Dundee fleet in 1859 which brought new life to the industry. But demand for whale oil had to withstand competition from American exports of sperm oil and the steady increase of petroleum products.[96]

The first sperm whale killed in the Pacific Ocean was harpooned in 1789 by the Nantucket mate of the British whaler *Emelia*, owned by the London firm of Enderby & Sons.[97] The British did much pioneering work in this way but did not reap the rewards which were gathered so plentifully by American whalers. The Indian and Pacific Oceans were known as the 'southern whale fishery' in Britain and it was for this that Sir Robert Wigram ordered the *Walker* from the Blackwall yard. She was built in 1799 of 341 tons, at a cost of £3753 or £11 per ton.[98] Later, in 1821, the British whaler *Syren* jointly discovered the Japan Grounds with the Nantucket ship *Maro*.[99] A painting of the *Syren* by Walters, made in 1823 showing the ship off Dover, depicts a vessel with all the appearances of a West Indiaman and very similar to the *Medina*.[100]

Another South Seas whaler was the *William Nicol* of 408 tons built at Greenock in 1834 as an ordinary merchant ship, but sold to Wilson & Co of London in 1843 and converted to a whaler. An oil painting shows a ship with eleven painted ports and three whaleboats hung from davits on the port side; like the brig *Hoffnung*, the boats are all painted green with black gunwales.[101] British ships sailing from Great Britain remained in this trade until the middle of the century, but many of the British ships were commanded by Nantucket men and several firms specialised in this trade, such as Enderby & Sons, and Green, Wigram & Green. The latter built several whalers in their own yard at Blackwall in the 1830s. The Southern Whale Fishery Company was organised by Charles Enderby in 1849 from a base in Auckland Island, south of New Zealand, but the business was wound up four years

Fig 84. Unnamed whaler. Lines plan reproduced from original plan formerly in the collection of the late Harold Wyllie, and reputed to have been owned by Enderby's. Dimensions inscribed on plan: extreme length 110ft 0in, extreme breadth 28ft 4in, height of wing transom 17ft 9in, [length of] keel for tonnage 88ft 6in; tonnage 377⁸⁷/₉₄ om.

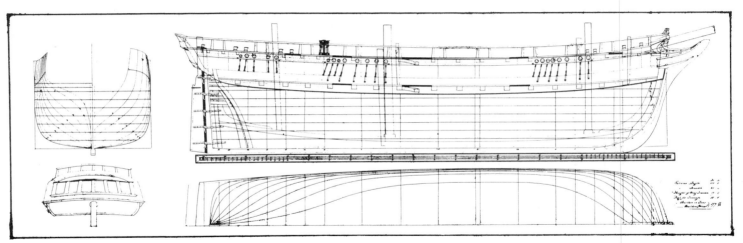

Fig 85. The American whaler Canton *hove-to. Of only 239 tons with a length of 103 ft she was cluttered up with a lot of gear for a voyage of several years. She was built at Baltimore in 1835. (MacGregor Collection)*

later after severe losses. This terminated the Enderbys' long connection with whaling in the southern hemisphere.[102]

There is an unrigged model of one of Enderby & Sons' later ships, the *Samuel Enderby*, at the National Maritime Museum, Greenwich. This ship was built in 1834 at Cowes by Thomas White and measured 422 tons. The model to $\frac{1}{2}$in scale shows a flush-decked vessel with her windlass abaft the foremast and one capstan; there is a fair amount of deadrise and a clean run, but a fullish entrance. A contemporary aquatint depicts her in 1834 as a full-rigged ship with trysails on all three masts and the foremast stepped well forward; the spritsail yard is fitted on top of the bowsprit; one pair of heavy timber davits is shown on the port quarter and nine ports are drawn each side at deck level. From a stern view on the right-hand side of the picture, the topgallant and royal masts appear to be in one piece.[103]

American whaling ships ranged the Atlantic, Indian and Pacific Oceans in their search for whales and were frequently away from home on long three- or four-year voyages which required them to provision themselves amply against every conceivable situation. This resulted in broad, bluff-bowed ships with maximum stowage capacity, both for their own provisions and for the whale oil they hoped to obtain. Size varied from 200 to 400 tons and the rig was usually that of ship or barque. The princi-

pal difference between American whalers, and European ships confined to the Arctic, was that the former rendered-down the blubber on board and stowed it in casks, while the others took it back to port. American ships boiled the blubber in two huge iron cauldrons or 'trypots' and the oily smoke soon blackened the sails.

New Bedford and Nantucket were the principal whaling ports in New England, but whalers also operated from New London, New York and Philadelphia. Schooners and brigs were used for whaling in the Atlantic and coastal waters, but in the South Atlantic and far distant oceans it was the full-rigged ship that was generally employed, although barques became increasingly popular after about 1840. Many of the ships were old packets or merchant vessels, but specially designed ships were also used and these were often given a fair amount of deadrise with slack bilges in order to make the hull roll more easily when cutting-in a whale.[104]

Whales were cut-in on the starboard side, abreast of the main rigging and part of the bulwarks could be removed for this purpose. Although a boat was carried on the starboard quarter, it was on the port side that three boats

Fig 86. Pencil drawing attributed to George C Wales of a whaler under easy sail with one of the whale boats pulling towards her. According to Robert Weinstein, the whaler could be the Lagoda (1840), or the Rousseau (1801), or the Desdemona (1823). (Peabody Museum, Salem)

Fig 87. The Jireh Perry lying rigged-down at a New Bedford wharf. The qualities of a wooden hull are well portrayed. She was built at Newburyport of 435 tons in 1851 and her first voyage lasted from 4 July 1852 to 16 June 1856. Photograph taken by Joseph C Terrill and given me by Howard I Chapelle.

88

were carried, slung from wooden davits 10 feet high. The try-works were erected on deck between the fore- and mainmasts and were built of brick with a furnace below two iron trypots, each of which could hold 250 gallons. Around the brick base was a wooden upstand, inside which sea water could flow freely to prevent the deck catching fire. A tank to cool the oil and a spare trypot were placed close to the try-works and the whole was roofed over.

There was a short forecastle and right aft there were usually two small deckhouses tucked into each quarter with the roof connected overhead to shelter the helmsman. A staircase leading down to the after cabins was placed in one of these houses and the other would contain the galley. Some of the whale ships were painted black, others had painted ports.

The heyday of American whaling was 1820 to 1850 and Alexander Starbuck gives some useful statistics in his two-volume work.[105] In 1840 there were 496 ships and barques and 59 brigs and schooners engaged in the trade; ten years later the figures were 502 and 51 respectively. When a whale ship became full of oil on a long cruise, the master would put into some port and ship it back home or perhaps to London. For instance, the *Envoy* of New Bedford sailed in 1848 under the command of Captain W T Walker, the ship having just been rescued from being broken up after being condemned. After cruising in the North Pacific she took 2800 barrels of oil in 55 days of which 1800 barrels and 40,000lbs of bone were shipped to London from Manila; in another cruise that year, a further 2500 barrels of oil were taken, and the ship was put into San Francisco where some of the oil was sold at $1 per gallon and some at half that price. Finally, $6000 was offered for the *Envoy*.[106]

One survivor from this age is the *Charles W Morgan* which was built at New Bedford in 1841 of 351 tons. On her first voyage lasting from 4 September 1841 to 1 January 1845 she brought back 1600 barrels of sperm oil, 800 barrels of whale oil and 10,000lbs of whalebone.[107] Built as a full-rigged ship, she was converted to a barque with double topsails in 1876 and returned with her last catch of whale oil in 1921 after an active life of 80 years. She was preserved under the auspices of Colonel Green in a sand berth at South Dartmouth, Massachusetts, until 1941 when, after six years of neglect through lack of money following his death, she was acquired by the Marine Historical Association and towed to Mystic. Here she has been restored and been given regular attention over the years, so that she now forms an impressive exhibit. The various skilled trades needed to fit out a whale ship and the method of hunting the whale are all displayed ashore in the reconstructed Seaport.

Fig 88. Deck view aboard Charles W. Morgan *in 1964 looking forward to tryworks with skids above them and foremast beyond.* (Author)

Fig 89. The Charles W. Morgan *in her berth at Mystic Seaport in 1964.* (Author)

89

3

SQUARE RIG AND FORE·AND·AFT 1835·1850

INTRODUCTION

In spite of the forces of change that were at work in the shipping industry there were still cargoes to be carried, freights to be earned, new ships to be built and older ones repaired. At scores of small ports, builders and owners might read of gold discoveries at the opposite sides of the world or the launch of some mammoth steamer in their own country, but for them, ships had to be as sturdy and reliable as ever and this meant the repetition of successful designs which had been proved and evolved over the years.

Whatever may be said of the swift clippers and their fast passages, it was the ordinary cargo carriers that formed the core of the shipbuilders' work. As the carrying trade of nations increased in international waters, so did the competitive spirit and the awareness of the economic factors controlling successful participation. In particular it was the attitude of the builders, owners and masters which affected the issue and the manner in which they dealt with the various problems thrust on them, not least being the increasing amount of regulations and legislation. It was certainly a complex field in which ship design was to develop.

An examination of the plans reproduced here indicates that by the beginning of the 1840s a definite trend was emerging for the cargo carrier and that its chief characteristics, when compared with earlier vessels, were less sheer, greater length in proportion to depth and breadth, more balanced ends, flatter floors, and less extremes of curvature in the hull. The plan of the barque *Arab* (1839), reproduced in figure 93, is a good example of the type which was continued throughout the period during which wooden ships were constructed. Meanwhile those built of iron, after first imitating their wooden counterparts, gradually altered to take advantage of the greater length which the new material made possible. The biggest single improvement to the ship's equipment was probably the fitting of purchase levers to the windlass instead of hand-spikes, and this arrangement remained virtually unchanged until the end of commercial sail in the present century. This 'Armstrong Patent' windlass was employed in vessels of up to 1500 tons, although various types of geared capstans were introduced which were especially suitable for large ships. Examples and illustrations were given in *Fast Sailing Ships*, pages 162–63.

Important alterations in the method of measuring tonnage became law in 1836, in which depth was measured for the first time. This tonnage figure became known as 'new measurement', often abbreviated here to 'nm'; the tonnage figure produced by the method it superseded was known as 'old measurement' or 'om'. The ways in which tonnage was measured and its implications in design are fully convered in *Fast Sailing Ships*, pages 104–5 and Appendix I. Basically the result was that excessively deep ships were no longer built and that vessels gradually became longer to compensate for the stowage capacity lost in the reduced depth.

Fig 90. Heaving up the anchor by means of the pump handles fitted to the old style windlass barrel. The combination was called an 'Armstrong patent'. Drawn by T W Ward.

Fig 91. The Armstrong patent windlass stands on the foredeck here, and the main topmast stay, which has split into two to go each side of the foremast, passes close above the windlass barrel. Some of the deck cargo of lumber has come adrift and fallen to leeward, but the deck fittings and houses can be clearly seen. This is the Emigrant *in the River Avon, Bristol, in 1905, when she was almost sixty years old. Built at Bremen in 1846, she was subsequently re-built in 1877. She had dimensions (in 1905) of 131.6ft × 32.1ft × 20.1ft and 567 tons net. (Nautical Photo Agency)*

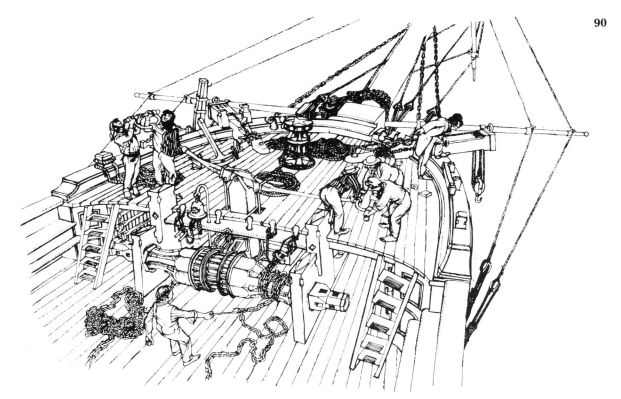

91

JAMES GEDDIE AND THE *ARAB*

In Morayshire, the River Spey enters the sea by the quiet village of Kingston and a short distance up the river, on rising ground, lies the larger community of Garmouth. It was at Kingston that the Geddie family were prominent shipbuilders for much of last century; other builders were William Kinloch, John Duncan and Young Brothers. Many ships are ascribed to James Geddie and his son, but several branches of this family bore the same Christian name. James (1820–95) emigrated to South Africa in 1879; William Geddie (1785–1863) was a shipbuilder and had a son James (1809–82).

A portfolio in the Science Museum contains the original plans of thirty-eight vessels built by the Geddie family and were donated by James Geddie, son of James (1820–95). The majority of the plans undoubtedly represent vessels built by his father, but several drawings in an older style and with a watermark of 1818 must be the product of an earlier generation. (See figure 38.) Through the kindness of B W Bathe, who was then in charge of the Water Transport Collection, it has been possible to study these plans in detail which now permits one to speak authoritatively about the Geddie ships. The drawings are all painstakingly done in ink on cartridge or Whatman paper, usually to ⅜in or ½in scales, with the spar dimensions carefully inscribed, proving that James Geddie was an artistic and methodical man. The drawings contain

Fig 92. A barque on the beach at Swansea. Although she has a flying jibboom rigged out and there are either stunsail booms or the gear for setting them on lower and topmast yards on the fore, and topmast and topgallant yards on the main, no fore royal is crossed because the topgallant mast is too short. There is a timber port for loading into the 'tween decks and another for loading into the hold. She has a full entrance with long straight sides and a deep hull. Inside her is a double-ended smack or trow with outside rudder, and further up the beach is a clinker-built lighter. (Robert S Craig)

Fig 93. Arab. Redrawn and reconstructed by the author from tracing made of builder's plan in the Science Museum, London. Built in 1839 by James Geddie at Garmouth. Dimensions scaled off plan: 91ft 2in × 24ft 1in × 17ft 0in (approx); tonnage was 269. Reconstruction, based on plan of deck beams and a few principal deck fittings in elevation: deck layout, elevation of each deck fitting.

Fig 94. Arab. Sail plan reconstructed by the author from spar dimensions written on builder's lines plan. No lengths were given for royal yards and those for the topgallant yards were listed as 14ft which looked far too short. So, this length was assigned to the royals and new lengths calculated for the topgallants which came out at 24ft. These agreed with Hedderwick's proportions. The following were not given in the builder's list and were calculated by Hedderwick's rules: all diameters of masts and yards; rake of masts; lengths of lower mast and topmast heads; length of jibboom housing; yardarm lengths. All sail outlines reconstructed as well as all stunsail booms and yards. No staysails set from mizzen as it was deemed too close to the mainmast. Cooke's etching in fig 35 of the barque Henry has the mizzen close to the main.

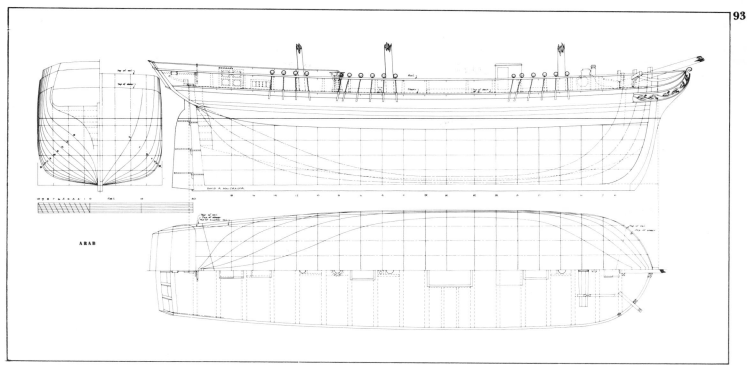

ARAB

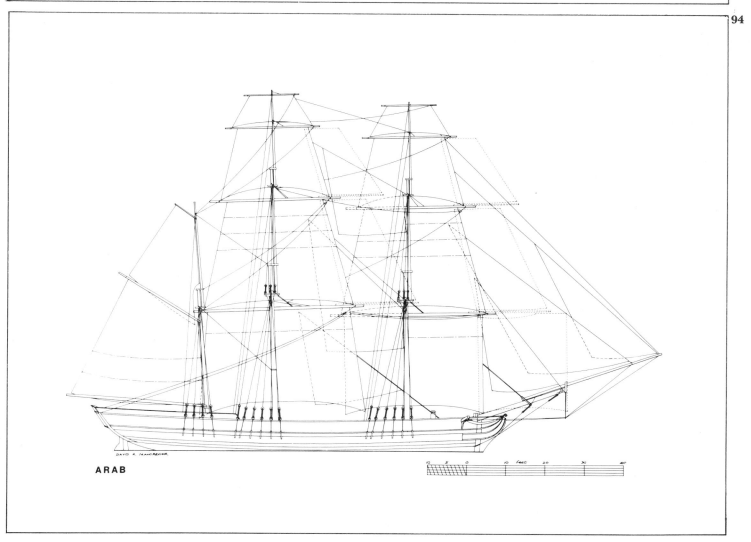

ARAB

many personal touches, such as the steering wheel shown in perspective. The hull-form of the ships as well as the style of draughtsmanship remained constant for some thirty years.[1]

Due to ample supplies of timber which were rafted down the river, Kingston was most prolific in building brigs and schooners, and several hundred were launched here. The shipbuilding boom of the late thirties was probably responsible for the construction of the barque *Arab* in 1839 in a yard predominantly accustomed to build smaller vessels, but it is not known if she was built on speculation or under contract. (Two other barques built in this yard were *Florence Barclay* in 1866 and *Northern Chief* 1873.) The *Arab* was owned by Wemyss at nearby Fraserburgh and was placed in the Mediterreanean trade, but she was a low-classed ship of only 5 A1. She registered 269 tons and had dimensions, scaled off the plan, of 91ft 2in

Fig 95. This watercolour of the straight-stemmed barque Venus *of Newcastle shows a main and mizzen close together. The absence of a fore royal was common practice. There is a trysail mast with its own small hoops close abaft the main, but the artist has failed to colour it above the gaff, although it is drawn. (Parker Gallery)*

Fig 96. Indianer. Outline sail plan reproduced from plan drawn by G Hillmann and dated Copenhagen 1861. The skysail masts with their long pole heads are stepped abaft the royal masts. The lines plan shows she is no clipper. (MacGregor Collection)

(length from fore part of stem to after part of sternpost aloft), 24ft 1in (moulded beam), and 17ft 0in (approx depth of hold). Her hull was appreciably deeper than Geddie's other vessels of this period although she had nicely formed lines with a fine run. *Arab's* plan was originally drawn in the same style as the *Violet's* (figure 134), but has been redrawn to provide a better comparison with other plans in this book (figure 93).

The *Arab* has a flush deck of conventional arrangement. The galley, forecastle scuttle, cathead, pumps and capstan are reconstructed but other fittings are traced from the original as also the deck beams on plan. Although no boats are drawn, the longboat would have been stowed on top of the main hatch and the gig slung from stern davits or from iron davits on the quarter. A good illustration of a barque of this date may be seen in a photograph of the *Santiago* which was built in Guernsey in 1845 and measured 255 tons (figure 114).

The sail plan of the *Arab* (figure 94) was developed from the spar dimensions listed on the shipyard plan and shows a variation on the accepted form of barque rig, which has already been referred to in Chapter Two when tracing the story of the barque. In this sail plan, spar diameters, mastheads and yardarms are reconstructed from Peter Hedderwick's rules in his *Treatise on Marine Architecture*.[2] The closeness of the mizzen to the main makes the *Arab* resemble a snow with the trysail mast stepped rather far aft. Other examples of a somewhat similar nature can be

95

found without having to look far, such as E W Cooke's etching of the barque *Henry* shown in figure 35. No trysail gaffs are listed for the *Arab* and the close spacing of the main and mizzen masts makes the setting of staysails almost impossible, which is why they have been omitted here.

Further east at Peterhead the principal shipbuilders in the forties and fifties were Lunnan & Robertson; they were strongly influenced by Aberdeen fashions and were launching a number of small clipper-bowed craft in the late forties.

ALEXANDER HALL'S SHIPS

At Aberdeen the chief builders were Alexander Hall & Sons, William Duthie Bros (restyled Alexander Duthie & Sons after 1840), Walter Hood & Co (established in 1839), John Ronalds & Co, and Nicol & Reid; but we know most about Hall through the survival of the yard accounts.[3] From the inception of the new measurement tonnage rules in 1836, Hall entered particulars of his ships according to the new system, beginning with the brigantine *Earl of Fife*, yard No 72. The last vessel he measured in this way was *Schomberg*, yard No 195. The *Sea Star*, No 196, was the first vessel measured by the 1854 Act. There was a short-lived boom in shipbuilding throughout the country between 1838 and 1841, and during these few years Hall's

yard received an increase in orders for vessels of all types. Perhaps the order for the clipper schooner *Scottish Maid* was placed as a result of this boom. That many prospective owners were late in taking the decision to order a new ship may be assumed from the fact that more tonnage was launched in 1842 than in any other year of this boom period, although in some parts of the country the shipbuilding boom had already collapsed by then. In this year Hall launched ten ships totalling 2652 tons averaging 265 tons per ship. This average size was not exceeded until 1848 when six ships averaged 286 tons. The total annual tonnage of 1842 was not exceeded until 1855 when 4136 tons were launched. In 1844, which was a particularly slack year, only three ships totalling 450 tons were built. After 1849, the average tonnage jumped from 294 in that year to 418 in 1850, because the size of ships was on the increase in the fifties.

In Chapter Four of *Fast Sailing Ships*, there are two lists which separate clippers from cargo carriers for the period before 1850, and the hull-form of some of these cargo ships is assessed. In particular the *Thomas Arbuthnot* and the *Glentanner* are compared. These two ships were built in 1841 and 1842 respectively and were the biggest vessels built by Hall in these years. Their dimensions indicate that their proportion of beams to length was approximately 5 to 1, which would doubtless assist their sailing abilities. Figure 102 in *Fast Sailing Ships* illustrates *Thomas Arbuthnot*'s full-bodied hull.

96

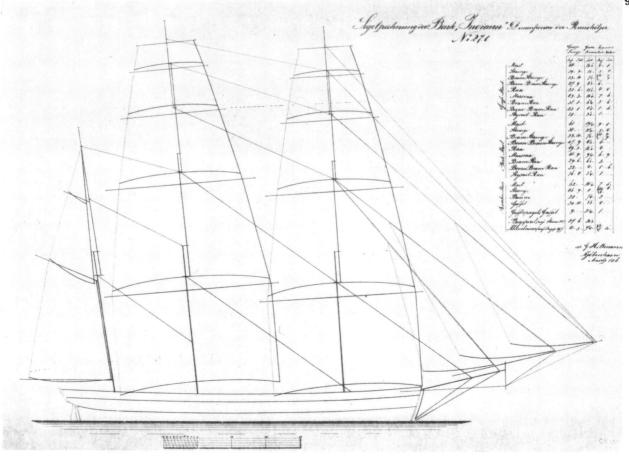

97

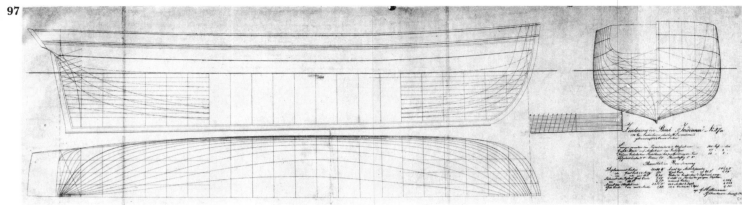

98

An example of the latter's speed is afforded by a passage of 102 days in 1850–51 between Portsmouth and Sydney, considered 'a fine run' at the time. On her return passage, she sailed from Sydney on 3 June 1851 and arrived off Beachy Head on 24 September, 113 days later, although she does not appear to have reached London until 5 October. She had every reason to carry her canvas on this passage as she had on board the first consignment of Australian gold ever to leave those shores – 253oz of it – and her master must have wanted to arrive home before any other ship, a feat which he successfully accomplished.[4] It was reported that some of the crew of HMS *Acheron*, then at Sydney, were supplied to the *Thomas Arbuthnot* to assist her in making a good passage, as many of the latter's crew had deserted for the gold-fields.

The full-rigged ships and barques built by Hall in the forties which were not clippers are shown by their spar dimensions to have been very lofty with large sail plans: the ships *Thomas Arbuthnot* and *Humayoon* carried skysails on all three masts; the barques *Ann Smith*, *Lord Western* and *Trio* had skysail masts and yards on fore- and mainmasts; and the barque *Cynthia* carried two skysail masts, although no yards are listed. This trend towards very lofty masts stepped on short hulls was in vogue in Europe until about 1850, and was recorded by many marine artists in their paintings. Such an example of an unidentified barque from a painting by William Clark is reproduced in figure 98 and shows the vast number of flying kites set, which include a main moonsail, a ringtail, watersails under the lower stunsail and the spanker, and no less than three sails on the mizzen above the big jackyard topsail. The date would probably be the late 1840s.

A comparison of *Thomas Arbuthnot*'s spar dimensions with those scaled off the sail plan of Peter Hedderwick's 500-ton ship (figure 20) reveal that the mast heights were about the same but that the former was somewhat squarer aloft, with longer yards all the way up. John Wards's lithograph of a full-rigged ship running before the wind

Fig 97. Indianer. *Lines plan reproduced from plan drawn by G Hill-mann dated Copenhagen 1861, and photographed from original at Mariners Museum, Newport News. Full-bodied hulls such as this needed big sail plans to drive them along. (MacGregor Collection)*

Fig 98. In this oil painting by William Clark (1803—83) of an uniden-tified barque, a number of flying kites are set: watersail, moonsail, ringtail, mizzen royal and skysail set from gaffs, watersail under the spanker boom. The ports in the bulwarks are painted green inside, and so is the inside of the house on the poop with its coved sides. (Private Collection)

Fig 99. Princess Royal *was a popular name for ships in 1841 after the birth of Queen Victoria's daughter. This ship was built at Aberdeen in that year by Alexander Duthie. Inventory from collection of I M Barl-ing.*

99 **For Sale by Private Contract,**

THE SPLENDID FAST-SAILING SHIP,

PRINCESS ROYAL, A1

637 467/1000 Tons N. M. and 564 23/94 Tons O. M.

Inside & 30ft outside

Length 132 ft. 5/10 —Breadth 27 ft. 4/10 ×—Depth 20 ft. 4/10; built at Aberdeen in 1841, of the best seasoned Materials, under particular inspection. This fine Vessel was built expressly for the India Trade, and has beautiful Accommodations for Passengers; she has made Two Voyages, and has just com-pleted the second out and home to Madras and Calcutta in less than nine months, eighty-three days of which were expended in port. She is well found in Stores of every description.

Now lying in the St. Katharine's Docks.

Hull, Masts, Yards, Standing and Running Rigging, with all faults as they now lie.

INVENTORY.

ANCHORS.		COOPER'S STORES.	1 looking glass
1 best bower	300 ditto tacks		2 sets of castors
1 small ditto	6 bags nails	1 deep sea lead reel	4 candlesticks
1 sheet	1 cross cut saw	1 hand lead	1 cabin bell
1 stream	1 pair copper scissors	1 ditto line	2 pair snuffers
2 kedges	1 pitch pot	1 log	1 foul plate basket
1 grapline	1 grindstone and trough	1 ditto reel	2 bread baskets
	Hatch bars complete	1 ditto line	10 table knives and forks
	Tarpaulin ditto	3 ditto glasses	12 desert ditto ditto
CABLES.	Handspikes ditto	1 hour ditto	1 knife box
	Capstan bars ditto	1 speaking trumpet	30 cups and saucers
1 best bower chain	6 padlocks	1 signal lanthorn	10 table spoons
1 small ditto ditto	6 hen coops	2 hand ditto	12 tea ditto
1 stream	1 oak plank	1 ensign	17 desert ditto
1 hawser	2 bundles oakum	1 jack	12 egg ditto
1 towline	1 ship's skeet	1 burgee	26 ditto desert ditto
1 warp	24 chain hooks	1 set Marryat's signals	2 ditto gravy spoons
	7 spare sheets of copper	1 ditto Telegraph Vocabulary	2 ditto ladles
SAILS.	2 pair grains	1 spy glass	29 tumblers
	2 shank painters	2 copper pumps	37 wine glasses
1 flying jib	3 pair boat's gripes	2 brass binnacles	2 champagne ditto
2 standing ditto	Quantity of old iron	1 pair steelyards	36 claret ditto
1 fore staysail	2 crow bars	1 set weights and scales	16 liqueur ditto
2 ditto topmast staysails		1 bread sieve	8 salts
3 foresails		4 paint brushes	2 pickle glasses
2 ditto topsails	BOATSWAIN'S STORES.	1 ship's bell	1 water decanter
2 ditto topgallant sails		6 paint pots	75 table cloths
1 ditto royal	2 cat ladles	6 oil cans	1 tureen and ladle
1 fore spencer	3 top ditto	2 shark hooks	4 sauce tureens ladles and
1 fore and aft mainsail	3 iron-bound snatch ditto	1 patent filters	stands
3 main topsails	1 signal halyard	1 medicine chest, with medicine	132 plates
2 ditto topgallant sails	2 fish hooks, runner, and tackle		8 dishes
1 ditto royal	1 fish pendant		2 corner dishes
2 mizens	Belaying pins, complete	COOPER'S STORES.	2 pie ditto
2 ditto topsails	6 double blocks		56 towels
1 ditto topgallant sail	6 single ditto	3 butts	2 funnels
1 ditto royal	2 bumkin ditto	27 puncheons	1 brass cock
2 square mainsails	2 burton ditto	2 harness casks	6 dish covers
1 wind sail	1 spunyarn, winch, and bolt	1 oil cask	1 wash hand bason
2 lower steering sails	1 winch handle	1 vinegar cask	2 black jacks
4 topmast ditto	Mats for rigging	2 steep tubs	1 water jug
3 topgallant ditto	2 serving mallets	3 mess kids	2 coffee pots
3 ditto royals	1 dozen scrapers	1 nun buoy	1 pepper mill
3 jolly boat's sails	½ dozen marline spikes	18 buckets	2 tea pots
1 quarter deck awning	24 hooks and thimbles		6 milk ditto
1 poop ditto	2 tar brushes	COOK & CABIN STORES.	1 coffee mill
6 bolts canvas	2 ditto buckets		4 butter boats
12 bundles twine	2 cask tar	1 patent troop's hearth	2 cabin lamps, with 10 chim-
	½ barrel black varnish	1 Winchester's patent cabouse	nies and 2 shades
CARPENTER'S STORES.	4 pair can hooks	house	1 cork screw
	1 ditto man ropes	1 shovel	1 hearth brush
1 pump hook	1 ditto side ropes	2 frying pans	1 dust pan
3 ditto brakes	4 cork fenders	2 tormentors	set of spirit measures
3 ditto spears	6 ballast shovels	5 saucepans	1 meat safe
3 lower boxes	2 deck stoppers	3 stewpans	1 steel
6 pump bolts	6 pair handcuffs	1 cook's axe	
1 sounding rod	12 leg irons	2 steamers	
2 spare topmasts		1 tea kettle	BOATS.
2 ditto lower yards		2 baking pans	
3 ditto topgallant masts	SHIP CHANDLER'S	1 copper ditto	1 long boat
1 ditto topsail yard	STORES.	1 dripping pan	1 pinnace
1 ditto jib boom		3 cabin tables	1 skiff
2 lower steering sail booms	2 brass compasses	3 table covers	1 gig
4 topmast ditto ditto	1 brass hanging compass	3 trays	
4 topgallant ditto ditto	1 wood ditto	2 swinging ditto	
3 royal ditto	1 deep sea lead	2 chairs	
10 steering sail yards	1 ditto line	4 stools	
1 piece pump leather		4 curtains	

The Ship and her Stores to be taken with all faults as they now lie, without any allowance for length, weight, quality, quantity, or any defect whatever.

For further particulars, apply to

HENRY & CALVERT TOULMIN,

8, George Yard, Lombard Street.

probably dates from about 1840 and shows a vessel simi-lar to the *Thomas Arbuthnot* with three skysails set and stunsails out both sides (figure 19).

Some idea of the profitability of a vessel such as this can be had from the account book of the barque *Cynthia*, which I purchased some years ago from a book dealer. This vessel was launched by Alexander Hall in October 1842 and measured 96.2ft × 20.7ft × 16.0ft, 242 tons om and 251 tons nm. The contract price was £2300 and extras added £67 2s 1½d, but the first cost to the owners was £2640, which would have included a basic outfit of equipment and hardware. Her sixty-four shares were divided unequally between four shipowners of Kincar-dine, who retained possession from 1843 to 1852 during which time ten voyages were made to the Mediterranean; the last and eleventh was made to South America. The profit and loss account between construction of the ship and her sale in 1852 may be summarised as follows:

Net profits on 10 voyages	£2914 17s 5d	
less loss	138 13 6	(seventh voyage 1847–48)
	2776 3 11	
owner's credit at sale of ship	929 18 10	(ship actually sold for £1050)
	3706 2 9	
less first cost of ship in 1842	2640 0 0	
TOTAL net profit	£1066 2s 9d	

The first cost of the ship was not actually cleared until the end of the last voyage, but had the loss on the seventh voyage of 1847–48 been replaced by only a small profit of, say, £100, the first cost would have been cleared two years earlier.

Full suits of stunsails were always carried although it is rare to find the lengths of the booms and yards given. An exception was made by Hall in his yard book entries for the barque *Lord Western*, launched in 1840 and measuring 118.4ft × 25.5ft × 19.5ft, 445 tons nm and 530 tons om. She was Hall's first vessel for London registration, and was heavily rigged with a mainmast measuring 127ft 0in from deck to truck, mainyard 56ft 0in and main skysail yard 16ft 0in. Hall's normal practice at this date was to make the lengths of the yards on the mainmast identical to those of the fore, but in the case of the *Lord Western*, the yards on the mainmast are slightly longer. The resulting sail plan prepared from the spar dimensions appears in figure 100: it will readily be noticed how square the stun-sails are, and also the tremendous projection of spars at each end of the hull. The length from the knightheads to the tip of the flying jibboom measures 72ft 0in, which is well over half the length of the ship.

The *Lord Western*'s contract price was £7300 or £13 15s 3d per ton om for building, fitting out and finishing to a class of 9 A1. There was a charge of £25 14s for carving, and the figurehead cost £1 8s 2d to be fitted. Clement Tabor of Essex was the sole owner and it was unusual to find a single individual owning all the sixty-four shares in a ship.

The half-model of the barque *Alexander Hall* has survived and a small photograph of it was reproduced in *Fast Sailing Ships* (figure 102) and reveals, not an extreme clipper as many might have wished from the association of the name, but a bluff-bowed, full-bodied vessel with excellent cargo capacity; in fact, the acme of all that was considered good in the way of construction, strength and profitability.

William Duthie (1789–1861) founded the shipbuilding firm in Aberdeen and his brothers Alexander (1799–1863) and John (1792–1880) took it over in that order. They were building a mixture of brigs, schooners and barques in the 150 to 300 tons range with an occasional ship of larger size. Many were for their own use and several were in the North Atlantic trade; they also sent ships to Peru for guano.

ALEXANDER STEPHEN OF ARBROATH AND DUNDEE

Shipbuilding flourished all down the east coast of Scotland and members of the Stephen family were actively engaged in it; by about 1820, Alexander Stephen (1795–1875) had joined his father William at his Aberdeen shipyard. But in 1828 his father was declared bankrupt through the failure of his eldest son, William, who

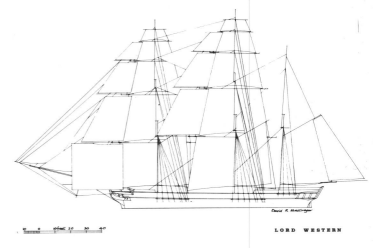

LORD WESTERN

Fig 100. Lord Western. *Sail plan reconstructed by the author from spar dimensions listed by builder, which included stunsail booms and yards. The assistance of James Henderson is gratefully acknowledged in providing these measurements. Reconstruction: hull profile, sail outlines, standing rigging.*

Fig 101. *The brig shown entering Malta harbour is the* Circassian *of 180 tons which William Duthie & Sons built at Aberdeen in 1836. The artist is unknown.* (City of Aberdeen Museums)

Fig 102. *Engraving from Arthur Young's* Nautical Dictionary *to illustrate the entry of BARQUE. This work first appeared in 1846 and was published in Dundee. A list of works consulted is given in the introduction. The barque has a bentinck boom and trysails on fore- and mainmasts — he terms them 'spencer' for each mast.*

101

PLATE III.
BARQUE.

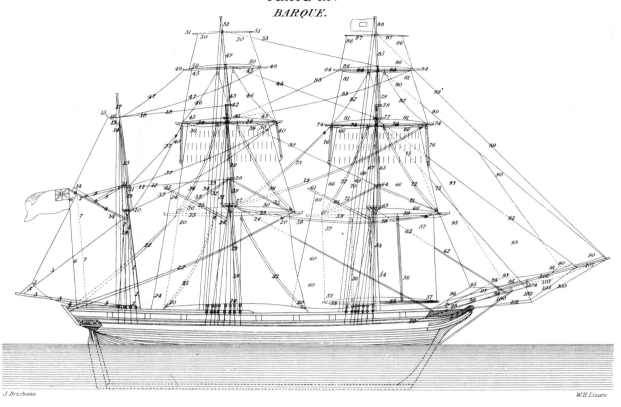

J.Brisbane   W.H.Lizars

NUMERICAL INDEX TO BARQUE.

1 **MIZEN MAST.**
2 Spanker.
3 Spanker Boom.
4 Spanker Sheet and Block.
5 Spanker Boom Topping Lift.
6 Signal Halyards.
7 Spanker Vangs.
(There are also Vangs for the Main and Fore-Spencers, not laid down in Plate.)
8 Spanker Gaff.
9 Peak Halyards.
10 Mizen Cross-trees.
11 Mizen Cap.
12 Mizen Stay.
13 *Mizen Topmast.*
14 Gaff Topsail.
15 Gaff Topsail Gaff.
16 Gaff Topsail Halyards.
17 Mizen Topmast Pole.
18 Mizen Topmast Stay.
19 **MAIN MAST.**
20 Mainsail.
21 Main Clue Garnets.
22 Main Braces.
23 Main Yard.

24 Main Spencer.
25 Main Spencer Gaff.
26 Main Stay.
27 Main Top.
28 Main Cap.
29 *Main Topmast.*
30 Maintopsail.
31 Maintopmast Backstays.
32 Maintopgallant Backstay.
33 Main Royal Backstay.
34 Signal Halyards.
35 Main Lifts.
36 Maintopsail Cluelines.
37 Maintopsail Braces.
38 Maintopsail Yard.
39 Maintopmast Stay.
40 Maintopsail Reef-tackles.
41 Maintopmast Cross-trees.
42 Maintopmast Cap.
43 Maintopgallant Mast.
44 Maintopgallant Stay.
45 Maintopgallant Sail.
46 Maintopgallant Cluelines.
47 Maintopgallant Braces.
48 Maintopgallant Yard.
49 Main Royal Mast.
50 Main Royal.
51 Main Royal Yard.

52 Main Royal Pole.
53 Main Royal Stay.
54 **FORE MAST.**
55 Bentick Boom.
56 Fore Bentick Clue Garnets.
57 Fore Sail.
58 Fore Braces.
59 Fore Yard.
60 Fore Spencer.
61 Fore Spencer Gaff.
62 Fore Stay.
63 Fore Top.
64 Fore Cap.
65 *Fore Topmast.*
66 Fore Topsail.
67 Foretopmast Backstays.
68 Foretopgallant Backstay.
69 Fore Royal Backstay.
70 Signal Halyards.
71 Fore Lifts.
72 Foretopsail Cluelines.
73 Foretopsail Braces.
74 Foretopsail Yard.
75 Foretopmast Stay.
76 Foretopsail Reef-tackles.
77 Foretopmast Cross-trees.
78 Foretopmast Cap.
79 Foretopgallant Mast.

80 Foretopgallant Stay.
81 Foretopgallant Sail.
82 Foretopgallant Cluelines.
83 Foretopgallant Braces.
84 Foretopgallant Yard.
85 Fore Royal Mast.
86 Fore Royal.
87 Fore Royal Yard.
88 Fore Royal Pole.
89 Fore Royal Stay.
90 Flying Jib.
91 Flying Jib Sheet.
92 Jib Stay.
93 Jib.
94 JibSheet.
95 Foretopmast Staysail.
96 Foretopmast Staysail Sheet.
97 Ridge-ropes.
98 Bowsprit.
99 Bowsprit Shrouds.
100 Bobstay.
101 Martingale Back-ropes.
102 Martingale.
103 Martingale Stays.
104 Bowsprit Cap.
105 Footrope of Jib-Boom.
106 Jib-Boom.
107 Flying Jib-Boom.

NOTE.—The fore, main, and mizen masts of a SHIP are rigged in the same way as the fore and main masts of a *Barque*, but on a *ship's* cross-jack yard, which is the lowest yard on the mizen mast, no lower square sail is generally set. A BRIG is rigged in the same way as the fore and main masts of a *barque*, but the fore-and-aft sail called a *spencer*, which is set upon or abaft the main mast of a barque, in a *brig* or in a *snow*, gets the name of a *fore-and-aft mainsail*, or a *trysail*, respectively.

103

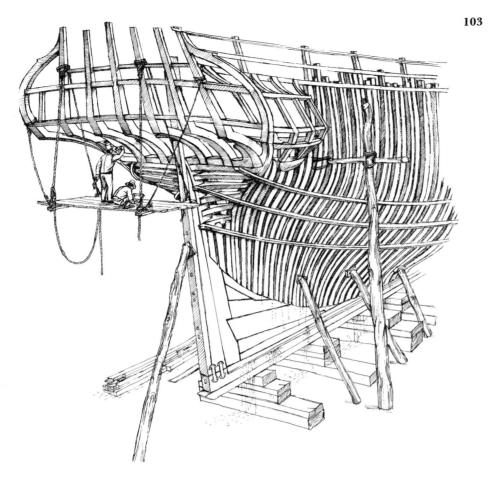

105

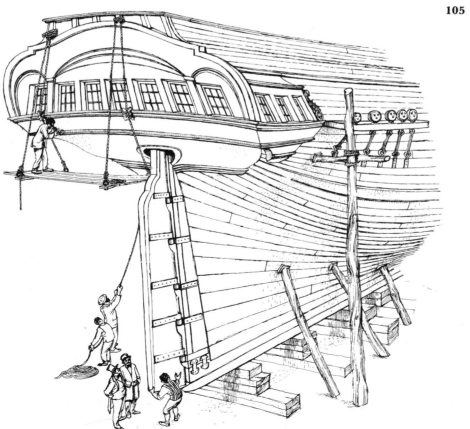

Fig 103. Drawing by T W Ward showing the framing at the stern for a ship or barque based on contemporary plans. This shows how the counter timbers rested on the wing transom and the great load it received.

Fig 104. Stern of a wooden ship in drydock photographed in the late 1840s by the Rev Calvert Jones. There is much to interest one here such as the mouldings on the stern, the long quarter gallery and what appear to be lids to stern windows.

Fig 105. As Fig 103 but from the starboard quarter with the planking on and the stern moulding and quarter gallery in place. Drawn by T W Ward.

was building ships at Arbroath, and Alexander took over his father's Aberdeen yard, renaming it Alexander Stephen & Sons. In 1830 he moved to Arbroath, into the yard previously occupied by his elder brother William, where he built thirty-three vessels in the years 1830–43, the general size ranging from 100 to 220 tons. Most of the vessels built were brigs and schooners, but there were four barques, and one full-rigged ship of 402 tons.[5]

Alexander Stephen commented in his diary on his activities during 1837:

Shipbuilding has on the whole been tollarabble [sic]. I have had for D [avid] Grant of 197 tons, masts, spars and ironwork for rigging and blocks as usual, £10.7 per ton. The *Hamille Mitchel* 167 tons compleat for sea £2045. The *Ann* to be launched of 206 tons, masts, spars and blocks £10 16s per ton. Copper fastened the whole three vessels. I have 20 apprentices, 12 jurnimen [sic], 4 sawers, 3 joiners and 3 blacksmiths and 2 boatbuilders and 1 blockmaker. I have paid for yellow pine 1s 7d; red pine 2s 1d; elm 1s 11d; Stettin oak 1s and 1s 2d free on board. The price of ships this year has rather advanced on the whole. I am about to erect 6 horse power steam engine in my yard to drive circular saws, grind stone, smith forges, block and smith's turning laths, and grind stone, and steam planks in stove. The Dundee Railway comes through my yard.[6]

The *David Grant* was a snow, the *Hamille Mitchell* a schooner, and the *Anne* a barque. These spellings accord with those given in Alexander Stephen & Sons' history and *Lloyd's Register of Shipping*.

Alexander Stephen moved to Dundee in 1843 and continued there for the next fifty years. In 1849 he erected a roof over one of his building slips which measured 170 feet long and 46 feet wide, with a height of 55 feet at the centre and 40 feet at the sides. The cost was about £450. This would allow vessels built under it to obtain an extra year's class at Lloyd's Register. The following year, he was ambitious enough to open a yard on the Clyde at Kel-

104

vinhaugh and work began there in 1851, although the first ship was not launched until the following year. Alexander Stephen was an energetic and capable man, and sufficiently far-sighted to adopt iron shipbuilding in his Clydeside yard from the start.

At his Dundee yard he built the barque *Asia* on speculation in 1847, but being unable to secure a purchaser was obliged to send her to sea on his own account. He finally sold her in 1850 for £5000. She registered 548 tons nm and was the first vessel he had built of more than 400 tons; yet in the same year he sold the *Amazon* of 667 tons om to Somes Brothers of London for a price of £18 per ton, complete and ready for sea at a class of 16 A1.[7] Alexander Stephen confirms this trend towards larger vessels, by writing in his diary: 'A leaning to build larger vessels than formerly has been growing of late throughout the country.'[8] In the four years 1844–47, ten vessels were built in his Dundee yard with an average tonnage of 250; in the following four years, 1848–51, six vessels were constructed with an average tonnage of 530. The end of the forties marked another important step for Stephen, as it was in 1848 that he sold his first ship to such a far-away port as London, all his previous vessels having been sold to local owners at Dundee, Arbroath and Aberdeen, apart from a few to Glasgow.[9]

The whole-hull model of the *Ann Miln* in the Dundee Museum indicates the probable shape of ships and barques built at Dundee in the thirties and forties. This ship was constructed in 1841 by Thomas Adamson and the large model was made to a scale of ⅜in to 1ft by his apprentice, Robert Simpson, later of Brown & Simpson. I took off the lines in June 1961. The hull of this ship is deep with wall sides above very rounded, slack bilges; the entrance is short, full and convex, but the run is longer with very square quarters in order to support a broad, square stern. The bulwarks are six feet high and so the full poop and topgallant forecastle do not project above the rail. The headrails are concave on plan as they sweep up to the figurehead; if straight, they would have projected unnecessarily outside the stem.

In the *Ann Miln's* model, the break of the poop is decorated with pointed arches, which is an unusual feature since, although the Gothic revival was all the rage ashore, classical mouldings and pilasters are generally found aboard sailing ships. The model of the extreme tea clipper *Spindrift* also has pointed arches around her deckhouse.

T & J BROCKLEBANK AND OTHER SHIPBUILDERS OF NORTH-WEST ENGLAND

At Whitehaven, Thomas and John Brocklebank operated a shipyard which built almost exclusively for their own requirements for trade to Newfoundland, the West Indies, South America and the East. From 1836 to 1849 they constructed a variety of barques, brigs and schooners each year, but the full-rigged ships only appeared at

106

Fig 106. Bow of a wooden ship in drydock photographed by the Rev Calvert Jones in the late 1840s. The number of small oval-section mouldings which together form the hair rail and the bulwark rail are in contrast to the plain rounded mouldings to be seen on the Cutty Sark today.

Fig 107. Susanna, ex-Druid. Sail plan redrawn by the author from tracing made of builder's plan when it was in possession of T & J Brocklebank. Reconstruction: upper deadeyes, shrouds, backstays. Remainder as the original. Schooner built 1838 at Whitehaven.

Fig 108. Oil painting of the Brocklebank ship Tigris, which they built at Whitehaven in 1836 of 422 tons. During the 1860s she was voyaging to Batavia and Manilla. The ship on the right with an American eagle on her stern and an American flag appears to be flying Marryat's code no 2 over 2189 which is the steamer Vesta. All Brocklebank ships of the 1840s probably looked like this. (Merseyside County Museums)

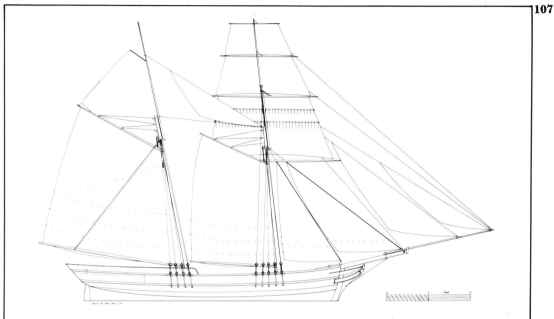

107

108

intervals of two or three years and were much larger in size than the others. The last smack for their own use was built in 1837; the last schooner in 1840; and the last brig in 1845. Much of the change from small to bigger ships stems from the hand of Thomas Fisher, who changed his surname to Brocklebank in the mid-forties when he assumed control of the firm. Thereafter the size of individual ships rose, as indeed it did generally throughout the shipping industry. In the four years 1844–47, Brocklebank's launched five vessels of an average tonnage of 423; in the following four years 1848–51, they built three ships of an average tonnage of 571 tons.[10]

The process of building several vessels from the same set of offsets with only minor variations was continued during the 1840s. For instance the schooners *Susanna* ex-*Druid* (built 1838, yard No 118), *Industry* (built 1840, No 122), and *Rowland Hill* (built 1844, No 130), with tonnages varying between 63 and 65, were all built from the same offsets and had the same spar dimensions. A sail plan, traced from the Brocklebank original, is given in figure 107. Three other vessels similarly treated were the barques *Horsburgh* (built 1838, yard No 116), *Santon* (built 1839, No 117), and *Aden* (built 1839, No 119). Nos 117 and 119 had similar spar dimensions but those of No 116 were a little shorter. All three were built from the offsets of No 116, but the number of deadflats varied, *Aden* having five.[11] The latter traded to China for twenty years like their *Patna* but neither made any record passages. Both were sold in 1868. I have listed all their passages made from 1847 in my recent edition of *The Tea Clippers*.

The *Patna* (built 1842 of 362 tons yard No 127) had this entry amongst the particulars in the builder's yard book: '...the moulds of No 125 and 126 were used for the vessel with this alteration, she had...additional flat frames, seven in number and the Room and Space widened ½ inch making the Space 2–2½ inches Room and Space'.[12] No 125 was *Valparaiso* and No 126 was *Lannercost*. The third regular China trader built in the 1840s was the *Crisis* of 395 tons om and 426 tons nm, built in 1847. She is reputed to have made a fast passage of 95 days from Shanghai to Liverpool in 1853–54, but the date of departure is in doubt by a month.

Any lines plans of Brocklebank ships examined for the period 1820–50 show very similar hull-form which any offsets that have been plotted confirm, only the amount of deadrise varying slightly. The vessels listed above were therefore probably a cross between the barquentine *Bonanza* (figure 79) and the *Harold* (figure 109). The latter was built in 1849 and probably represents about the last of the fleet to be designed on arcs of circles. The *Aracan* of 1854 has quite a different hull-form which corresponds to that commonly adopted by most other shipyards.

A lines plan of the *Harold* of 588 tons om and 666 tons nm shows a vessel designed with maximum carrying capacity having a full convex entrance, 25ft of parallel middle body, and a full run especially in the quarters. In the midship section there is appreciable rise of floor with very slack bilges which round up into vertical sides. The deck is flush from stem to stern, and as the fore hatch is abaft the foremast, the only open deck space on which a deckhouse might be situated is between the after hatch and the mizzen. The *Arachne*, built two years later, was stated in the builder's yard book as having an 'improved' model to the *Harold*. Between them came the small flush-decked barque *Petchelee*, yard No 136, built in 1850 with dimensions of 118.8ft × 22.7ft × 17.5ft and tonnages of 393 om and 357 nm.

Although there is no lines plan of *Petchelee* in the Brocklebank archives, the longitudinal section with which is combined the spar and sail plan provides sufficient interest to include it here as figure 110. The draughtsmanship of the hull on the original plan has been traced without any alterations, but some beams had to be re-positioned to suit the foremast. Several obvious deck fittings are omitted such as the fore hatch, a deckhouse or galley, and a steering wheel; the figurehead is also missing. Dimensions of some of the stunsail booms and yards were written on the original and so all such spars with their respective sails have been reconstructed.

There are actually two spar plans of her in the Brock-

109

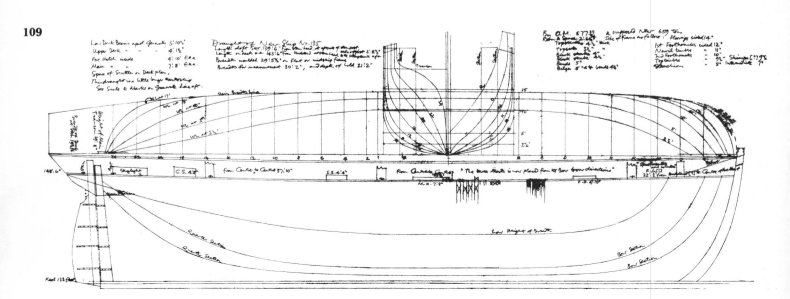

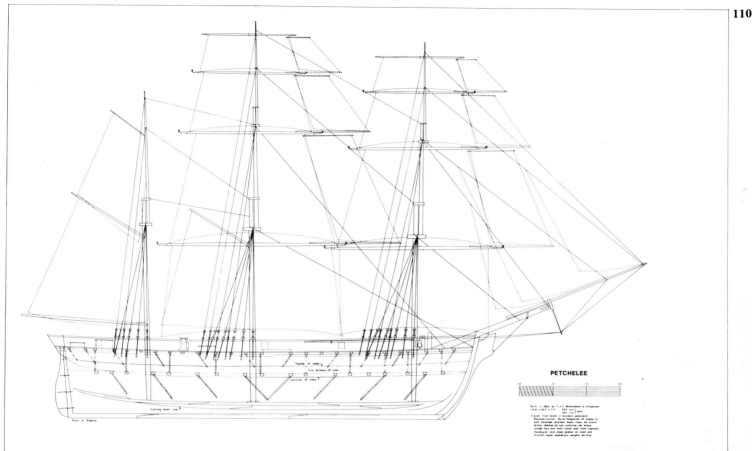

PETCHELEE

Fig 109. Harold. *Lines plan traced from builder's plan in 1955 when in possession of T & J Brocklebank. Built in 1849 at Whitehaven. Original drawn in sepia ink and in an old style; all the notes copied off the original. Measurements listed on plan: length aloft 'Sqr.' 139ft 6in; rake of sternpost 2ft 2½in; length on deck oa 143ft 6in 'from huddend at stem head to the stern plank aft'; breadth moulded 29ft 5½in; depth of hold 21ft 2in. Tonnage 577⁸⁰/₉₄ om; 'supposed new 659 tons'.*

Fig 110. Petchelee. *Longitudinal section, spars, sails and rigging plan. Redrawn in ink by Paul A Roberts from tracing made by the author from plan when in possession of T & J Brocklebank. Built in 1850 at Whitehaven by T & J Brocklebank for their own use, with dimensions of 118.8ft × 22.7ft × 17.5ft and tonnages of 393 om and 357 nm. Reconstruction: all sail outlines, dolphin striker, most of jibboom, all stunsail booms and yards which are drawn dotted, all stays except fore and main lower and main topmast stays, deadeyes and chainplates on main and mizzen.*

lebank archives in the Liverpool Museum, one as a ship and the other as a barque, and the differences between the two are quite interesting, but as she began life as a barque it is uncertain whether the alterations to a ship were ever put into effect, and they may never have got beyond the drawing board stage. The foremast is stepped five feet further forward in the barque rig and is approximately one foot shorter; the mizzen lower mast is now longer so that the heads of the main and mizzen lower masts are level, as indicated by a line on the original. From deck to truck, the mizzen as a barque is one foot shorter than as a ship. Another slight difference concerns the main trysail gaff: as a ship it measures 24ft 0in; as a barque it is only 20ft 6in with a higher peak. The length of the jibboom is unknown because on the Brocklebank plan the edge of the paper occurs just foward of the bowsprit cap. As drawn, the arrangement of the diagonal iron riders is typical of a constructional method that was becoming fairly widespread by this date. The *Harold* had a square stern and probably the *Petchelee* also. With a crew of seventeen, the latter traded at first to India and in 1854 sailed out to Calcutta in 85 days; later she was diverted to the South American trade.

Another Whitehaven shipbuilder was Lumley Kennedy who had been manager of Brocklebank's shipyard for nearly twenty years when he left in 1835 to start his own business. His shipyard was known as Lumley Kennedy & Co and he was the managing partner, being described at that time as a 'draughtsman and mechanic'.

There were eight other partners. The firm built sixty-six vessels of all rigs between 1835 and 1864, but mostly of under 450 tons. In 1857 Kennedy wanted to modernise the yard at a cost of £5000 by erecting sheds for building ships under, by providing steam power and saw mills, and by giving the yard the capacity to build iron ships. This did not take place, presumably because the landlord, the Earl of Lonsdale, from whom Kennedy rented the yard on a yearly basis, did not agree. The lease of the yard and change over from wood to iron were problems which brought about the termination of the business.

A large number of small vessels in the 100 to 275 tons range were produced by this yard in the boom at the end of the 1830s: five in 1837, three in 1838, four in 1839, seven in 1840, and three in 1841. Thereafter not more than two were launched in any one year in the forties and fifties, except for 1852 and 1859 in which three were launched.[13]

Lumley Kennedy & Co's largest ship was the *John o'Gaunt* of 871 tons, built in 1855; but a more typical example was the barque *Ennerdale* of 343 tons nm, built in 1842. She made some voyages to India in the forties and in 1851 took 89 days on a passage between the Downs and Adelaide, having originally sailed from Leith. This was 54 days quicker than the *Symmetry* which had sailed from Leith about a month before. A sail plan of the *Ennerdale*, prepared in 1872 at Whitehaven probably for the purposes of sailmaking, shows double topsails on fore- and mainmasts, single topgallants and royals; the main spencer is to be superseded by mizzen staysails; and the jib is to be divided into two. A plain bow is shown without any head and the stern appears to be square; the foremast is stepped well forward and the bowsprit is a correspondingly long spar measuring 22ft 10in outside the knightheads; the length of the lower yards is 44ft 0in. The arrangement of stays on the mainmast suggests that a fore trysail gaff was originally fitted. Dimensions of the barque in 1872 were 104.7ft × 25.7ft × 17.4ft.[14]

A third builder at Whitehaven in these years was Robert Hardy who launched eighteen ships between 1825 and 1852, most of which were brigs and schooners.

At the National Maritime Museum, Greenwich, is a contemporary mast and rigging plan, drawn to 1/8in scale, of the full-rigged ship *Meg of Meldon*, which is signed: 'W E Parkinson, rigger, Oct 1840'. This ship was built at Liverpool in 1840 of 377 tons om for the India trade and classed 12 A1. The plan shows three-piece masts with four yards crossed on each mast; between the royal and skysail stays there is sufficient space to set sails, but no skysail yards are drawn. Dimensions are written against each spar. The mainyard measures 53ft between the cleats and each yardarm is 2ft 6in; the spanker boom is 40ft. Like Alexander Hall's ships, she is lofty with a long projecting jibboom and flying jibboom, and the height of the mainmast from deck to truck equals the length on the load waterline from cutwater to after part of rudder. The main and mizzen masts are so close together that the yardarm of the main lower yard projects astern of the mizzen lower mast by 1ft.

Joseph Steel & Son were builders at Liverpool and their wooden ship *Jhelum* has survived as a hulk in the Falkland Islands. She was built in 1849 and measured 466 om and nm tons; by 1864 she was listed as a barque of 428 tons with dimensions of 123.1ft × 27.1ft × 18.1ft. In 1870, overloaded and leaky, she put into Port Stanley from Cape Horn, was condemned and sold as a hulk. The photographs obtained by many who have visited the Islands give an excellent idea of the massive timbers employed in shipbuilding, together with the iron knees and pillars then in use. One of the photographs appears as

figure 112. Those who have seen the hulks of sailing vessels around the world will quickly recognise the massive nature of the timber structure.

Between 1831 and 1859, Joseph Steel and his son produced twenty-eight ships but after 1843 the majority were built for their own shipowning interests. The father died in 1854 at the age of seventy-four.[15] It is curious that another of their vessels, the *Tinto*, lasted well into the present century. Built in 1852 of 466 tons om she was at first in the China trade, but by 1913 had found her way into Chilean ownership, and towards the end of the First World War she was sailed back to Norway in 122 days by twenty-eight Germans who came from interned ships. On arrival at Drontheim she was converted into a barge, in which disguise she lasted for some time.[16]

WOODEN SHIPBUILDING IN SOUTHERN AND SOUTH-WESTERN ENGLAND

The traditions of ship design which Henry Adams took from Buckler's Hard were employed again at Poole where he worked in the yard of his brother-in-law, Richard Pinney, as described in the last chapter. There are four plans in the Longstaff Collection at the National Maritime Museum which are very similar in style to the plans of ships built by Edward Adams at Buckler's Hard,

Fig 111. The brigantine Woodville *seen here under full sail was originally built as a brig in 1839 and as such would have had single topsails on both masts and probably also royals, or at least on the main. She is therefore exhibiting a cut-down rig here, and double topsails have replaced the single ones. But the long bowsprit is original and the straight-stemmed heavy hull would be out of fashion when she was photographed. She was built at Whitehaven by Scott with measurements of 75.0ft × 22.8ft × 13.0ft and 136 tons net.*

Fig 112. Hulk of the Jhelum *at the Falklands Islands, photographed in April 1976. The run of the planking helps to indicate her shape, and a small portion of the doubling with which she was once sheathed below the load line has remained, just under the bow port. (Hilton Matthews)*

and it may be that Edward's son Henry drew them and even designed the ships. The plans are of the following vessels:

1836, *Emerald* (bk), 216 tons om
1838, *New Express* (bk), 277 tons om
1843, *Great Britain* (ship), 392 tons om; lengthened 1845 and then measured 467 tons om
*c*1843, unnamed ship, 486 tons om

In general, the shape of the midship section of the Buckler's Hard ships was repeated at Poole, although there was no proportionate increase in breadth and depth. In the above four plans, the ends are more balanced with practically no hollows in the waterlines. As a result of the 1836 tonnage law in which depth was measured for the first time in one hundred and twenty years, these plans show that to obtain greater size, the ship's length was increased but the breadth and depth remained unaltered.

Compare the dimensions of these two ships, both probably designed by the Adams family, but twenty-five years apart:

Name	Dimensions by om rules	Tons om	Tons nm	L/B	L/D
Thalia (1818)	99ft 0in × 28ft 8in × 19ft 9in	357	-	3.45	5.01
Great Britain (1843)	109ft 0in × 28ft 2in × 18ft 0in	392	433	3.97	6.05

A lines plan of *Thalia* appears as figure 31. In the design of *Great Britain*, the big sheer is gone and so are the bluff bows and the very hollow run; the sternpost is almost vertical. Raised quarterdecks are now popular and the construction is of the highest grade. The framework and external planking are of English oak to obtain Lloyd's highest classification and the surveyor at Poole commented that the *New Express*, in conjunction with the barque *Maurition*, was 'considered to be superior to any yet built in this port'.[17]

The *Great Britain* was launched on 3 December 1842, but as she was not completed until January 1843, this year appears as her date of building. The date of her first registration was 20 January. The thickness of her external planking was: 3½in keel to bilge; 3½in, 4½in and 5in bilges; 4½in to 3½in bilge to wales; 5in wales; 2½in topsides. The height in the 'tween decks was 6ft 4in from the top of the lower deck beams, and these beams were only decked over at the forecastle and the after accommodation.

The Lloyd's Register survey report on the *Great Britain* lists the following sails:[18]

2 foresails	2 jibs
2 mainsails	1 flying jib
4 topsails	1 fore trysail
2 mizzen topsails	1 main trysail
4 topgallant sails	2 spankers
2 mizzen topgallant sails	2 lower stunsails
2 royals	4 topmast stunsails
1 mizzen royal	4 topgallant stunsails
2 fore topmast staysails	2 windsails

All sails were made in London by Daniel Burn & Son.

It is obvious that the topsails, topgallants and royals on the fore- and mainmasts were of similar size; also that there were spares for a number of the principal sails. The trysails on fore and main appear to have replaced all staysails between the masts.

113

It is odd that only two years after her launch she was lengthened amidships by the addition of 16ft 7in, which increased her tonnage to 467 om. According to Lloyd's Register, the lengthening was occasioned by no change of ownership or trade, nor in two years had her 12 A1 classification terminated – any of which reasons might have caused this major structural alteration. At this date she was engaged in trade to Montreal.

Many square-rigged ships were below two hundred tons and one such example is the *Steadfast* of 178 tons, built at Bristol in 1839 by Hilhouse, Hill & Co. Her lines show her to have the same basic hull-form as the ships built at Poole. Dimensions figured in pencil on the original draught give length 81ft 1½in, breadth 21ft 8in, and depth 13ft 9in. It is interesting to note that her design is really a scaled-down version of a larger ship, although she is not quite so deep in relation to length. Yet the parallel midships body, which formed such a feature of the Hilhouse ships, is still present. Other plans of Hilhouse ships at this date, such as the *Princess Royal*, show that the full hull-form had been retained, with deep vertical sides, and that the entrance and run were short and full, thus maintaining maximum cargo capacity. An illustration of just such a ship can be seen in the photograph of the barque *Maria*, reproduced as figure 113. She was built at Bristol in 1842 and measured 107.2ft × 24.4ft × 18.6ft and 354 tons; Hilhouse, Hill & Co were not her builders. She appears to have been a flush-decked vessel and the after deckhouse would have contained accommodation for the master, officers, steward, and perhaps two or three passengers.

Fig 113. The street behind this quay in Bristol is The Grove and the photographer must have stood on Redcliffe Parade, just as one can today, to obtain this splendid view of the barque Maria. *She was built in Bristol in 1842 and measured 354 tons. The after deckhouse through which the mizzen passes is not too common for British ships, according to most illustrations. It is worthy of note that* Maria *has a Colling & Pinkney's roller-reefing single topsail on the foremast, but Cunningham's roller-reefing gear on the mainmast. The photographer was probably Fred Little. (Bristol Museum)*

Fig 114. The barque Santiago *of Middlesbrough is here photographed hauled out for repairs. This could not be on the slip just before launching because the topsail yards have Colling & Pinkney's roller-reefing gear which was not introduced until about 1864. There are two men working aloft. (Peter Barton)*

114

107

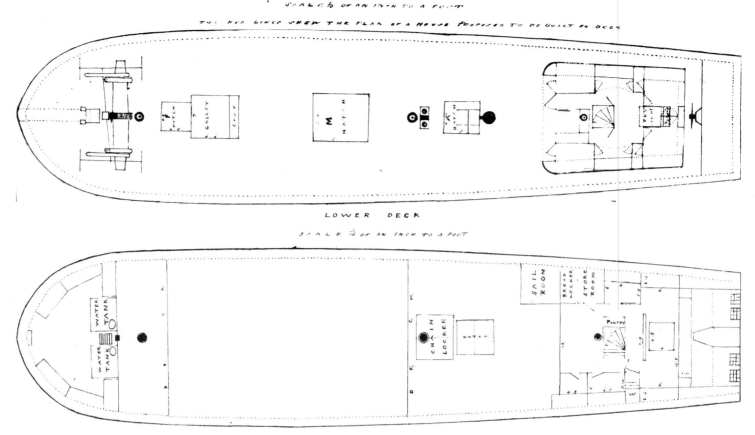

Another typical small barque was the *Santiago* (figure 114), built in Guernsey in 1845 of 255 tons om, which in 1847 rounded Cape Horn on a voyage to Chile. The vast length of the jibboom contrasts oddly with the short deep hull and stumpy foremast; the bentinck boom is hoisted up and the lack of a fore royal is typical of many small barques of the last century. Here the main royal yard is a small spar. Pictures and lists of sails carried in ships of this date suggest that the fitting of fore and main trysails largely replaced the use of any staysails between the masts.

The shipbuilding industry on the Thames gradually contracted during the forties and fifties, as prices for London-built ships remained high, due no doubt to the necessity of importing most raw materials. The firms that had lived by the construction and repair of East Indiamen lost much of their business in 1834 when the old monopoly was revoked; but the Blackwall yard continued to build for the partners, as related in Chapter Four, and many fine passenger frigates were launched throughout the forties. There were a number of engineering firms of high repute and this assisted the building of steamers and marine engines. But many of the yards were fully and profitably occupied in repair work and there were numerous drydocks and slipways for this purpose.

In the Isles of Scilly, Thomas Edwards had launched the 338-ton barque *Monarch* in 1844, and she slid down the ways fully rigged, with topgallant and royal yards crossed, all sails bent, and the hull coppered.[19] This was obviously a practice followed in the Scilly Isles and James Gibson has a photograph of the barque *David Anterson* ready for launching in 1870, with yards crossed and sails bent. This procedure was adopted when the vessel was built on the beach and no harbour existed nearby in which to fit her out, and shipyards in other parts of the country used this method at various times. In 1850 Thomas Edwards launched the barque *Cassiterides* of 414 tons for owners in Scilly. Classed 12 A1, her first voyage was around the Horn to California, presumably to take advantage of the gold boom. More and more British ships were rounding Cape Horn on regular passages to the west coast of South America for copper ore and nitrate, possibly taking out coal or manufactured goods.

One such vessel was the ship *Admiral Moorsom*, built at Whitby in 1827 of 392 tons. She sailed from London for Valparaiso in February 1849 and the sailing instructions handed to her master could have applied to any of the small British ships bound to the Pacific ports. Aboard the *Admiral Moorsom*, Captain Joseph McGill would have opened the letter from his owner and read:

You will cross the line anywhere most convenient between 20° and 28° West and keeping your vessel full run down boldly along the coast of the Brazils. Pass Cape Frio, say from 50 to 150 miles distance; make your westing in low latitudes and cross the Parallel of 40° in 56° and then shaping a course for the entrance of Straits of Magellan, taking care to hold your westing when on the Parallel of 50°S inside the Falkland Islands, shape a course for Staten Island and if convenient pass through the Straits le Maire. Do not go far south of Cape Horn and do not be frightened by the bad name it bears. Make sail on your ship whenever you have a chance. I should have remarked that when you get down to 50°S get all your studding sails unbent and put below except topmast and lower s[tudding] sails. Send down your main topmast and topgt stuns'l booms and unreeve the gear and make your ship as snug as possible.

The weather off the Horn is not as bad as generally represented. The prevailing winds are from SW to NW but the heaviest gales that I experienced blew from South, varying a point each way, say, S by E to S by W.[20]

Fig 115. Two deck plans of Admiral Moorsom *copied from her log-book when under the command of Captain Joseph McGill. In the case of the* Maria *(fig 113) I remarked it was unusual for a British ship to have a large deckhouse aft with the mizzen passing through it; but here is another example. The foremast is close abaft the windlass; then comes fore hatch and galley; next main hatch, mainmast, pumps and after or booby hatch; finally the deckhouse with stairs down to cabins on lower deck. This is actually a proposal and not yet built. There are figures here giving sizes of rooms. (L E Evans)*

Fig 116. Brig. Lines, midsection and frame elevations reproduced from the 10th Annual Report of the Royal Cornwall Polytechnic Society, 1842, plate 4, as submitted by William Hutchins. Brig not identified. Accompanying text given here in full.

The *Admiral Moorsom* finally took her departure from St Helen's Roads, Isle of Wight, on 26 February 1849; she was off Tierra del Fuego on 23 May and reached Valparaiso on 17 June, 111 days after leaving the Isle of Wight.

The hull-form and innovations in construction of a brig which appeared in the Royal Cornwall Polytechnic Society for 1842, are quoted here in full and the accompanying drawings are reproduced in figure 116. It is certainly rare to find such detailed information about a mere merchant brig of 271 tons, and the frame elevation is particularly valuable. I should like to acknowledge the assistance received from Mr H L Douch of the Royal Cornwall Institution in obtaining the report.

THE MODEL OF A MERCHANT VESSEL
By Mr William Hutchins
To which the Society's Gold Medal was awarded

The mode of framing in this model was different from that usually adopted in the Mercantile Navy, as to the shifts of timber, which are so arranged as not to have any butts in the same range of the square body, nearer than every fourth timber; this arrangement, which may be readily seen on the drawing of the disposition of the frame, increases the strength of the vessel very considerably, especially for taking the ground, as three timbers in every four, must cross the keel as floors.

The after body is framed without transoms; by this system the upper and lower stern is connected much better than by the old system, which was evidently a very bad one, as all the counter timbers were stepped on the wing transom, which also received the ends of the bottom plank, and thus became the only connection between the upper and lower stern, and often proves to be insufficient, as a heavy sea striking the

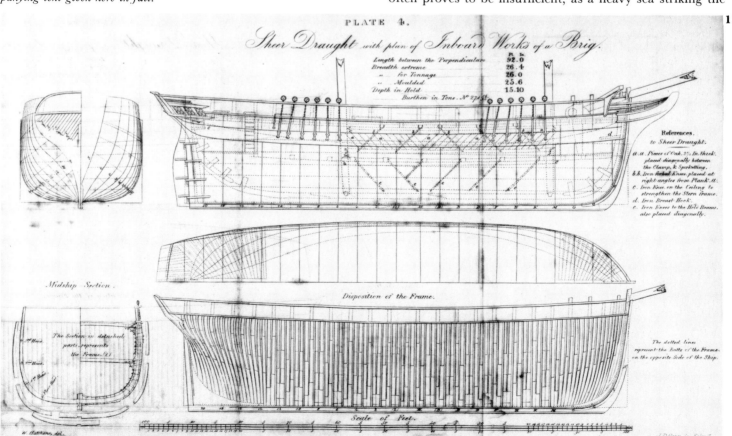

PLATE 4.

Sheer Draught with plan of Inboard Works of a Brig.

	Ft. In.
Length between the Perpendiculars	92.0
Breadth extreme	26.4
" for Tonnage	26.0
" Moulded	25.6
Depth in Hold	15.10
Burthen in Tons. No 271

Midship Section.

Disposition of the Frame.

Scale of Feet.

117

118

vessel in the stern frequently causes a leakage there, water finding its way immediately into the cabin, and endangering the safety of the ship and cargo. The proposed system effectually remedies this evil, as it firmly connects the whole stern throughout, and gives a squarer fastening, and consequently better security for the plank in the run.

In the profile drawing of in board work, is shewn a suggestion for diagonal ceiling between the upper deck clamp and spicketting, the object of which is to prevent the hogging of the ship; the iron knees are also placed diagonally in order that their bolts may be distributed into different timbers, for when all the bolts of a knee go through one timber, that timber is greatly weakened, and frequently splits the whole of its length, and when the outer plank is removed, these timbers through which the bolts are driven, frequently present that appearance, especially in the upper part of the ship where the scantling is small. This diagonal arrangement forms a complete truss frame. *See Plate 4.*

The extent to which Mr Hutchins' plan was adopted would be interesting to discover, but many such projects appear to fall on deaf ears. Diagonal iron trussing was certainly in use and was soon insisted upon by Lloyd's Register, but framing the after body without a wing transom was another matter in the days of square sterns.

SHIPBUILDERS IN CANADA

Of the increasing number of ships built in Canada for British registry, the Quebec shipyard of George Black played a prominent part, because fifty of their fifty-four vessels were destined for British owners. The yard was operating from 1819 to 1846 and a total tonnage of 23,645 was the result. Situated at Cape Cove, the yard lay immediately under Wolfe's monument on the Plains of Abraham. George Black seldom built for his own account and never undertook ship repairing which was a stand-by for many yards. His last ship, the *Omega*, built in 1846 of 1278 tons, was also his biggest; his son, George, built for three more years until the yard closed down and was taken over by W H Baldwin. George Black Snr died in 1854 at the age of seventy-six.[21]

Fig 117. Ships lying at the Cattle Pier in Cossack Bay, Balaclava, from a photograph taken in March 1855 by Roger Fenton. The ship in the foreground bears the figure '11' on the white band of her painted ports at both bow and stern. In October 1855, transport No 11 was the St. Hilda. This ship was built in 1849 at Quebec, was of 791 tons nm, and was owned in Liverpool by Nicholson. The ship in the photograph could well be her. The topgallant masts here have been sent down and the lower yards cock-billed; there is a full-length female figurehead standing. Several masts of other ships are of the polacre type, without tops but with fidded topgallant masts; these include a mast on the left, and a lofty mast between the main and mizzen masts of ship No 11. (Library of Congress)

Fig 118. The barque Tay taking in sail on the Clyde, as pictured by William Clark in 1844. She was built in 1832 by John Owens at Saint John, New Brunswick, and measured 512 tons. There are skysail gunter poles fidded abaft the royal masts; the flag at the fore truck is a white 'S' on a blue ground. There are topsail and topgallant gaffs on the mizzen. (Richard Green Gallery)

The emphasis in the yard was always on square rig and only three schooners were ever built: *Julia* in 1825, *Lion Hill* in 1828, and *Thomas Tucker* in 1830. There was a single brigantine, the *John Brenner* of 1827 for Quebec owners. There were only five brigs, of which the *Eleanor* (1821) was the largest with a tonnage of 271 register. Of two steamers, the PS *Royal William* built in 1831 of 364 tons achieved fame by her crossing of the Atlantic under steam in 1833 between Nova Scotia and Cowes – a crossing which has largely been ignored by historians.

Of the square rigged vessels produced by George Black, eleven barques were built of which the *Junior* of 1845 was the biggest with a tonnage of 677 and dimensions of 128ft 0in × 28ft 0in × 20ft 0in, being first registered in Liverpool; thirty-six full-rigged ships were built of which the *Omega* of 1846 was the largest with a tonnage of 1278 and dimensions of 156.8ft × 33.3ft × 24.9ft. Of the other full-rigged ships, only the *Theodore* of 1849 exceeded 1000 tons being of 1064 tons. In the 1820s, the size was mostly in the 300 to 400 tons region with the *Onondoga* of 568 tons in 1829 being by far the largest; in the thirties, the size was on the increase, seven ships of over 600 tons, one of 746 tons (*Jessie Logan* of 1836), and one of 876 tons (*Mangalore* of 1837).

Up to 1831, the ports of first registry were predominantly London, Waterford, Cork and Dublin, but from 1832 Liverpool takes over as the first port of registry.

George Black launched more vessels in 1829 than in any other year, namely 2433 tons in all with seven vessels; in 1840 he produced three vessels totalling 2032 tons, but generally he built only one or two vessels per year. As his rate of production gradually declined, that of other Quebec yards increased, such as the Jeffreys, John J Nesbitt, David Gilmour, John Munn, and Thomas H Oliver. During the forties, ships of over 1000 tons were regularly being launched from Canadian shipyards at Quebec, New Brunswick, Nova Scotia and other areas.

Saint John was the principal shipbuilding centre in New Brunswick and from the beginning of the 1820s the business of building tonnage for export increased rapidly, with Glasgow, Greenock, Liverpool and London taking the majority of vessels. Prior to 1850, the highest numbers of ships were launched in the years 1825 and 1840 with totals of 19 and 34 respectively. The totals in numbers and tonnage may be summarised for these three decades as follows:

SHIPBUILDING AT SAINT JOHN 1820–1850[22]

Years	Number of Vessels	Total Tonnage
1820–29	81	25,833
1830–39	155	75,801
1840–49	162	111,680

The boom and depression experienced in Great Britain was echoed in Canadian shipyards as orders increased or collapsed, and times were hard in the mid-1840s. At Saint John there were a number of prominent shipbuilders such as John Owens who built 53 vessels in the years 1820–51; William James and Isaac Olive and their sons from 1818 until the 1880s; John Haws who constructed 32 vessels in the years 1824–49; William and James Lawton who built 25 vessels in the period 1832–45; George Thomson whose

Phebe of 1834 was the first ship of over 800 tons and who died in 1841 after building about 27 vessels; he is said to have taught William and Richard Wright the art of shipbuilding, and these two brothers constructed 30 vessels in the years 1830–55 with an average tonnage of 972, and their largest ship before 1850 was the *Dundonald* of 1372 tons, launched in 1849. This ship fetched £11,500 at Liverpool in 1854.

The first ship of over 1000 tons to be built at Saint John was the *York*, constructed in 1839 by the brothers Francis and Joseph Ruddock as the first vessel to be launched from their yard. They died in 1881 within a few days of each other, having altogether built 41 full-rigged ships and 2 barques, with an average tonnage of 1002, their last vessel having been built in 1868. The shipbuilder James Smith, who achieved fame because he built the *Marco Polo*, was not related to the other Smith families in Saint John. His first vessel was the barque *Ocean Queen* of 235 tons built in 1836 and he built schooners and brigs as well as two ships of over 1000 tons in the 1840s. The barque *Burita* built in 1854 was his last vessel but his son, James Thomas, continued in the yard, the father dying during the 1870s. John W Smith was another builder of the same surname. Altogether 14 ships of over 1000 tons each were sent afloat by Saint John yards before the end of 1849, of which the largest was the *Forest Monarch* of 1542 tons, constructed in 1847 and lost two years later.[23]

During the 1840s, newly-built Canadian ships were sold at £7 to £12 per ton depending on the quality of the timber and the extent of the outfit. In the case of the Wright Brothers, Richard was often master on the trans-Atlantic crossing and acted as his own agent for selling the ship, thus cutting out the middleman's commission. To be builder, master and owner reduced expenses considerably.

Ships built in Canada somewhat resembled American ships in their size, hull-form, type of timber employed, speed, good qualities at sea and, owing to their comparative cheapness, proved valuable to British shipowners who were trying to resist the growing competition of American shipping, which was attempting to dominate the worldwide carrying trade. The Canadian shipyards turned out much larger vessels than could be built in Great Britain where much of the timber had to be imported, and these large Canadian ships were ideal in the booming freight markets at the end of the forties and the early fifties.

SOME BRIGS COMPARED

In spite of the hundreds of brigs that were built, there is little scope for selection due to the paucity of complete sets of plans, and although lines plans or sail plans do exist they rarely appear to combine in one vessel. Indeed few complete sets have been discovered outside those presented in this work.

The plans of the brig *Black Prince* (figures 120 and 121), built at Maryport in 1838, make an interesting comparison with those of the *Neilson* (figures 32 and 33), which was launched fourteen years earlier at Buckler's Hard.

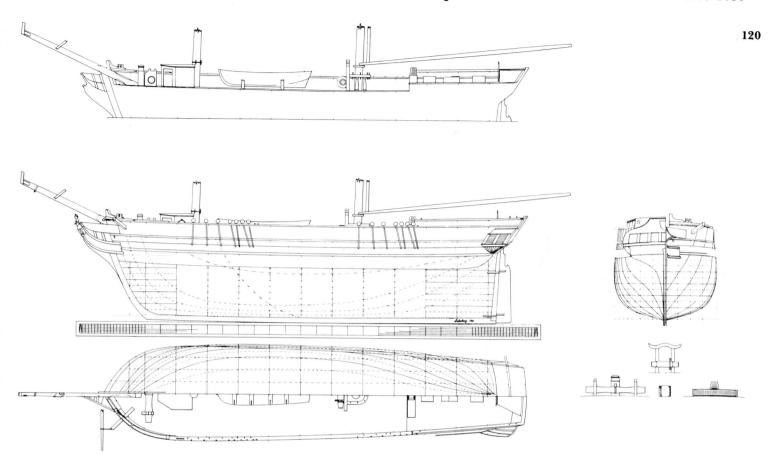

The plans of the *Black Prince* were drawn by William Salisbury from a contemporary rigged model in the Liverpool Museum and it is through their courtesy that the plans are reproduced here.

The Maryport brig is of a sharper model than the *Neilson* with a finer entrance and greater deadrise, but the run is similar; it is interesting to note the slight rocker given to the keel. Both brigs have a raised quarterdeck, square stern and quarter galleries, and a fairly similar disposition of the necessary deck fittings. In the *Black Prince* the galley is situated on the fore side of the foremast and its front has been splayed each side to permit easier working of the windlass; the crosspiece above the winch has the traditional gallows shape; the longboat is stowed on chocks on the main deck, keel down. Although no hatchways are shown there would have been two or three and these would have been placed in positions similar to those aboard the *Neilson*. The *Black Prince* might well have looked like the brig *Bee*, built at Workington in 1830, of which a stern view appears in figure 111 in *Merchant Sailing Ships 1775—1815*.

The *Black Prince* has a tonnage of 298 om, and dimensions scaled off the plan give 127ft 6in (length for om tonnage), 33ft 3in (extreme breadth), and approx 23ft 0in (depth of hold). This makes her a deep vessel. Throughout the forties she traded to South America, sometimes rounding Cape Horn to ports on the West Coast. Whereas the sail plan of the *Neilson* has been reconstructed from various sources, that of the *Black Prince* is from the contemporary model and no reconstruction has been neces-

Fig 119. In the River Avon at Rownham Ferry, Bristol, the Mary Ann Peters *was photographed on 31 March 1857 stranded on the mud. This barque was built at Richibucto of 545 tons in 1835. Judging by the shape of her fore deck, she was very bluff forward. (Reece Winstone, Bristol)*

Fig 120. Black Prince. Lines and general arrangement plans drawn by William Salisbury from measurements taken off rigged model in Liverpool Museums. Built at Maryport in 1838 with dimensions scaled off the plan as 127ft 6in (tonnage length) × 33ft 3in (max breadth) × 23ft 0in (approx depth of hold); tonnage 298 om. (Merseyside County Museums)

sary. There are several interesting points about the *Black Prince*'s sail plan.

Firstly, as regards the spars and their fittings, the trysail mast is not stepped on the deck but on the boom and so would pivot slightly as the boom swung. A similar arrangement is to be seen in the photograph of the small brig at Wisbech (figure 45), the head of whose trysail mast, unlike the *Black Prince*, projects above the top. The dolphin striker of the *Black Prince* is positioned four feet inboard from the bowsprit cap, an arrangement which may be observed in numerous photographs of old vessels. Iron trusses were being fitted to lower yards by 1840 and they are shown in this sail plan, the yards being slung from the hounds by chain; the earliest trusses appear to have been of this semi-circular pattern. The spritsail yard has been transformed into a pair of whisker booms for

spreading the jibboom rigging and there is an iron arm from the cathead in which the boom rests, which was standard practice; when in port, the iron ring was hinged open to free the boom, which could either be topped up, as shown in a photograph of the *Countess of Bective* taken at Swansea in 1845,[24] or laid to rest parallel with the bowsprit.

Secondly, the run of the stays from the mainmast of the *Black Prince* varies somewhat from general practice. The mainstay actually sets up on the bowsprit and inevitably crosses the foremast so high up that there must have been considerable chafe to the bottom half of the fore course. The main topmast stay is taken to the fore top; the main topgallant stay would normally be expected to set up somewhere on the fore topmast head, but here it drops down to lead through an eye on the fore lower masthead; the main royal stay follows suit and goes to the fore topmast head, rather than to the fore topgallant mast.

Thirdly, none of the yards have standing lifts which one would have expected to see by this date, certainly on the royal and topgallant yards.

Apropos the royal yards, which in brigs of under seventy-five tons must have been very small, R Morton Nance recalls an incident on a tiny West Country brig in which the master, 'on seeing a member of his crew mounting aloft with the main topgallant yard under his arm, cried, choking with indignation, "Lay down there, you lubber, and send up that yard in a proper manner".[25]

Many of the brigs spread their fore course on a bentinck boom which would allow them to save a hand or two in the crew, as this boom greatly simplified the setting of the sail. When the sail was furled, the boom was hauled up close below the yard, but when in port the boom was often disconnected from the sail and laid to hang in its gear a few feet above the rail. Numerous illustrations here show bentinck booms in use on brigs. As the century wore on, the British brig could usually be distinguished from Contiental brigs by the omission of the fore royal yard.

Photographs taken by the Rev Calvert Jones at the end of the 1840s in the Swansea area show two different brigs. In figure 123 the *Ellen Simpson* of 1847 has her bentinck boom hanging clear of the rail as she lies remarkably upright at some distance from the quay; the dolphin striker has been swung back; there is a wooden-stock anchor at each cathead; the lower shrouds and backstays set up on the main rail which broadens out for this purpose; below it the chain plates are formed of chain across the bulwarks and then fastened to plates bolted to the ship's side.

The other brig appears in figures 124 and 125 where she is lying bow on to a shingle beach with a topsail schooner alongside. On the brig's hull, the drainage from four small scuppers suggests the curvature of the body and from the run of the planking it will be seen that she has a full entrance and broad quarters turning into a hollow run. Externally, there are double channels for the rigging; a bumpkin projects through the trailboard, in a greatly fore-shortened view, with a block lashed to the outer end for the fore tack, below which two guys are taken to the hull to hold down the bumpkin.

Fig 121. Black Prince. Sail plan drawn by William Salisbury from measurements taken off rigged model in Liverpool Museums. Plans of tops and of crosstrees at top left; also of some yards. A plan of the bowsprit rigging is placed below the bows. (Merseyside County Museums)

Fig 122. Lithograph by John Ward of brigs close-hauled on the starboard tack in a light breeze while another is at anchor in the foreground. All appear to be similarly rigged. (MacGregor Collection)

Fig 123 A dramatic photograph of a brig said to be the Ellen Simpson *and taken by the Rev Calvert Jones around Swansea at the end of the 1840s. The bentinck boom is hanging just clear of the bulwarks. She was built at Sunderland in 1847 of 310 tons nm; Lloyd's Register has her with the rig of barque in 1848 but allots that of brig by 1851. (National Maritime Museum, Greenwich)*

123

A remarkable amount of detail of the brig's deck can be picked out from the photograph: the anchor has an iron stock; the windlass is on the fore side of the foremast; the main hatch is open; the galley is placed between the main hatch and the mainmast; there may be a harness cask on the fore side of the galley, under the coil of rope; an old-fashioned wooden pump casing (presumably one of two) can be seen close abaft the mast with its standard in position and a long handle fitted; there is a capstan abaft the pump, and close to the after hatch. Across the break of the raised quarterdeck there is a rack for capstan bars, which are stowed vertically; on the port side there is a tall companionway with the doors hinged back, which presumably gives access to the after accommodation down a short ladder (it is unlikely that it was the heads); on the starboard side steps ascend to the quarterdeck and there are probably similar steps to port. On the quarterdeck there is a companionway with a sliding top and windows at its forward end; hen coops are placed each side of it; the tiller ropes are led around the barrel mounted on the wheel axle, in the normal manner; below the axle is something like a skylight; due to the low height of the stern rail, the axle must have been mounted on some suitable support at its after end; two timber davits project out over the stern for a jollyboat; surrounding the quarterdeck is a light metal railing. Aloft, there is a black-painted trysail mast on the main and what looks like one on the fore lower mast, although it may really be an upper yard sent down as there is no gaff fitted. Some of the clearest rigging details are on the bowsprit where it can be seen that the double forestay no longer employs the old-fashioned collar around the bowsprit, a change that was being adopted about 1840. Such details as these are typical of many vessels of under 300 tons irrespective of their rig which other contemporary illustrations will confirm.

A few interesting items occur in Alexander Hall & Sons' yard books, such as the spelling of the word 'caboose' (galley) which is sometimes written as 'cab-house' and at other times as 'camboose'. Admiral Smyth certainly allows the latter as a variation in his dictionary.[26] Barques and ships almost invariably carried trysail gaffs on the fore- and mainmasts as many of the illustrations show. Referring to the barque *Crusader*, launched in 1840, Hall used the word 'main-spencer' rather than 'main-trysail'. He had not employed this word before and as he continued to refer to trysails in succeeding ships, it may be conjectured whether he here implied some special significance. According to the *Shorter Oxford English Dictionary* (1959), the first use of the word 'spencer' in its maritime connotation is dated 1840. Hall was still describing vessels as 'brigantine' when the spar dimensions showed that they were brigs or snows, and the first occasion in which he employed the word 'brig' in both the builder's certificate and the contract statement was the the *Princeza* of 1849. The number of brigs he built after 1840 declined markedly in favour of schooners, as the table in Chapter Two demonstrated.

An interesting comparison occurs between the brig *Tartar* and the barque *Crusader*, both of which were built by Alexander Hall in 1840, with almost identical measure-

ments of tonnage, hull and spars, the only valid difference being the presence of a third mast in the barque. It is a matter for calculation whether the fractionally longer spars on the brig would have given her the same area of canvas as was to be found on the barque, which was a similarity that Peter Hedderwick recommended.[27]

COMPARISON OF MEASUREMENTS AND SPAR LENGTHS OF A BRIG AND A BARQUE[28]

	Tartar (brig)	*Crusader* (barque)
tonnage om	211	210
tonnage nm	203	224
dimensions (ft)	87.8×20.6×14.7	86.4×20.7×14.8
contract price	£2100	£2101
finished price	£2178	£2101
fore lower mast above deck	42½ft	37ft (head 8½ft)
main lower mast above deck	42½ft	39ft (head 8½ft)
fore and main topmasts	28ft	27½ft (head 4½ft)
topgallant masts	15ft	15ft
royal masts	9ft	10ft
skysail masts	6ft	5½ft
fore and main lower yards	42½ft	42ft
topsail yards	33½ft	34ft
topgallant yards	23½ft	24ft
royal yards	18ft	16ft
skysail yards	[none listed]	[none listed]
fore gaff	16ft	19ft
main gaff	28ft	18ft
mainboom	40ft	–
mizzen gaff	–	20ft
boom	–	38ft
lower mast above deck	–	39ft (head 7½ft)
mizzen topmast	–	31ft
topmast pole	–	10ft
bowsprit outside knightheads	20ft	20ft
jibboom	24ft oa	30ft
jibboom pole	–	3ft
flying jibboom	16ft	10ft outside
whisker booms	–	15ft
martingale	–	9ft

The length of the 'head' where given above occurs within the length of its mast, which is an overall length; this is standard practice.

Plans of an unnamed Danish brig of about this date, from the collections at Kronborg Castle, illustrate a craft of broader and shallower proportions than the *Black Prince* with measurements of 78.4 (Danish *fod*) from rabbet to rabbet on the load waterline, 24.0 (Danish *fod*) moulded breadth, and 11.0[?] (Danish *fod*) depth of hold. The lines

Fig 124 Broadside of a brig photographed in the late 1840s; the deck fittings and other details are described at length in the text. The imitation painted ports are on the bulwarks rather than below the sheer strake. She has not been identified. (National Maritime Museum, Greenwich)

Fig 125. Bow view of brig on right (seen in Fig 124) and a topsail schooner. No names are visible. (National Maritime Museum, Greenwich)

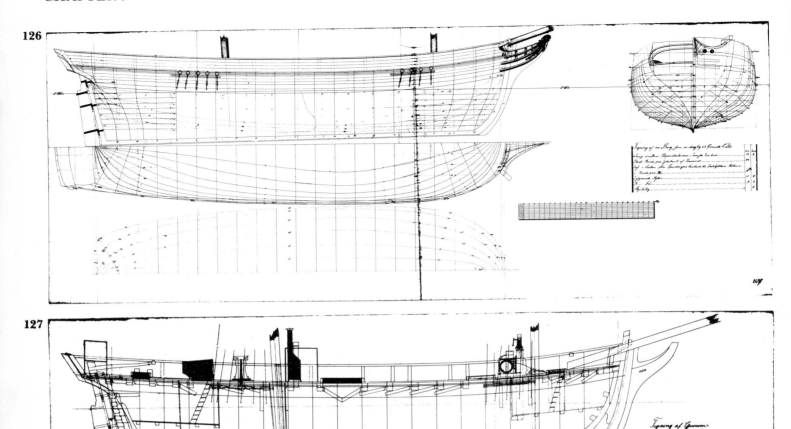

Fig 126. Danish brig. Lines plan reproduced from original in Maritime Museum at Kronborg Castle through the courtesy of the Director, Hans Jeppensen. Unidentified.

Fig 127. Danish brig. Longitudinal section and deck plan reproduced from original plan in Maritime Museum at Kronborg.

Fig 128. Danish brig. Outline sail plan reproduced from original in Maritime Museum, Kronborg. Each gaff sail has its own trysail mast. The fold in the paper running up the foremast should be ignored, if possible. The plan is undated,

show a full entrance with the maximum beam placed well forward from which the body tapers into a longer run, although it remains full at the load line. There is a fair amount of deadrise and the floors round up into very slack bilges with slight tumblehome. There is a drag aft of about 1.5 Danish *fod*; in the bows, a long and heavy head supports a richly carved fiddlehead.

The brig is flush-decked and as the foremast is stepped right up in the bows, the handspike-operated windlass is situated abaft it. No scuttle is drawn above the hatch leading to the forecastle but the main companionway is surmounted by a high scuttle; the galley is placed between the main hatch and the mast, and a capstan is abaft the mast; the brig is steered with a long tiller, and the rudderhead is covered with a small house which might contain the heads on one side and a store locker on the other.

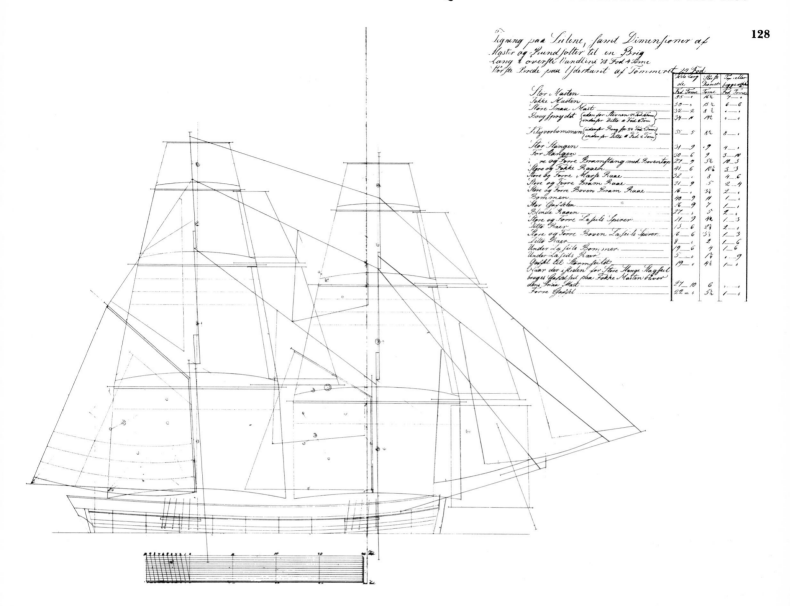

The outline sail plan, figure 128, provides a conventional disposal of canvas, with four yards on each mast. Points of interest are that the top half of the large fore trysail is overlapped by a four-sided main topmast staysail; the main trysail boom is as long as the head of the main course, which makes the trysail the largest sail in the brig; the three headsails are cut very long on the foot which gives them considerable overlap; a jib-headed topsail is drawn above the main trysail gaff, the head of which reaches almost to the top of the main topgallant mast; a spritsail yard is drawn; there are only four shrouds to the foremast but five to the mainmast.

Hull-form of moderately full waterlines but with appreciable rise of floor was a feature of many Continental vessels from northern Europe. Brigs continued to be built in America down to the middle of the century and even later in some districts. In his report on shipbuilding in the United States, published in 1884, Henry Hall listed numbers of ships according to their rig that were built at Portsmouth, New Hampshire. Of brigs and snows, 18 were built in the 1820s; 7 in the 1830s; 5 in the 1840s; 4 in the 1850s; 4 in the 1860s; and 2 in the 1870s.[29]

On the Merrimac River, Massachusetts, which includes the ports of Newburyport, Salisbury and Amesbury, the totals are as follows:[30]

	1810-19	1820-29	1830-39	1840-49	1850-59	1860-69
Sloops	11	1	-	-	-	-
Schooners	121	93	108	55	47	34
Brigs	70	19	14	15	2	6
Ships & Barques	45	30	46	65	79	52

129

130

Fig 129. Although stunsails were in common use up to the mid-1870s, they were rarely photographed, but here the brig Ornen *has five of them set as she creeps along ready to drop her anchor, the wooden stock of which is just above water. She is in the process of lowering her main topgallant stunsail to starboard. Built at Kragero in 1836, she was owned at Fredrikstad, Norway, when photographed in 1870.* (Nautical Photo Agency)

Fig 130. The Byron, *painted as entering and leaving Palermo, was built in 1824 at Scituate, Mass, and was of 178 tons. The lofty rig given to high-sided, full-ended brigs was common.* (Peabody Museum, Salem)

Fig 131. The fact that this American brig carries some guns on deck suggests she may have been a survivor of the 1812 Naval War, or else that she was a Baltimore-built vessel used in the West Indies trades where self-protection was important. I bought this small lithograph in Copenhagen; the sprit-rigged double-ended boat in the foreground makes the picture. (MacGregor Collection)

Howard Chapelle gives the lines plan of the brigs *Powhatan* and *Pocahontas* which were built at Newburyport between 1829–30. His plan is drawn from lines he took off the builder's half-model in the Smithsonian Institution. These show a full-modelled hull with bluff entrance, a short hollow run, rounded bilges with little deadrise, and a deep hull with flat sides. The square stern is wide and the headrails support a figurehead. Dimensions are 113ft 0in (moulded length at rail), 26ft 4in (moulded breadth), 17ft 6in (moulded depth), and a tonnage of about 268. These brigs were in the North and South Atlantic trades under the ownership of John N Cushing.[31]

In 1832 Cushing added the brig *Palos* to his fleet with dimensions of 109ft 0in (moulded length at rail), 24ft 0in (moulded breadth), 20ft 0in (moulded depth), with a tonnage of about 277 om. Developed from the earlier model, she had a kettle-bottomed hull-form with great tumblehome and a deep narrow hull. Being able to load a cargo equivalent to twice her register tonnage, she proved a successful and profitable vessel, and no less than fifteen other brigs were constructed from the same half-model, most of them built by Stephen Jackman. The last of these was the *Keying* which was built in 1845 at a cost of $22,264. There is a painting by Frederick Roux of the *Salisbury*, one of this fleet, showing that she carried skysails and stun-

131

sails on both masts. With such a full-bodied hull, a large suit of sails must have been required to push her along. The spar dimensions which are listed for the *Palos* have fore- and mainyards 46ft long and topsail yards of 36½ft.[32]

The lines plan of a brig given by Lauchlan McKay in *The Practical Ship-Builder* of 1839, plate 4, is also for a vessel with full hull-form, having a very bluff entrance, some deadrise and slack bilges, but all the waterlines are convex without any hollows.

Clipper brigs with big deadrise and fine waterlines were occasionally designed and built for specialised trades where speed irrespective of cargo capacity was required, and Baltimore was still favoured. Some of the trends and examples of such craft were reproduced in *Fast Sailing Ships*.

BARQUENTINES

As described in the last chapter, the *Bonanza*, built in 1830 at Whitehaven, is the earliest example of a conventional barquentine so far discovered and this is authenticated by the existence of the builder's spar dimensions which have been used to reconstruct the sail plan in figure 80. The next example is the Canadian *Loyalist* which was launched in October 1838 at Yarmouth, Nova Scotia, from the yard

of Dennis Horton with measurements of 87.1ft × 20.9ft × 11.8ft, 219 tons om and 186 tons nm. Her builder's certificate listed her rig as that of a brigantine with three masts. This leaves really no doubt that she was a barquentine unless, of course, there were square sails on the main topmast. Two years later she was altered from a brigantine to a barque.[33]

An engraving in the *Illustrated London News* in 1845 illustrates the auxiliary American screw steamer *Marmora* with a conventional barquentine rig (figure 132). Although there is a fore gaff, no sail is bent to it.[34]

In the Northern Maritime Museum at Groningen, John Lyman saw an oil painting executed in 1854 of the *Christine Jacquelin* which was a galliot built in 1848 at Galjvot. She was rigged as a barquentine with a fore royal and also carried a fore trysail.[35] No doubt other examples of the rig existed in the world at this time which have not been recorded.

Anomalies are always to be found, and engravings, sketches and drawings occasionally show a brig or brigantine with a lug sail set from the big ensign staff carried on men o'war, but it is difficult to determine whether a temporary expedient had any influence in producing a new rig. Cutters which did this eventually discarded their long booms and made the mizzen a permanent feature, and this form of rig, called a 'dandy', became a ketch.

132

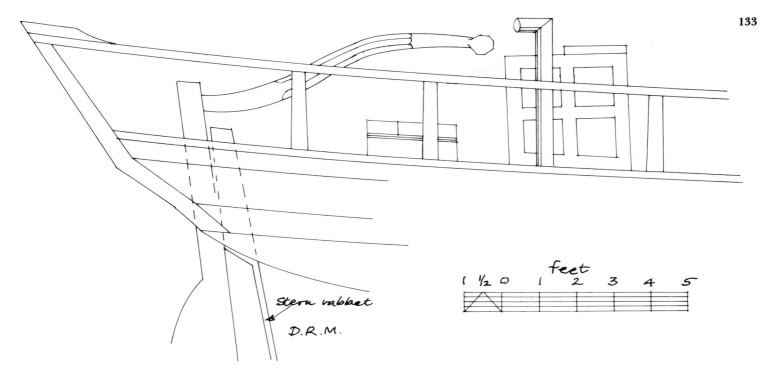

Stern rabbet

D.R.M.

THE *VIOLET* AND OTHER BRIGANTINES

The hull-form of brigantines was identical to that of brigs or schooners and the various remarks made about deck layouts on brigs apply equally to brigantines. The main-mast of a brigantine was generally placed a few feet further forward than on a brig, as the mainsail was a fore-and-aft sail. This rig became more popular as falling freights forced greater economies on all classes of vessels, and it was found that there was a definite saving of crew, gear and spars by converting brigs into brigantines or building them thus from the start. Alexander Hall's first brigantine was the *Matilda* of 1829 and the next was the *Buchan* of 1835; two brigantines were built by him in 1836, two in 1838, one in 1839, two in 1841, and then no more until the *Juan de la Vega* thirty years later. However, the experience of one builder is by no means indicative of all and James Geddie at Kingston, near Garmouth, was alternating the building of schooners with that of brigan-tines from 1838 until 1874. One of his early brigantines was the *Violet*, built in 1839, plans of which appear in figures 134 and 135.

Amongst the collection of Geddie's plans at the Science Museum, London there are seven lines plans of brigan-tines for which spar dimensions are inscribed on the draft, and the *Violet* was chosen as she was one of two fitted with a bentinck boom.[36] As she also had a foreboom and gaff and no fore trysail mast is listed, the distinction between her and a schooner becomes less defined, and one might pardon contemporary builders for labelling such a rig as 'schooner'.

There are seven vessels in the Geddie Collection at the Science Museum whose plans are closely related at this date:

Fig 132. Auxiliary steamer Marmora *rigged as a barquentine. This engraving appeared in the* Illustrated London News *on 4 October 1845. She was built at Bath, Maine, in 1845 of 323 tons with a length of 145 ft.*

Fig 133. Detail of tiller and deck fittings adjacent for a two-masted vessel. Redrawn from a plan by James Geddie traced at the Science Museum, London, (no C/7/29D).

Date	Name	Tonnage	Rig
1838	*Reliance*	90 om	sch or bgn
1838	*Brutus*	135 om, 116 nm	bgn*
1839	*Violet*	74 om	bgn*
1839	*Arab*	269 om	bk*
c1839	*Patriot*	(watermark 1836)	bgn*
1841	*Brothers*	100 om, 82 nm	sch or bgn
1844	*Vigilant*	78 om	sch†

* all spar dimensions written on plan
† lengths of lower masts only written on plan

All the above plans are drawn in the same style and are of much the same hull-form and deck arrangement. The plans of *Arab* and *Brutus* alone have buttock lines pro-jected, and then only in the run. The *Reliance* is fitted with channels, but the other six have the lowest deadeyes set up on the rail with twisted wires or chains stretching across the bulwarks to the chain plates which are bolted to the hull.

The lines plan of the *Violet* – spelt 'Vilot' on the buil-der's plan – has been traced from the original and drawn in exactly the same manner to show the style of draughts-manship used. No buttock lines are employed, but diagonals give additional fairing to the body plan and as they are drawn in solid lines, they may have been consi-dered more important than the waterlines, which are dotted. If a comparison is made with the lines of Peter Hedderwick's schooner *Glasgow* in figure 52, it will be

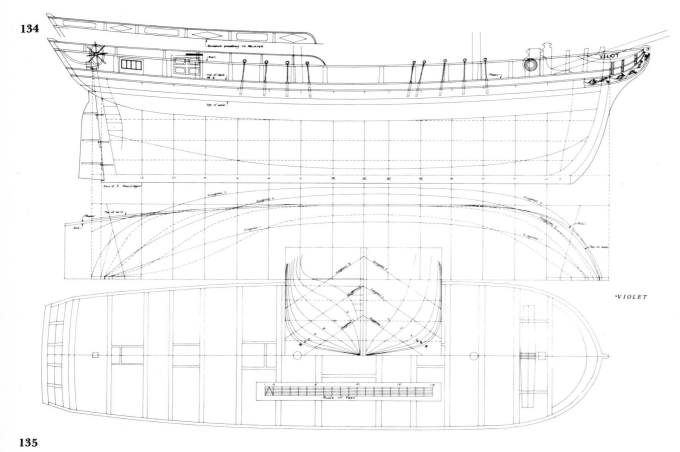

VIOLET

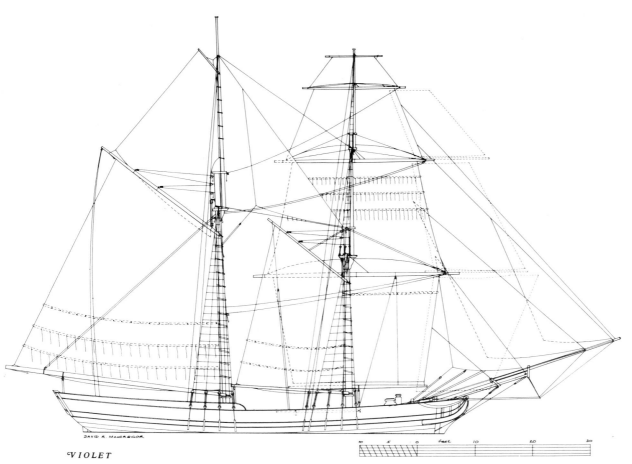

DAVID R. MACGREGOR

VIOLET

immediately apparent that Geddie is influenced by Hedderwick in the layout of his plan and the quality of line he employs. Likewise, the general hull shape forms a close parallel. Hedderwick often placed his body plan on the sheet so that the centre line of the half-breadth plan formed the load line on the body plan; this method has been employed when determining a suitable load line for the *Violet* and the result looks correct. *Violet*'s plan was originally drawn to $\frac{1}{2}$in scale, which is rather on the large size. Measurements scaled off the plan give 62ft 0in length from the fore side of the stem to the after side of the sternpost, 18ft 9in moulded breadth, and approximately 9ft 0in depth of hold; the tonnage in *Lloyd's Register of Shipping* is 74 om, the class is 6 A1, and the hull is partly fastened with iron bolts.

The builder's drawing does contain a plan of the deck beams, hatchways and windlass, and there are elevations of the latter in addition to the cabin skylight, after companionway, wheel and tiller, but some reconstruction was desirable in the deck layout and this has been concentrated in William Ward's drawing of her, reproduced in figure 136. In this perspective view, the known fittings have been elaborated somewhat, such as the tiller ropes and binnacle on the cabin skylight; various other fittings have been added in accordance with contemporary practice such as stern davits, pumps, cargo winch, galley between fore and main hatchways, channels, pinrails, catheads and so on.

In the matter of masts, sails and rigging, William Ward has brought the sail plan alive. The fore royal yard is such a short spar that it was judged unnecessary to rig it with braces, lifts or footropes and it would probably be furled in with the topgallant, similar to the billy-boy *Lively* at Whitby (figure 55). As no diameters, doublings or yardarms are listed amongst the spar dimensions inscribed on the plan, these have been calculated in accordance with Hedderwick's rules.[37] Slight hollows are given to the fore topsail leeches to ensure that the lower reef cringle is vertically under the reef pendant. Hollow leeches in topsails were common in colliers.[38] The bentinck boom shortens the foot of the fore course and also of the lower stunsail. Like much of the detail in the deck fittings, the rigging has been reconstructed, but there are several contemporary paintings which yield excellent information.

Of other pictures illustrating brigantines, one of the most helpful is a water-colour painted by D A Teupken of Amsterdam in 1846 depicting the Norwegian brigantine *Christine* in two positions. Figure 137 shows this spirited painting. The chief difference between her and the *Violet* is that she has a fore trysail mast, but otherwise the rigging details were found most applicable. The halliards on the fore gaff hook on to the outer end and so permit the head of the sail to be hooped to the gaff; thus when the sail is brailed in, the head hoops slide down the gaff. This practice was widely adopted. A water-colour drawing by the Marseilles artist, Honoré Pellegrin, which passed though the hands of the Parker Gallery about ten years ago, depicts the *Scotia* of Bowness in 1845: she is rigged in an identical manner to the *Christine*, and her fore royal yard has neither lifts nor braces.

Fig 134. Violet. Lines and beams plan traced from original builder's plan (no C/7/5) in the Science Museum, London, and redrawn in identical way to show style of draughtsmanship. Built in 1839 at Garmouth by J Geddie with a tonnage of 74 om. Dimensions scaled off plan: 62ft 0in × 18ft 9in (moulded) × 9ft 0in (approx). No reconstruction.

Fig 135. Violet. Sail plan reconstructed from spar dimensions listed on builder's lines plan. Reconstruction: all sail outlines, all rigging, diameters of all spars, lengths of yardarms, lengths of doublings, length of main topmast head. No fore trysail drawn because none listed on plan, although some brigantines had them; leech to fore topsail drawn curved sufficiently to place cringle on the lowest reef band vertically below the reef pendant. Principal sources: Hedderwick, books by Kipping, other Geddie plans, Biddlecombe's Art of Rigging.

Fig 136. Drawing by William Ward of Violet based on plans I have drawn, and with additional details added. The deck planking was intentionally omitted to save confusion with other lines.

137

138

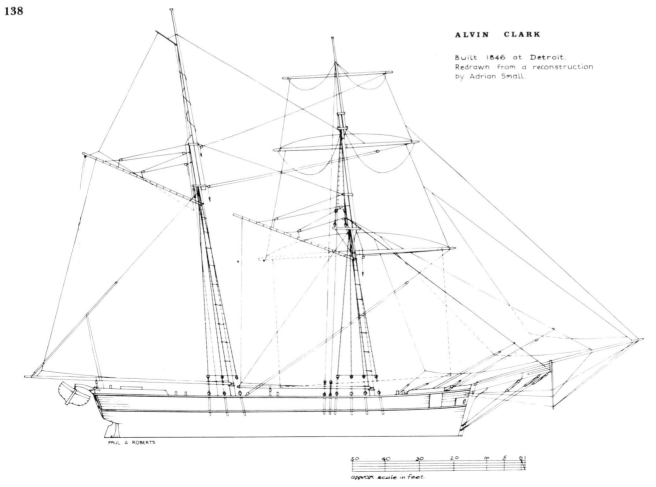

ALVIN CLARK

Built 1846 at Detroit.
Redrawn from a reconstruction
by Adrian Small.

PAUL A ROBERTS

approx scale in feet

Another example of fairly similar rig is the *Alvin Clarke*, which was raised from the bottom of Lake Michigan in 1969 by Frank Hoffman and a team of volunteers. She is now preserved at Menominee, Michigan. She had been built in 1846 on the Detroit River at Trenton, Michigan, by John P Clark with dimensions of 105ft 8in × 25ft 4in × 9ft 4in and a tonnage of 218. She sank in a freak storm in 1864 but when found she was fitting upright on the bottom. She was fitted with a large centreboard, the massive trunk of which is set to starboard of the keel; the windlass is the Armstrong patent variety, and at least one of the handles has survived.[39]

Adrian Small made some drawings of the *Alvin Clark* in 1971 and his reconstructed sail plan has been redrawn for reproduction as figure 138. She has a three-piece foremast which together with the fore top indicates a brigantine rig. Gaffs and booms for each mast survive, and so does the foreyard, bowsprit and jibboom. There is an iron truss for the foreyard. The fore topsail and topgallant yards are reconstructed, as are the sails. She has a heavy square stern with the transom kept low. Her reconstructed rig is very similar to the 'schooner' illustrated by Arthur Young as plate IV to his *Nautical Dictionary* of 1846, and the mass of such illustrations indicates the popularity of this rig on both sides of the North Atlantic, because there were so many sail combinations available. The three-piece foremast is the chief reason why this form of rig has close connections with a 'brigantine' as well as a 'schooner', and the separately fidded topgallant mast is part of a brigantine's rig; however, the fore lower mast and gaff foresail definitely belong to a schooner. The Continental term 'schooner brig' is a good definition of this type of rig,

Fig 137. Brigantine Christine, *built in 1846, and here flying the Norwegian flag, in this watercolour painting by D A Teupken of Amsterdam. (*National Martime Museum, London*)*

Fig 138. Alvin Clark. Sail plan reconstructed from drawings made by Adrian Small, and drawn in ink for reproduction by Paul A Roberts. Built at Trenton, Michigan, in 1846 and of 218 tons. Described in text. Scale computed from hull length.

Fig 139. The Ranger *of Padstow was built in Prince Edward Island in 1845 and was of 123 tons. Watercolour by Francois Carlebur (1821—93), inscribed 'Dordrecht 1848'. (*Richard Green Gallery*)*

although 'schooner-brigantine' is ever better. Such an example may be seen in the plan of a Dutch kof or galliot reproduced in figure 140. The foremast is a three-piece mast but the lower mast is not much shorter than the main lower mast; the fore gaff and boom also provide a sizeable sail. The sail outlines are dotted with the exception of the fore course, but there is the bunt of a sail furled on this yard and bowlines are drawn which lead to the bowsprit. Bowlines are also shown from the topsail and topgallant, leading down to the bowsprit and jibboom respectively. No royal yard is crossed, but there is space for one on the mast, and it was almost certainly carried.

This galliot has a slightly finer entrance in the lower body than the three-masted galliot illustrated in figure 28, but at the load line the waterlines remain very full. The tumblehome has been reduced, compared with earlier years, and the sides are now almost vertical, but there is

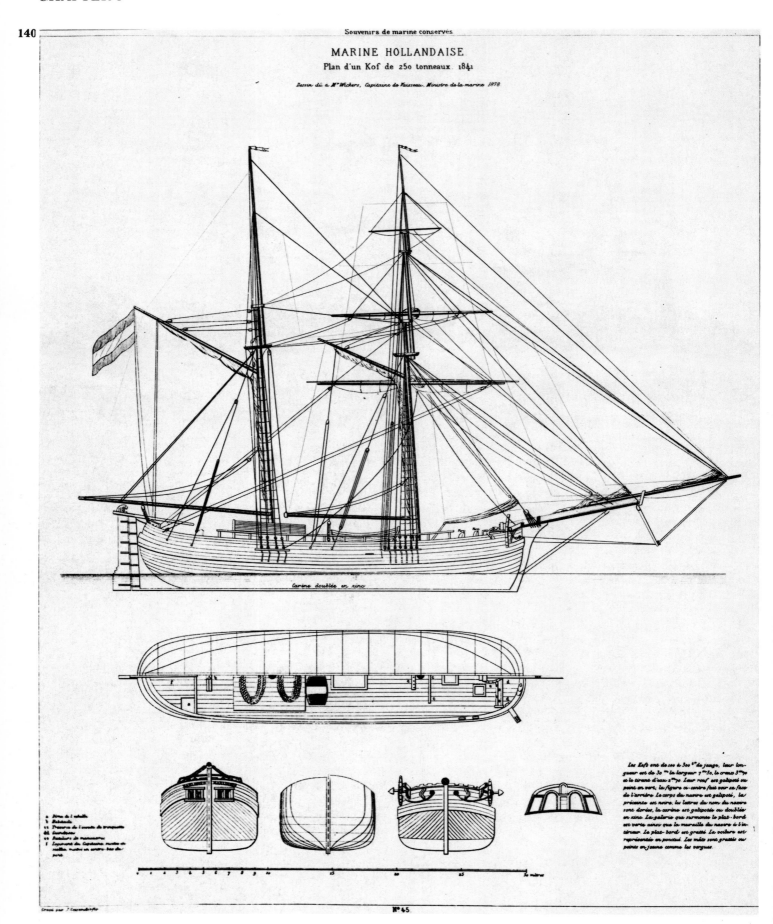

MARINE HOLLANDAISE
Plan d'un Kof de 250 tonneaux. 1841

Dessin dû à Mr Wickers, Capitaine de Vaisseau, Ministre de la marine 1878

Carène doublée en zinc

N° 45.

still the round stern and outside rudder with a long tiller coming in over the top of the bulwarks. This plan, taken from *Souvenirs de Marine*, represents a galliot of 1841 and of 250 tons. No actual dimensions are specified, but by scaling the plan we get 30.0m keel, 7.5m breadth below wale, and 1.5m light draft of water. A note on the hull states that the underwater body is sheathed in zinc.[40]

The *Kezia Page*, photographed off Folkestone deep-

Fig 140. *Dutch kof. Lines, sails and deck plans. Reproduced from Adm Paris,* Souvenirs de Marine, *pl 45. Design dated 1841 for kof of 250 tons. The sail outlines are dotted but the mainsail is feint.*

Fig 141. *The* Kezia Page *approaching Folkestone Harbour under easy sail with her anchor awash ready to be dropped; the luff of the mainsail has been triced right up to spill the wind and the halliards are being slacked off. She was probably laden with coal. She was built at Sunderland in 1846 and had a tonnage of 152. She was a schooner by 1881 but was out of the Register by 1884.* (MacGregor Collection)

laden with coal in about 1880, was a typical brigantine, but the passage of time has caused her single topsail to be divided into an upper and lower one, as can be seen by the illustration in figure 141. She was built at Sunderland in 1846 and latterly measured 152 tons, being a regular collier sailing into Folkestone.

It has not been satisfactorily resolved at approximately what date the word 'brigantine' was applied unequivocally to a vessel that was square-rigged on the foremast and fore-and-aft rigged on the mainmast. In 1841 the surveyors to Lloyd's Register described Alexander Hall's brigantine *Wave* as a 'schooner', but due to the existence of her spar dimensions we know otherwise. In the first edition of his *Nautical Dictionary*, published in 1846, Arthur Young defined what we should call a brigantine as a 'hermaphrodite brig'. But in his edition of 1863 he gave this definition:

'A *Brigantine* properly signifies a brig without her square mainsail. The term *Brigantine* is now applied to what have been hitherto called *square-rigged schooners*, or *hermaphrodite brigs* (Fr. *Brigs goëlettes*), have the foremast rigged as a brig's, and the mainmast rigged as a schooner's.'

141

Fig 142. *Watercolour drawing of unnamed brigantine aground after tide has receded, but lying upright due to her flat bottom. The main topmast is missing. There are two men working aloft. Painting dated 6 December 1836.* (MacGregor Collection)

This is the modern sense of the word and Young's definition implies that its use was already well-established by the mid-fifties, although subject to localised interpretation. (It was observed earlier that Alexander Hall employed the terms 'brig' and 'brigantine' interchangeably.) By the middle of the forties and throughout the fifties, the word 'brigantine' was appearing in Lloyd's Register survey reports with increasing frequency which indicates that the modern type of brigantine was increasing in popularity, and there is an instance of the schooner *Earl of Mulgrave* (1838) being converted to this rig at London in 1854.[42] There is no pictorial evidence to show that the old brigantine with square sails on the mainmast had survived in British waters.

POLACRES

Before leaving the subject of brigs and brigantines, a word must be said about the polacre in northern Europe because it carried these two rigs. The polacre in Great Britain has been the subject of considerable discussion in *The Mariner's Mirror*, much of it stemming in recent years from the definitive article by Vernon Boyle.[43] This rig first appeared in the Mediterranean about the middle of the eighteenth century, its distinctive feature being that the square-rigged masts were in a single stick or pole from heel to truck without crosstrees, and that the upper yards lowered close down to the lower yard. This rig in a Mediterranean chebec is illustrated in figures 22 and 23 in *Merchant Sailing Ships 1775—1815*, and for a brig in figure 143 here. The latter drawing was specially prepared to clarify the rig: on the foremast the sails are set, but on the main they are furled and the two upper yards lowered close down on to the mainyard; down-hauls are provided to the topsail yards; there are neither tops nor crosstrees; and there is a rope ladder beside the mast from the head of the shrouds to the topmast rigging.

Pierre Ozanne's published engravings of brigs, schooners and sloops which appeared in France in about 1770, include some brigs which possess the characteristics of polacres in that they have a pole foremast and lower their fore topsail yards close down on to the foreyard, although there is an ordinary fidded main topmast. In one of the two examples, the main topsail yard is also lowered below the lower mast cap. These brigs are small craft without jibbooms or topgallant yards and with very short doublings, but they could set two headsails, two staysails between the masts, and on some there was a boomless fore-and-aft mainsail. It is difficult to tell if any of them carry a square mainsail, but it appears unlikely.[44]

Two such examples could suggest a possible line of development leading to the north Devon version. In Chapter Two of *Merchant Sailing Ships 1775—1815*, the French pole-masted cat was described although no direct English counterpart had been discovered. Early examples of polacres under British ownership were prizes, and between 1788 and 1803 three such craft were registered at Liverpool.[45] The following pointers suggest that the polacre rig was first employed in British-built vessels between 1790 and 1830.

Firstly, the underwriters' version of *Lloyd's Register* added the abbreviation 'Pl' for 'polacre' between 1828 and 1830, which suggests an already well-established form of rig.

Secondly, many of the vessels classed as polacres in the Custom House Registers of the Bristol Channel ports were built between 1790 and 1830 and it is not unreasonable to suppose that they began life with the same rig they possessed in 1836, which is the first year the term 'polacca' was assigned to any vessel in these registers.[46] However, as certain vessels known to be polacres on the evidence of paintings are not shown as such in the Statutory Registers, some may question the reliability of these registers to record the exact rig demanded by an overstrict posterity for identification purposes.

At the National Maritime Museum, Greenwich, is a rather crude engraving dated 1822 and entitled 'Scotch Smack and Prussion Snow': the snow is a polacre rigged like the *Newton*, with a pole foremast and two-piece mainmast.[47] So polacres were in use in northern Europe by 1822 and were visiting British ports too.

Another contemporary illustration entitled 'Two Schooners' is a lithograph drawn on zinc by J R Jobbins from an original by W M Grundy being plate 9 from a *Sketch Book of Shipping and Craft*. Although the vessel on the right might well be a schooner, that on the left is a polacre, with a pole foremast and a two-piece mainmast. She is in fact a brigantine. The rough hulls are well indicated, but as in all Grundy's works there are no people to be seen.

In Great Britain the polacres appear to have been concentrated in the Bristol Channel area to judge by surviving evidence, much of which emanates from the Bideford district. Here the local name was 'muffie', apparently a contraction of 'hermaphrodite'. Most were built as brigs but many were later converted into brigan-

tines. In their original form they followed the masting and rigging to be seen in the plan of the *Newton* (figure 144), in which the polacre rig is confined to the foremast.

This plan has been reconstructed from a water-colour drawing owned by Basil Greenhill who encouraged the attempt at drawing a sail plan to scale from it. The painting is dated 1844, at which date the *Newton* measured 54 tons nm on dimensions of 53ft 4in × 15ft 6in × 8ft 8in, having been built in 1788 at Cleave Houses on the River Torridge, below Bideford. Her fore course is set on a bentinck boom with the gear peculiar to that spar; her fore topsail is a lofty sail and the yard is rigged with special

Fig 143. Polacre brig. Sail and rigging plan drawn by the marine painter, Francois Roux, in 1876. Reproduced from the original plate in Souvenirs de Marine, *pl 26, vol I. Brig unnamed.*

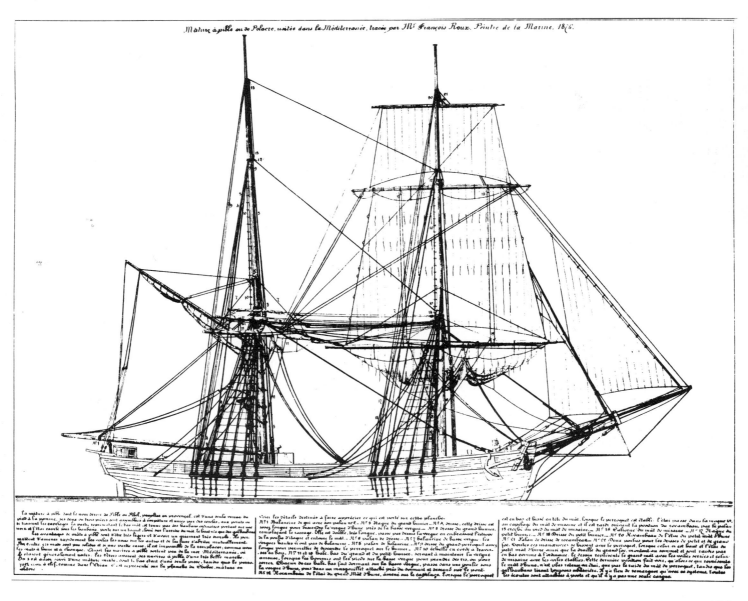

144

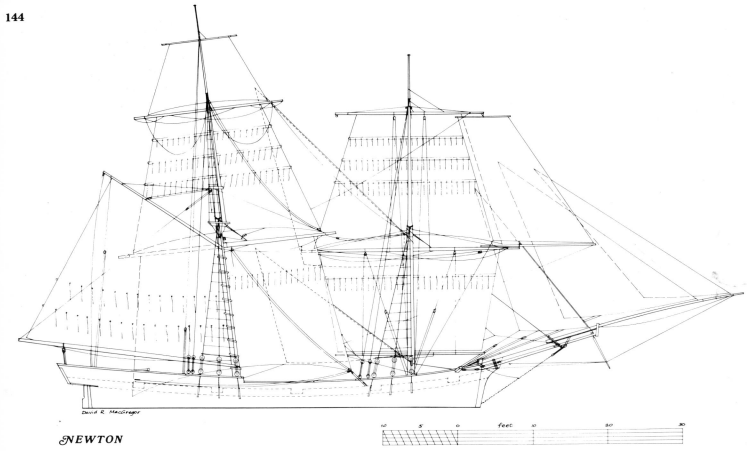

David R. MacGregor

NEWTON

10   5   0   feet   10   20   30

145

Fig 144. Newton. *Sail plan reconstructed by the author from painting dated 1844 owned by Dr Basil Greenhill. Built at Cleavehouses, River Torridge, in 1788; dimensions in 1837 by new measurement rules 53ft 4in × 15ft 6in × 8ft 8in and 54 tons. Hull scaled up to registered length. Reconstruction: doubling on mainmast increased in length; drift between deadeyes lengthened; tackle on boom topping lift placed at head by mast instead of by boom end. Foremast is almost vertical and the respective yards on each mast are of similar lengths.*

Fig 145. Pictured at Padstow in the 1850s is the polacre brigantine Peter and Sarah, *built in 1809 and with a length of fifty feet and a tonnage of 59. The single stick of her foremast is clearly visible. Her bows and hull-form indicate she was built for cargo-carrying. There is a barrel winch with gallows top forward of the mainmast, and she appears to be steered with a tiller. She dropped out of Lloyd's Register in 1855. A bluff-ended trading smack can be seen to the left with a tall topmast. On the right is a type of shallop or schooner-rigged open-decked lighter of the*

kind to be found at Padstow throughout the nineteenth century. Several pulling boats complete this interesting group. (Richard Gillis Collection)

Fig 146. A view at Stockton on the River Tees in the late nineteenth century, with two unidentified but probably German or Scandinavian vessels. The brig has the masts of a polacre below but fidded topgallant masts above. Although there are no tops, the topsails are not lowered down. To get aloft, there is a rope ladder abaft the mast from the head of the shrouds to the hounds. There is a short standing trysail gaff on the fore with trysail bent. She may be a Baltic trader, possibly loading salt. The brigantine is unlikely to be British, because of her deckhouse aft and tall foremast with a royal yard. The rake of her masts contrasts with those of the brig, and on her foreyard the stunsail booms are stowed underneath the yard. (Peter Barton)

146

down-haulers; a large fore topmast stunsail is set; particularly noticeable is the absence of a fore topgallant in spite of the long masthead, and the reason for such an omission has not yet been satisfactorily explained. These features were typical for most West Country polacres, although not all carried a bentinck boom. The *Newton*'s mainmast rakes aft as in one of Ozanne's brigs cited above and her main topgallant yard is not fitted with lifts or braces; again there is the long masthead, which many two- and three-masted vessels possessed in the eighteenth century. One use was that flags could be seen easily without the need to drop the yard below them. In 1851 when rigged as a brigantine, the *Newton* had a crew of only three.

A painting of the polacre brig *Sarah* shows that each mast is composed of a single spar, and a main topgallant stunsail is also set.[48] The photograph of a polacre at Padstow, identified by Basil Greenhill as probably the *Peter and Sarah* (figure 145), reveals the full-bodied hull which these craft appear to have had. This hull bears a strong resemblance to that of the small brig photographed at Wisbech (figure 45) and the hull-form probably conformed to that of other cargo-carrying craft such as the schooner *Glasgow* (figure 52) or the brigantine *Violet* (figure 134).

It should not be imagined that the polacre rig was really a common one in the Bristol Channel, as Grahame Farr was only able to compile a list of thirty-three such vessels described as 'polacca' by the Custom House Registers of Bideford and St Ives. Only one was larger than 100 tons and the *John* was only 37 tons; she was finally re-rigged as a smack.[49] These polacres traded all round the coasts and even across the Atlantic but they were most frequently employed in the carriage of coal and limestone from the ports of south Wales to the harbours of north Devon. Numerous lime kilns can still be located on these West Country creeks and rivers where limestone was burned for use on the land as a fertiliser. R W Stevens described these craft in his article on 'Limestone':

> Quantities of limestone are conveyed from Welsh ports to Bideford, in polacca-rigged schooners, which skillfully [*sic*] drop their lofty fore topsails when crossing the dangerous bar, and run to the mud near the kilns. A portion of the cargo is thrown on the deck, to give a list inward; and the discharge is soon accomplished by the help of women, shipped at Appledore on entering the Tor, and landed again on departure. Having the choice of three ports of loading, six trips are sometimes made in a week. The vessels are light-handed and worked by shares; about 80 tons are dropped each trip, and 20 retained for ballast.[50]

Polacre brigs from abroad visited the Thames during the 1860s, according to a Leigh bawley-man, who stated that they had pole masts and set courses, topsails and topgallants on each mast and that, although they lowered the topsail yards close to the lower yards, they kept the topgallant yards aloft.[51] This accords with another report that polacre brigs and barques were to be seen in German waters in the 1870s and 1880s; 'the lower masts and topmasts were in one piece without a top, but topgallant masts were fitted as in our vessels.'[52] This is the rig pictured at Stockton and reproduced in figure 146,

although the so-called benefits of the pole masts are not utilised as the topsail yards have not been lowered right down.

THE SCHOONER *VICTORIA*

With Queen Victoria's accession to the throne in 1838, the name 'Victoria' became very popular for new vessels and quite twenty new craft were so named in the years 1837–39. One of these was a West Country schooner whose rigged model in the National Maritime Museum, Greenwich, forms an interesting example of a small merchant vessel of this period. The model itself, built to $\frac{1}{2}$in scale, is a beautiful example of craftsmanship, particularly in the hull which is probably contemporary, and lines have been taken off to produce the plans in figure 147.

This model represents a schooner named *Victoria* which was built in 1838 by Joseph Alinock at East Looe and was registered at Plymouth, being employed as a coaster. Her register tonnage was 88. Measurements scaled from the plan give 73ft 6in length (fore side of stem to after side of sternpost), 18ft 6in extreme breadth, and approximately 11ft 9in depth of hold. The register length by the new measurement act would be about 71ft 6in and the beam about 17ft 0in. The bulwarks measure 4ft 10in high from deck at side to top of topgallant rail which is tall for a coasting schooner and suggests that she was intended for deepwater trade, a suggestion which is supported by the large area of square canvas on the foremast. She was lost in the Bristol Channel in January 1849.

The hull-form reveals well-balanced ends with an easy entrance and run, and the buttocks repeat the easy waterlines; but she is a deep vessel both in proportion to length and breadth, and her sides curve up all the way with maximum beam at deck level. The proportional ratios are 6.25 L/D and 1.57 B/D. The *Victoria*'s hull-form more resembles Steel's collier brig that was afloat in 1805 than the form we have seen developing in the designs of Hedderwick, Geddie or Adams with straight floors, firm bilges and greater beam, and suggests that her sections were partly built up with arcs of circles. She probably represents the local tradition of schooner design which was an attempt at compromise between the necessity to sit moderately upright when taking the ground in a drying harbour and the desire to achieve a fast, weatherly hull. An undated lines plan of a Mevagissey schooner with a 62-foot hull, a photograph of which is sold by the Science Museum,[53] probably dates from this period and confirms the very deep hull-form of Cornish schooners before they adopted the longer and shallower hulls which became popular in the 1840s.

On the *Victoria*'s model the deck fittings are very carefully executed, a good example being the alternate bulwark stanchions which are carved in the form of classical pilasters. No cargo winch is placed abaft the main hatch, nor are there any pumps or longboat, all important omissions of fittings that would undoubtedly have been carried. The rectangular planks let into the deck on each side

Fig 147. Victoria. *Lines plan drawn by the author from measurements taken off model in July 1965 by William Salisbury from a model in National Maritime Museum, Greenwich. Built 1838 by Joseph Alinock at East Looe; measurements scaled off plan give 73ft 6in × 18ft 6in × 11ft 9in (approx), but see text for comments. Tonnage was 88. Reconstruction: none.*

Fig 148. Victoria. *Deck plan and elevation of fittings drawn by the author from measurements taken off model by William Salisbury in 1965. Model in National Maritime Museum, Greenwich. Reconstruction: none.*

147

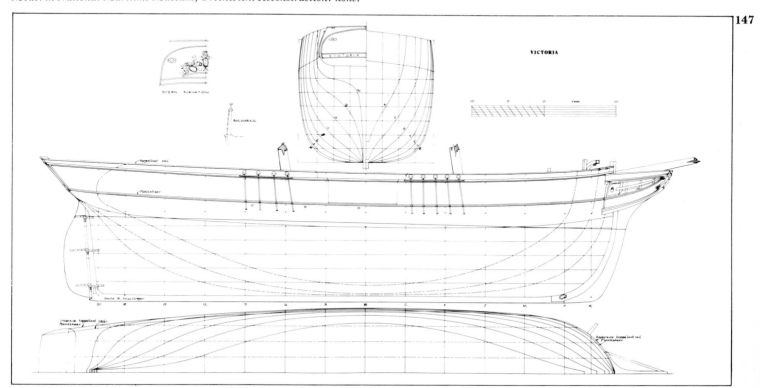

148

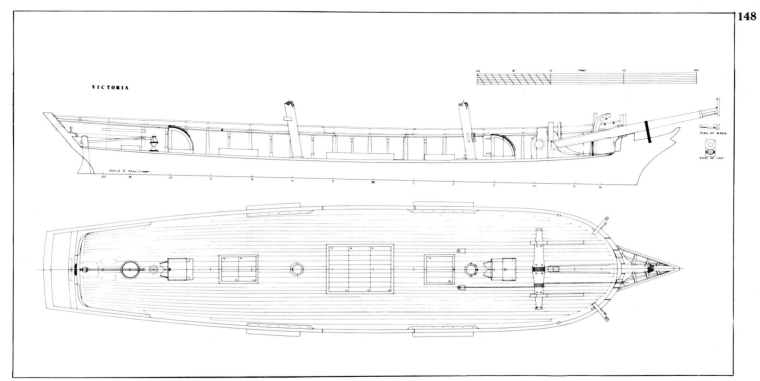

of the tiller suggest that at one time a wheel was carried or fitted in the model.

The workmanship of the model's spars was below the standard of the hull and deck fittings which suggested that the model had been masted and rigged at a later date. On this hypothesis the authorities at the National Maritime Museum decided some years ago to make new spars and re-rig her in the same manner as Hedderwick's schooner *Glasgow* (figure 53). The result is a fine example of the model maker's art, but we now have a south Cornish hull rigged like a Leith schooner and with masts somewhat shorter than those they replaced. However, the mast and rigging plan reproduced here in figure 149, shows how the model was originally rigged. The contention that the masts were too tall is not supported by contemporary evidence. Take for example Jacob Petersen's painting of another schooner named *Victoria*, which was built in Guernsey in 1837 (figure 150): she has very lofty masts and a similarly large fore topsail and sizeable topgallant. A painting of the Salcombe schooner *Lizzie Garrow* (1854) in figure 154 is also similar with a topsail that has two rows of reef points, and a square foresail with one row. John Ward's lithograph, done about 1840, of east coast schooners under various points of sail likewise portrays them with a deep fore topsail and two rows of reef points.[54]

One point about the model that is strange is the arrangement of the stays leading to the bowsprit. The normal practice would have been to have set two headsails from the fore crosstrees, with the forestay set up to the knightheads and a second to the bowsprit bees by the cap, as in the *Courier*. Of course, large schooner yachts did only set one large fore staysail. However, the lead of the stays complies more nearly with what one might expect to find in a brigantine. Although there was no evidence to indicate the authenticity of the rigging – assuming it to have been undertaken later than the hull – neither was there evidence to prove that it was totally unreliable, and many anomalies are to be found in the sparring and rigging of actual ships as the illustrations given here prove. No sails

Fig 149. Victoria. Sail plan drawn by the author from measurements he took off the model in 1965. Model in National Maritime Museum, Greenwich. Plans of bowsprit rigging, fore and main crosstrees, fore stay collar on bowsprit, and main cap also detailed. Reconstruction: sail outlines dotted. The fore topsail halliard tackle and also the topgallant halliard tackle both go to port.

Fig 150. Another Victoria *as painted by the Danish artist Jacob Petersen passing Elsinore. This schooner was built in Guernsey in 1837. Original painting made available to me for copying by J Attwood.*

Fig 151. Carrying a fore royal, a big square sail boomed out on a passaree boom, and two stunsails, the Dartmouth-built King of Tyre *shows what a lofty schooner looked like. Here she is passing Gibraltar in 1837, bound from Messina to London. She was built in 1836 to class 12 A1 and was of 82 tons. (Fairweather Collection)*

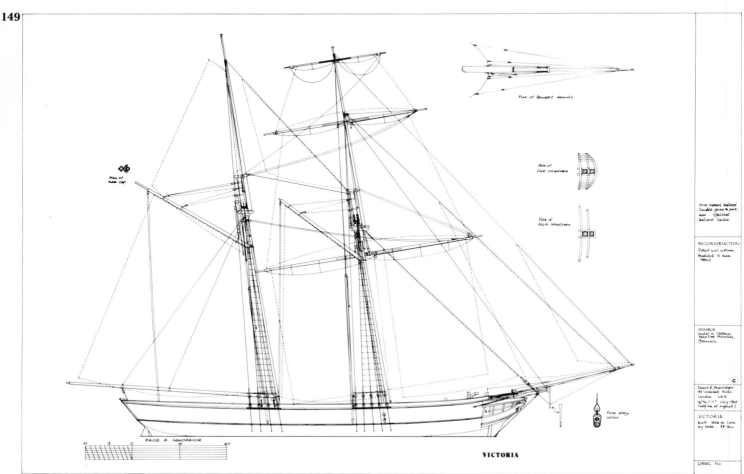

152

153

were set on the model, but their suggested outlines have been dotted on. Neither are stunsail booms provided, although the *Victoria* would undoubtedly have carried them to set topgallant, topsail and possibly even lower stunsails.

OTHER SCHOONERS

Clipper schooners of this period are covered fully in *Fast Sailing Ships*, Chapter Four, but after making due allowance for finer lines it will be found that the differences between them and ordinary bulk-cargo schooners are not large. During the 1840s, shipyards throughout Great Britain were building schooners in greater numbers than ever before and a photograph of one such craft under sail – again it is a West Countryman – shows the Bideford-built *Hope* in a very light breeze (figure 153). As already noted, schooners in Europe were rigged with a large amount of square canvas and the *Hope* is photographed when the stunsail boom irons on the lower yard have been removed and when the single topsail has been replaced with double ones. On the Continent, the brig and heavily rigged galleas or galliot was still preferred to the schooner, although the latter was gaining in popularity. Brigantines such as *Alvin Clark*, *Violet* and the Dutch kof of 1841 were little different from schooners.

Contemporary books on rigging and sailmaking do not give any straightforward directions on rigging a schooner in, say, 1845. Robert Kipping's book on sailmaking, which first appeared in 1847, gives rules for determining the sizes of sails for a schooner, but for one that is 'brig-rigged forward', or, in other words, is a brigantine. Kipping, who was sailmaker to T & W Smith of Newcastle, has two plates of schooners: plate 11 shows a craft that looks like a small naval schooner with raking masts and very short topmasts and two square sails; plate 17 is entitled 'Clipper Schooner' showing sails, spars, standing and running rigging, and it is ably drawn, apart from the terrible shape of the stem which might be construed to represent an Aberdeen bow.[55] George Biddlecombe's revision in 1848 of what was once David Steel's *Art of*

Fig 152. The Flensburg schooner Die Frau Lurewine, *painted in 1843, forms a useful comparison with British schooners. There are crosstrees above the topsail yard, even though the fore topmast is a single pole. (Maritime Museum, Kronborg)*

Fig 153. The schooner Hope *was built at Cross Park, opposite Bideford, by Thomas Waters in 1849, and would originally have been equipped with a single topsail and a topgallant above that. This photograph, taken later in life, illustrates her with double topsails. Four men are working about her decks and she appears to be steered with a tiller. (York Collection, Bristol Museum)*

Fig 154. The Kingsbridge-built Lizzie Garrow *entering Malta harbour; she was built by Date in 1854 of 174 tons nm. Her rig is compared in the text with that of the* Victoria *and likened to a 'schooner brigantine'. (Fairweather Collection)*

154

Fig 155. *Engraving for the entry 'SCHOONER' in Arthur Young's* Nautical Dictionary, *published at Dundee 1846. No square sail is drawn from the foreyard, but a schooner of this date would undoubtedly have set one.*

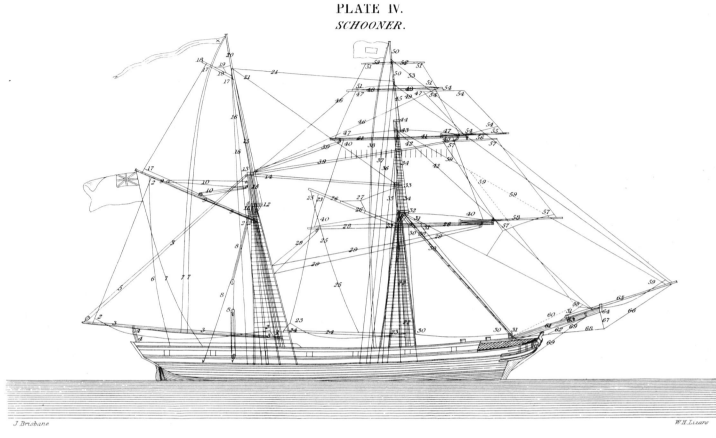

PLATE IV.
SCHOONER.

J. Brisbane   W.H. Lizars

NUMERICAL INDEX TO SCHOONER.

1 MAIN MAST.	25 Fore Spencer Vangs.	48 Foretopgallant Yard.
2 Main Sail.	26 Fore Spencer Gaff.	49 Foretopgallant Stay.
3 Main Boom.	27 Fore Peak Halyards (connected to Gaff by the *bridle*).	50 *Fore Royal Mast* and *Pole*.
4 Main Sheet (and M. S. Block).		51 Fore Royal.
5 Main Boom Topping Lift.	28 Fore Yard.	52 Fore Royal Yard.
6 Vangs of Main Gaff.	29 Fore Braces.	53 Fore Royal Stay.
7 Signal Halyards.	30 Fore Sail and Fore Stay.	54 Foretopgallant Studding Sail and **Yard**.
8 Runner and Tackle.	31 Fore Staysail (and Halyards.)	55 Foretopgallant Studding Sail Boom.
9 Main Gaff.	32 Fore Cross-trees.	56 Foretopmast Studding Sail **Yard**.
10 Main Peak Halyards.	33 Fore Cap.	57 Foretopmast Studding Sail.
11 Main Throat Halyards.	34 *Foretopmast.*	58 Foretopmast Studding Sail Boom.
12 Main Cross-trees.	35 Foretopmast Backstays.	59 Jib, and Jib Stay.
13 Main Cap.	36 Foretopgallant Backstays.	60 Jib Sheet.
14 Main Stay.	37 Fore Royal Backstay.	61 Bowsprit.
15 *Main Topmast.*	38 Signal Halyards.	62 Bowsprit Shrouds.
16 Maintopmast Backstays.	39 Foretopsail Braces.	63 Bowsprit Heart.
17 Gaff Topsail.	40 Foretopsail.	64 Bowsprit Cap.
18 Gaff Topsail Gaff.	41 Foretopsail Yard.	65 Jib Boom.
19 Gaff Topsail Halyards.	42 Foretopmast Stay.	66 Martingale Stay.
20 Pole of Main Topmast.	43 Foretopmast Cross-trees.	67 Martingale.
21 Maintopmast Stay.	44 Foretopmast Cap.	68 Martingale Back-ropes.
22 FORE MAST.	45 Foretopgallant Mast.	69 Bobstay.
23 Fore Spencer.	46 Foretopgallant Braces.	
24 Fore Spencer Boom.	47 Foretopgallant Sail.	

Fig 156. The American schooner Wm.L.Cogswell *in the Mediterranean starting to take in sail. The square sail below the foreyard is furled and the hoops which slide on the yard and secure the head have been hauled into the bunt, and the sail hangs like a tube down the mast. At the foot of the foremast, two passaree booms have been hinged up as the sail is not set.* (Parker Gallery)

Rigging includes a clipper schooner on the frontispiece, but his textual description of a schooner closely parallels Steel's original, and the ketch he describes is still an eighteenth century square-rigged ketch.[56] On the other hand the sketch of an 'English Merchant Schooner' in *Naval Costumes* depicts an ordinary schooner at the beginning of the forties; in addition to the gaff sails, there is a large fore staysail at the bowsprit end, a jib at the end of the jibboom, and a square fore topsail.[57]

It is clearly evident, from numerous examples, that there were many hybrid versions of the topsail schooner – versions which are a cross between a schooner and a brigantine, and the sail plan of the *Violet* with the gaff and boom fore trysail is a case in point. The Kingsbridge-built *Lizzie Garrow* (1854) has a two-piece foremast, in spite of crosstrees at the head of the topmast rigging, but the square foresail with its row of reef points looks like a brigantine's fore course. The 1846 and 1863 editions of Young's *Nautical Dictionary* give a sail plan entitled 'Schooner'; no course or square sail is shown, but there is a separately fidded topgallant mast, and altogether there are four yards on the foremast; and the foresail is set from a gaff and a boom. With so many rig variations in existence, the use of the term 'schooner' proved the least exceptionable word. Today the term 'schooner-brigantine' gives a finer shade of meaning.

An early example of a three-masted, two-topsail schooner was the yacht *Brilliant* of 393 tons whose owner, G H Ackers, sailed her with the Royal Yacht Squadron from 1839–62. She crossed royals and topgallants above single topsails on both fore- and mainmasts, although none of the illustrations of her show square sails set from the lower yards. The fore- and mainsails were boomless with standing gaffs and the sails brailed into the mast. The mizzen had a long boom and there was a big jackyard topsail. Booms were provided to set topmast and topgallant stunsails on both fore- and mainmasts. A wash drawing of her with this rig includes the description, 'Barque schooner'.[58] An oil painting by J Lynn dated 1843 depicts the *Brilliant* in company with other yachts of the Royal Yacht Squadron, and here she is also given four yards on her mizzen, thus making the mizzen similar to the other two masts.[59] This is certainly a unique case, but whether she began life with square sails on all three masts and later discarded them on the mizzen has not yet been ascertained.

In America, topsail schooners and brigantines remained popular in the longer coasting trips and for passages down to the West Indies, but for trading in shallower waters the fore-and-aft schooner without any square canvas was preferred. Centreboards were introduced into Chesapeake Bay schooners in the years 1815–25. Schooners were usually broad and of shallow draft with not much deadrise, but had rounded bilges, a full entrance and a hollow run; they retained headrails, albeit rather snub-nosed, and a wide square stern. Some had a raised quarterdeck with the after house projecting through it, and with a short forecastle; others had flush decks with all the accommodation in a house standing on the after deck, with or without a short monkey forecastle. A big sheer was common practice. Although schooners in the West Indies trade were up to 100ft in length and were often armed, those in the coasting trades were usually under 80ft long. Topsail schooners frequently set square topsails and topgallants, but a fore royal was rare.[60]

Schooners with three masts were built occasionally before 1850 on the American East Coast under the influence of the Baltimore clipper model and were usually of sharp model and so carried little cargo but were suitable as coastal packets and for other specialised trades. The Baltimore clipper had a wide range of influence and builders in Europe tried to copy it occasionally, but for use as a cargo carrier in peace time it was unsuitable. Some fine-lined schooners were built in Holland in the second quarter of the nineteenth century, but the influence of the Aberdeen clipper schooners was gaining in importance and various copies were made abroad.

KETCH, GALLEAS, SLOOP AND BARGE

In northern Europe, the galleas or galliot carrying four yards on the mainmast as well as a large boom-and-gaff

sail, and a tall mizzen with a slender boom-and-gaff sail remained a popular form of rig, as can be seen by many contemporary paintings, such as that in figure 157. This picture by D A Teupken is dated 1836 and portrays the galleas *Freund Georg* of Blankenese. The presence of a square lower stunsail set on a boom gives her no less than three stunsails on the mainmast. There were really few equivalents of this rig in the British Isles apart from the old square-rigged ketch or 'ship without a foremast'; but the ketch-rigged billy-boy had similarities with the galliot, both as regards hull-form and rig, and a few English yachts were so rigged.

A well-known yacht in her day was Lord Yarborough's *Kestrel* with which he replaced his ship-rigged yacht *Falcon*, when she was sold. The *Kestrel* joined the Royal Yacht

Fig 157. The galleas Freund Georg *was built at Blankenese in 1836 and was painted the same year by the Amsterdam artist, D A Teupken. The topsail yard hoisted on the doubling and the lower masthead is specially lengthened to increase the depth of the topsail. (Altonaer Museum, Hamburg)*

Fig 158. Jean Baugean's engraving of a galliot and a lugger. The galliot is double-ended with a round stern and outside rudder; she has big gaff sails on each mast as well as a main topsail gaff. Published 1817 as plate 84 in Recueil de Petites Marines.

Fig 159. Entitled 'Fishermen Returning to Brighton', the artist's name has been trimmed off by a previous owner of the print. The two-master is a Dutch galliot or a billy-boy and is discharging cargo. (MacGregor Collection)

157

Baugean del. et sculp.

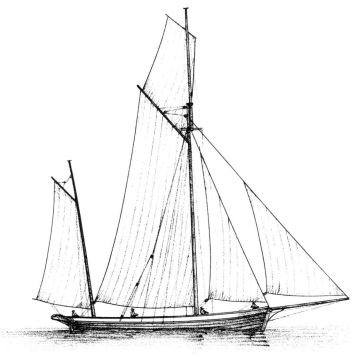

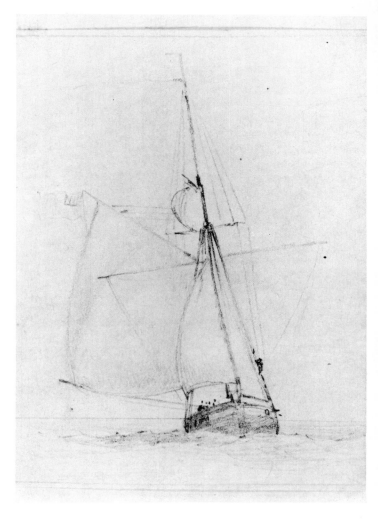

Fig 160. A 'River Ketch' in Naval Costumes by Admiral Symonds. The plates are unnumbered and there is no title page.

Fig 161. Pencil drawing by E W Cooke of a cutter or sloop running before the wind with the long main boom right out to starboard. It must be blowing fresh as the topsail has been taken in and a hand is going aloft to secure it. (MacGregor Collection)

Squadron in 1839, rigged as a ketch of 202 tons, but contemporary illustrations show that she could also set three square sails on the mainmast and big lower stunsails in addition. The mainmast was placed well forward and the sheet of the boomless mizzen had to be hauled out to a long outrigger. In 1845 the *Kestrel* was altered to brigantine rig.[61]

Lord Yarborough might well have seen the naval cutter *Arrow*, which was stationed at Portsmouth in the late thirties. A sail plan of her indicates that in 1838 she was ketch-rigged with gaff and boom mainsail and mizzen, together with three yards on the mainmast.[62] Like the schooner *Glasgow* (figure 53), the topsail yard hoists to the lower mast cap, but the square foresail and square topsail both have two rows of reef points. Although the mizzen is not lofty, the truck reaches above the level of the main crosstrees, which makes the rig approximately equivalent to that carried by the billy-boy on Brighton beach.

Another similarity to the Continental galleas is the drawing in *Naval Costumes* by Admiral Symonds of an 'English Ketch, close hauled on a Wind'. There are four yards on the mainmast and the mainyard is set some distance below the level of the mizzen crosstrees, which might have suggested a brigantine; but the mizzen gaff

sail is slender and the truck of the fidded topmast only reaches to the level of the topgallant yard. This makes her the nearest equivalent to the *Freund Georg* yet discovered.

But the tendency was for the ketch or galleas to lose its square rig after 1850 and to become purely fore-and-aft. Illustrations of the latter are found but rarely before this date, although it was obviously very common in rivers, estuaries and ports for cargo work. Admiral Symonds gives an example in *Naval Costumes* entitled 'River Ketch'. She is a purely fore-and-aft rigged craft without any yards and setting a boomless mainsail, a main jackyard topsail, two headsails from the main crosstrees, and a small boomless mizzen. By late nineteenth century standards the mizzen mast would be considered too short and stepped too far aft. But Calvert Jones' pen-and-ink sketch done in South Wales in August 1828 (figure 66) includes a ketch on the left of the picture. She has a much shorter mainmast with no fidded topmast and she looks a typical working boat with full hull and square tuck stern.

Although Arthur Young's *Nautical Dictionary* (1846) described a ketch as being 'rigged something like a galliot', this implied some recognition in print that the old English square-rigged ketch, or ship without a foremast, had at last died. George Biddlecome did not properly

Fig 162. The sloop-rigged billy-boy Angerona *had brought a cargo of coal to Cley Mill on the north Norfolk coast in 1886 when photographed, and was going to take away flour. Known as 'the Plumper', she was built in 1848. The Cley grocer and shipowner, V W Porrit, is sitting on the rail, just above the leeboard.* (Peter Catling Collection)

recognise this newer form of ketch in his *Art of Rigging*, published 1848, perhaps because he was bringing David Steel's old book on rigging up-to-date. To him, a fore-and-aft yawl was a 'dandy', or in other words, a cutter with a lug mizzen. He did not illustrate a ketch.

In the early part of the nineteenth century, a yawl was generally considered to be a man-of-war's boat like a small pinnace, and indeed Admiral Smyth gave this as one of his definitions in 1867. But he also referred to 'the yawl in the Customs Act' and defined this in the same terms as he did a dandy. Yachts and fishing boats were included in this yawl group.[63] The 59-ton *Railway* was described in 1853 as 'altered from a yawl to a schooner' when surveyed on the Thames after returning from a passage to St Michaels, where she had presumably gone for oranges. She was built in 1850 by Harvey at Wivenhoe.

On the Thames the ubiquitous flat-bottomed barge was being rigged in various ways: sometimes with a sprit mainsail or else with a gaff and boom sail, but both usually with a small sprit mizzen.

On the north-east coast of England, the billy-boy was the popular barge form and many were clinker built up to the sheer strake, such as the *Angerona*, seen in figure 162

discharging coal at Cley Mill in the early 1880s. She was built at Lincoln in 1848 of 47 tons and probably carried 90 tons of cargo. When first built, she probably carried a yard to set a square sail, because the massive blunt-ended hulls required a big sail area to push them along. She is fitted with leeboards which must have improved her ability to sail to windward. Billy-boys always received a variety of rigs. When surveyed at London in 1846 the *Wesleyan* was described as a 'billy-boy schooner' by Lloyd's Register surveyor who reported on her in this manner:

'This vessel is built carvel from keel to the bilges, clinker from the bilges to the wales and carvel from wales up. Is entirely iron fastened. Appears to have been carefully put together of good sound materials.'[64]

Like many of her kind, she was built at the inland port of Knottingley in Yorkshire and owned at Goole by her master, William Green, and in 1846 was about to begin a

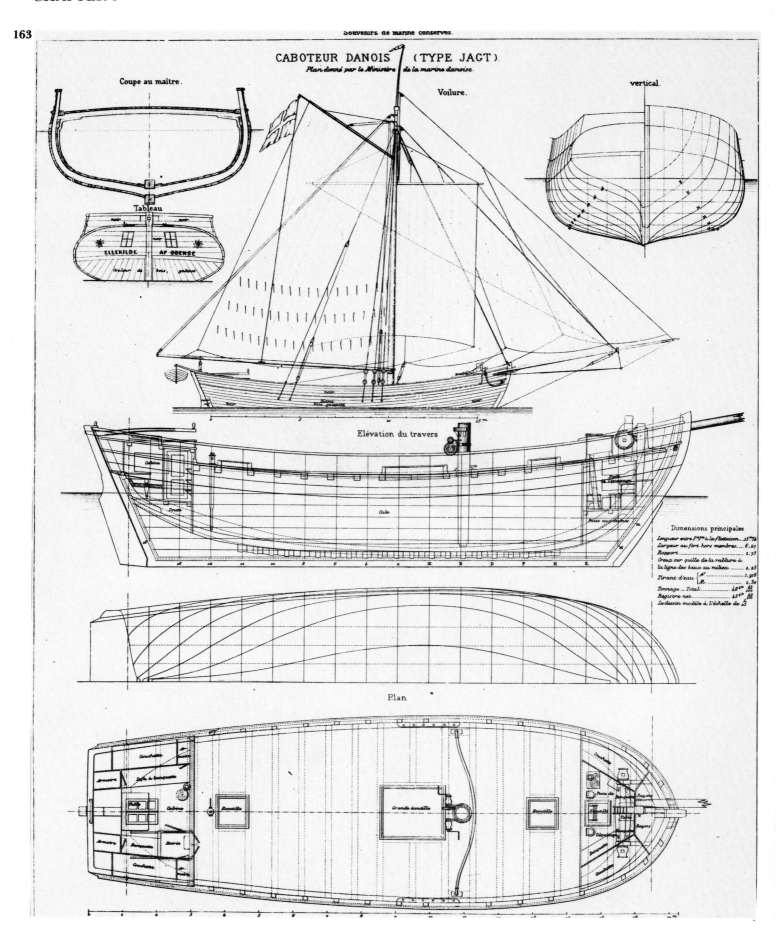

passage to Belgium. She measured 63.0ft × 18.0ft × 8.0ft, 75 tons nm and classed 7 A1. She was equipped with a winch but no capstan, a longboat, three iron pumps, hemp rigging and one suit of sails. There were eleven deck beams and two hold beams. The frame was of English oak, 7in moulded and 8in sided, with 21in room and space. From keel to bilge the plank thickness was 3in; at the bilge and up to the wales it was 2½in; the three wales were 3in thick, the two topside planks 2in thick, and the sheer strake 3in.[65]

IRON SHIPS AND THE *JOHN GARROW*

Before describing iron ships that fall within the scope of this chapter, a short résumé of their historical background will place them in true perspective. The first iron vessel is credited to the ironmaster John Wilkinson who constructed it in 1787 at Willey, Shropshire.[66] Richard Trevithick, who developed the high pressure engine, and

Fig 163. Danish jagt. Lines, general arrangement and sail plan reproduced from plate no 213 in Souvenirs de Marine *by Adm Paris. Name printed on stern elevation reads:* Ellekilde of Odense. *Register tonnage is given as 45 net. This type was in use for the middle half of the 19th century. There are bunks for four.*

Fig 164. The iron sailing ship Ironside *built in 1838 of 270 tons. The figures seem to be painted too small. Lithograph by Physick after Samuel Walters. (Parker Gallery)*

Robert Dickinson jointly took out a patent in 1809 to build in iron 'ships of war, East Indiamen and other large decked vessels'; also to make 'masts, bowsprits, yards and booms of wrought iron, out of plates rivetted together or screwed together in hollow or tubular form'.[67] This may have seemed wishful thinking to some, but it was to be realised in practical form within a short lifetime. Iron boats were constantly being built for canal and river use and in 1820–21 the first iron steamer, the *Aaron Manby*, was built at Tipton, near Birmingham, taken to pieces and reassembled in the Surrey Docks, London. Ten years later iron shipbuilding was firmly established on the Thames, Mersey and Clyde. The chief pioneers were John Laird and John Grantham on the Mersey; Thomas Wingate, and the partners David Tod and John MacGregor on the Clyde; David Napier, William Fairbairn, the firm of Maudslay, Sons & Field, and the partners Thomas J Ditchburn and Charles Mare on the Thames. In 1835 paddle steamers of about 275 tons were the maximum size for an iron ship.

Writing in the mid-1820s, the naval architect, J Bennett, commented on progress in the use of iron as a shipbuilding material:

Ballast of cast iron is now substituted for shingle; wooden casks are replaced by iron tanks; and the immense consumption of valuable timber, for the purposes of hanging and lodging knees, is avoided by the general introduction of iron knees; chain cables have been partially substituted for those of hemp; iron has also been applied in the merchant service, for beams, rigging, blocks, etc; and even vessels of considerable burden have been entirely composed of this material.[68]

164

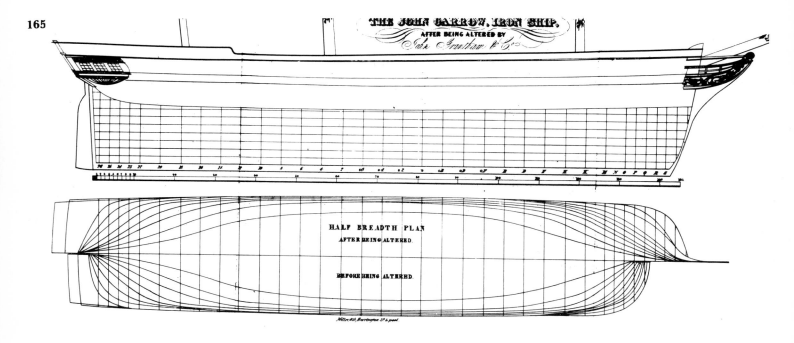

And he went on to describe how an iron mainmast and bowsprit were fitted to the 46-gun frigate *Phaeton*, prior to a cruise in 1825.

The first iron vessel included in *Lloyd's Register* was the 77-ton ketch *Goliath* built in 1836 at Liverpool, but the first vessel assigned a classification was the steamer *Sirius*, built in 1837 by Fairbairn & Co on the Thames.[69] In the same year John Laird launched the paddle steamer *Rainbow* which at 580 tons was easily the largest iron ship so far constructed. In 1838 the *Ironside* of 270 tons was launched at Liverpool by Jackson & Jordan as the first iron full-rigged ship. She measured 99.0ft × 23.6ft × 13.8ft and was fitted with an alligator figurehead, a square stern and sham quarter-galleries, and was placed in the Brazilian trade. A lithograph of the ship at anchor, drying her sails, yields some good details for a ship of this date, but fancy giving three skysail masts to a tiny full-rigged ship of 270 tons! Her maiden passage took her to Pernambuco in 47 days. John Grantham wrote of her that she was 'the first iron sailing vessel of any magnitude that was employed for sea voyages' and that she 'fully realizes all the advantages proposed in her construction'.[70] The integration of iron ships into the mercantile marine had now begun in earnest.

Three larger iron-built vessels were launched in 1840 from shipyards in Scotland. The barque *Iron Duke* came from the Clydeside yard of Tod & MacGregor and measured 108.5ft × 26.1ft × 15.6ft and 392 tons nm. After a return voyage to Calcutta and another to the Baltic she was driven ashore near Yarmouth in 1842. Another product of 1840 was the barque *Vulcan* of 298 tons om and 318 nm which was launched by Vernon & Co at Aberdeen with bottom plates ¾in thick.

The third iron sailing ship to make her appearance in 1840 was the *John Garrow* which was launched in March from the yard of John Ronalds & Co at Aberdeen. She had dimensions of 130.1ft × 30.0ft × 19.6ft and tonnages of 556 om and 711 nm. She was thus one of the largest iron ships yet constructed but her builders had obviously encountered difficulty estimating the iron scantlings commensurate with her size. The naval architect and engineer, John Grantham, was called in by her owners, Anderson, Garrow & Co of Liverpool, to advise on how best to improve the ship after her lengthy maiden voyage to India, and it is thanks to his written description in his monograph entitled *Iron, as a Material for Ship-Building*, that so much is known about her. This information includes detailed drawings of the midship section, connection of the deck and hold beams to the frames, sections of the keel and stem, and a lines plan showing her before and after alterations. Some of these drawings are reproduced here. The half-breadth plan exhibiting her form before she was altered reveals an exceedingly full entrance and run, and it is hardly surprising that she stowed 1500 tons of cargo on her passage out to Bombay in 1840 on a draft of 16½ feet. Her homeward passage proved to be very lengthy, due to the foulness of her bottom, a circumstance which was inevitable in the early days of iron ships before adequate types of anti-fouling paints had been invented.[71]

Her owners described the *John Garrow* as 'our experimental ship'[72] and John Grantham paid tribute to their determination to have the ship's form improved rather than to condemn her outright, a decision which would, he claimed, have curtailed the progress in iron shipbuilding. The *John Garrow* suffered on two scores: the hull was too full for sailing, and the iron framework was too light in construction. As regards her hull-form, the *Aberdeen Journal* had written prior to her launch that 'judging from her appearance she is a beautiful model';[73] but Grantham stated that she had 'an unusually bluff bow, full quarters and low transom – all militating against her speed', as an examination of her plan will confirm.[74] Newspaper

Fig 165. John Garrow. *Lines plan reproduced from* Iron, as a Material *for Ship-Building by John Grantham (1842). Built 1840 by J Ronalds & Co, Aberdeen, with dimensions of 130.1ft × 30.0ft × 19.6ft and tonnages of 556 om and 711 nm. The sheer elevation obviously shows the ship as altered. No body plan was published, but there is a half cross section.*

Fig 166. John Garrow. *Half cross-section reproduced from* Iron, as a Material for Ship-Building *by John Grantham.*

Fig 167, Fig 168, Fig 169, Fig 170. These four plates from Iron, as a Material for Ship-Building *by John Grantham show constructional details, but it is not specified in the text if they apply solely to the* John Garrow *or are Grantham's recommendations for iron shipbuilding.*

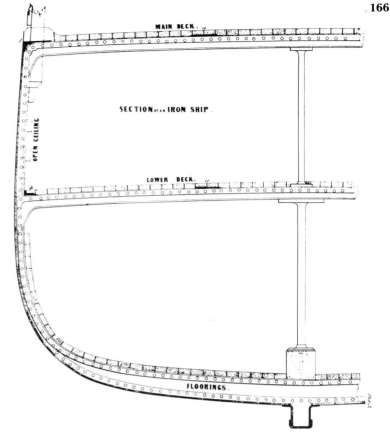

166

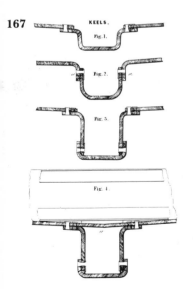

167

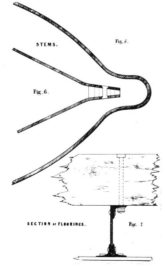

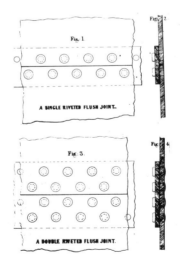

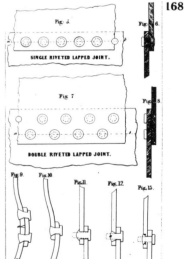

168

accounts of a ship's form are notoriously unreliable, a view that is promulgated more than once in this book. Grantham describes the construction in these words:

The iron framing was very light in proportion to what has been adopted in other sailing vessels, each frame consisting of only single three-inch angle-iron, and about two feet six inches asunder. The beams were formed by two pieces of angle-iron, rivetted together without any plates to stiffen them. The stancheons [sic] were of round bars, of about an inch and a half only in diameter, except where strengthened by angle-iron. These and the lower-deck beams were so slight as to be bent in all directions by the mere pressure of the cargo. The plates, however, were unusually strong. . .

This vessel, almost without internal support, and entirely without ceiling, except what covered the bottom, encountered a great deal of heavy weather, carrying a large cargo of dead weight, and all without an apparent strain of any kind whatever.[75]

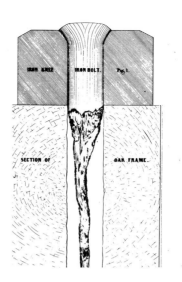

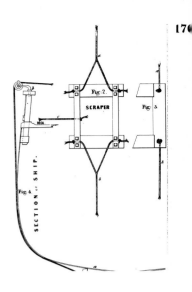

Particulars from the Lloyd's Register survey report at the time she was built are tabulated in Appendix II.

John Grantham describes the alterations which were carried out by his firm:

> The owners, with a view to remedy the several evils referred to, had an accurate model of her made while she was in the graving dock; and they subsequently gave orders for considerable alterations and improvements in her hull. The principal of these was, that she should be lengthened by about 14 feet, which enabled us to entirely remodel both ends, – reducing the heavy quarters, and raising the main transom about 4 feet; – and, also, in place of her original bluff bows, giving her a comparatively fine entrance.[76]

To make the above model, the *John Garrow*'s lines must have been taken off, and so this plan became available. It is highly instructive to be able to compare Grantham's comments on her hull-form with the actual plan (figure 165), and it provides a rare opportunity to discover just what a naval architect considered a 'bluff bow' in 1842. No body plan appears in his work, but this can be easily reconstructed, especially with the midship section available to give the deadrise. Unfortunately, no statement of cost is given to complete the story, but it is interesting to be able to compare the ship before and after the alterations were made. 'The form of the main body remained unaltered,' although the sides were 'let out in midships 6in on each side and the sheer of the deck has been much improved', wrote Grantham. Internally, the iron frames were doubled by rivetting reverse angles to take the ceiling; a new 18in deep keel was added; a 6in × 2½in angle was placed between the two 3in × 3in angles forming the deck beams, to stiffen them; and the stanchions, or as they were later called, hold pillars, were replaced with larger bars of 2½in to 3in diameter.[77]

John Grantham remarked that these alterations show 'with what facility iron vessels may be altered and strengthened at pleasure . . . Many of the plates and angle bars that were removed have been restored, . . . Not so with the wood work: scarcely any of it could again be made use of'.[78] If wooden ships were to be lengthened, they were usually cut in two, dragged apart to the required distance,

and a new centre-piece inserted, but it is not known when this was first done with iron vessels. The operation in this case involved the improvement of the vessel's form but was nevertheless an uncommon procedure. After she was lengthened at the ends, she measured 157ft 0in × 31ft 7in × 21ft 8in, 685 tons om and 849 tons nm. So well was the work done that the *John Garrow* was afloat until 1857 in the cotton trade between the southern ports of the United States and Liverpool.

No doubt pictures exist of the *John Garrow*, but so far neither they nor any spar dimensions have come to light. Some data on the wire standing rigging with which she was fitted has been preserved in a pamphlet by Andrew Smith, who patented the iron wire rope in question. He gives a table of wire rigging sizes which is reprinted in Appendix III. Andrew Smith allowed these tables to prove his point that wire rope weighed only 4180lbs compared with 13,204lbs for hemp rigging. The surface area of wire was about half that of hemp and the cost £112 as against £271. He also gave examples showing the greater durability of wire rope over hemp.

This detailed description has been given for the *John Garrow* because such accounts are rare for early iron ships; another useful source comprises the surveyors' remarks on construction which appear on the Lloyd's Register survey reports and which yield information on contemporary practice.

WIRE RIGGING

Perhaps a short digression into the introduction of wire rigging could now be made. John Grantham commented in 1842 on its virtues, adding that chain in place of hemp for halliards, topsail sheets and other running rigging was extensively used, having been found more slender than ropes of the same strength and that sheaves and blocks could become smaller. However, he linked these improvements with 'the opposition of seamen, who view innovations with an extraordinary degree of abhorrence'.[79]

By May 1841, Andrew Smith's patent wire rigging had

been fitted by Robertson & Co, his agents, to eight steamers, one iron ship (*John Garrow*), three barques, three schooners, two light-ships and a yacht.[80] In addition, some naval lighters were fitted with it; also the schooner *Marshall* which had been so rigged when built in 1836 at Grimsby. *Lloyd's Register* for 1837 has included in the latter's entry: 'Metal Cordage'! Andrew Smith's first patent for wire rope was dated 1835 and included a method of setting it up by means of a double screw thread. The schooner *Foig a Ballagh* and the barque *Q.E.D.*, both built of iron in 1844 at Newcastle by John Coutts, had wire standing rigging set up with a double screw thread, but no inventor's name was given.[81] Rigging screws were used aboard HMS *Ganges* at Portsmouth in 1831, as invented by James Pearce.[82] Setting-up rigging with various screw threads was tried out for some years, but it was not until about 1875 that a 'bottle screw' was perfected that could be used with absolute security.

Previously, patents for iron rigging, of which the earliest is dated 1804, had specified that it consist of chain or continuous iron rods, and in 1827 the American three-masted schooner *Pocahontas* had her standing rigging composed of continuous iron bars, served with rope yarn.[83] In 1839 the three-masted iron paddle steamer *Rio Doce* was rigged with ½in and ⅜in chain standing rigging. She was built that year by J B Humphreys at Northam, near Southampton, of 178 tons nm with a proportion of seven beams to her length.[84] Robert S Newall took out a

patent in 1840 for ropemaking machinery and his first patent for wire rigging, including setting it up with some form of screw thread, was dated 1848.[85] Dating from the early 1850s, most large British ships had wire standing rigging set up with deadeyes and lanyards.

Fig 173. This lithograph advertises the advantages of Newall & Co's wire rigging. It states they are the 'patentees of untwisted wire rope'. The ship is the William Connal *built in 1852 by William Simons at Greenock with a length of 148ft and a tonnage of 596 nm. On her second voyage, she sailed out to Hong Kong in 107 days, and returned home from Whampoa in 1853 in 113 days against the monsoon, but was wrecked in 1854 on the next passage out to India. The lithograph is from a painting by William Clark. The master, James Brown, is quoted on the bottom of the print as saying, in part: 'I would suggest that the whole should be galvanized throughout with no serving except at Mast Heads, and as far as the end is twined up through a roller attached to chain on top of rail . . .' He found that it became slack on the lee side when under a press of sail. Copied from lithograph through courtesy of Connal & Co. (MacGregor Collection)*

THE WILLIAM CONNAL. 600 TONS
RIGGED TO THE TRUCK WITH NEWALL AND Cº PATENT IMPROVED WIRE ROPE
JAMES BROWN ESQ. COMMANDER

171

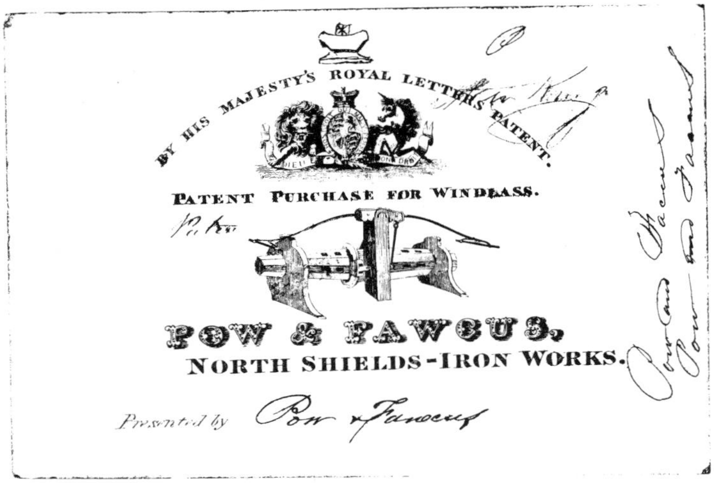
BY HIS MAJESTY'S ROYAL LETTERS PATENT.
PATENT PURCHASE FOR WINDLASS.
POW & FAWCUS,
NORTH SHIELDS-IRON WORKS.
Presented by Pow & Fawcus

Fig 171. Front of a trade card for Pow & Fawcus, well-known in their day. The windlass has the pump handles of the Armstrong patent variety. Size of original $5\frac{1}{4}$in × $3\frac{5}{8}$in. (MacGregor Collection)

Fig 172. Reverse of Pow & Fawcus trade card.

Fig 174. The Antelope *as lengthened and re-engined in 1853. She was designed by John Grantham and built in 1845. See table. This is an engraving from the* Illustrated London News *in 1853.*

172

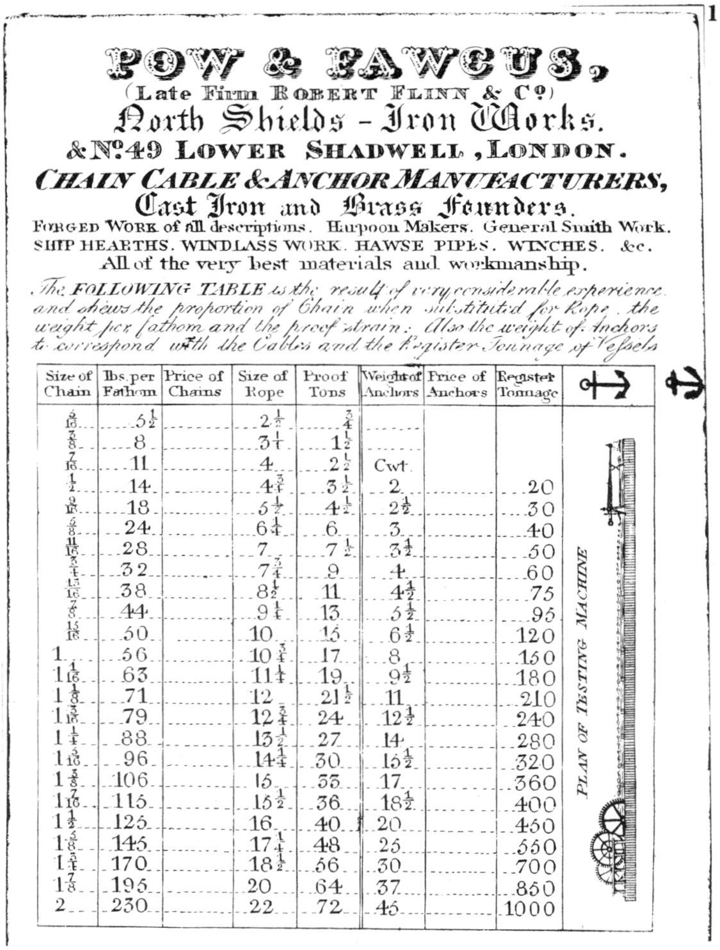

POW & FAWCUS,
(Late Firm ROBERT FLINN & Co)
North Shields - Iron Works.
& No. 49 LOWER SHADWELL, LONDON.
CHAIN CABLE & ANCHOR MANUFACTURERS,
Cast Iron and Brass Founders.
FORGED WORK of all descriptions. Harpoon Makers. General Smith Work.
SHIP HEARTHS. WINDLASS WORK. HAWSE PIPES. WINCHES. &c.
All of the very best materials and workmanship.

The FOLLOWING TABLE is the result of very considerable experience and shews the proportion of Chain when substituted for Rope, the weight per fathom and the proof strain: Also the weight of Anchors to correspond with the Cables and the Register Tonnage of Vessels

Size of Chain	lbs. per Fathom	Price of Chains	Size of Rope	Proof Tons	Weight of Anchors	Price of Anchors	Register Tonnage
$\frac{5}{16}$	$5\frac{1}{2}$		$2\frac{1}{2}$	$\frac{3}{4}$			
$\frac{3}{8}$	8		$3\frac{1}{4}$	$1\frac{1}{2}$			
$\frac{7}{16}$	11		4	$2\frac{1}{2}$	Cwt.		
$\frac{1}{2}$	14		$4\frac{3}{4}$	$3\frac{1}{2}$	2		20
$\frac{9}{16}$	18		$5\frac{1}{2}$	$4\frac{1}{2}$	$2\frac{1}{2}$		30
$\frac{5}{8}$	24		$6\frac{1}{4}$	6	3		40
$\frac{11}{16}$	28		7	$7\frac{1}{2}$	$3\frac{1}{2}$		50
$\frac{3}{4}$	32		$7\frac{3}{4}$	9	4		60
$\frac{13}{16}$	38		$8\frac{1}{2}$	11	$4\frac{1}{2}$		75
$\frac{7}{8}$	44		$9\frac{1}{4}$	13	$5\frac{1}{2}$		95
$\frac{15}{16}$	50		10	15	$6\frac{1}{2}$		120
1	56		$10\frac{3}{4}$	17	8		150
$1\frac{1}{16}$	63		$11\frac{1}{4}$	19	$9\frac{1}{2}$		180
$1\frac{1}{8}$	71		12	$21\frac{1}{2}$	11		210
$1\frac{3}{16}$	79		$12\frac{3}{4}$	24	$12\frac{1}{2}$		240
$1\frac{1}{4}$	88		$13\frac{1}{2}$	27	14		280
$1\frac{5}{16}$	96		$14\frac{1}{4}$	30	$15\frac{1}{2}$		320
$1\frac{3}{8}$	106		15	33	17		360
$1\frac{7}{16}$	115		$15\frac{1}{2}$	36	$18\frac{1}{2}$		400
$1\frac{1}{2}$	125		16	40	20		450
$1\frac{5}{8}$	145		$17\frac{1}{4}$	48	25		550
$1\frac{3}{4}$	170		$18\frac{1}{2}$	56	30		700
$1\frac{7}{8}$	195		20	64	37		850
2	230		22	72	45		1000

PLAN OF TESTING MACHINE

174

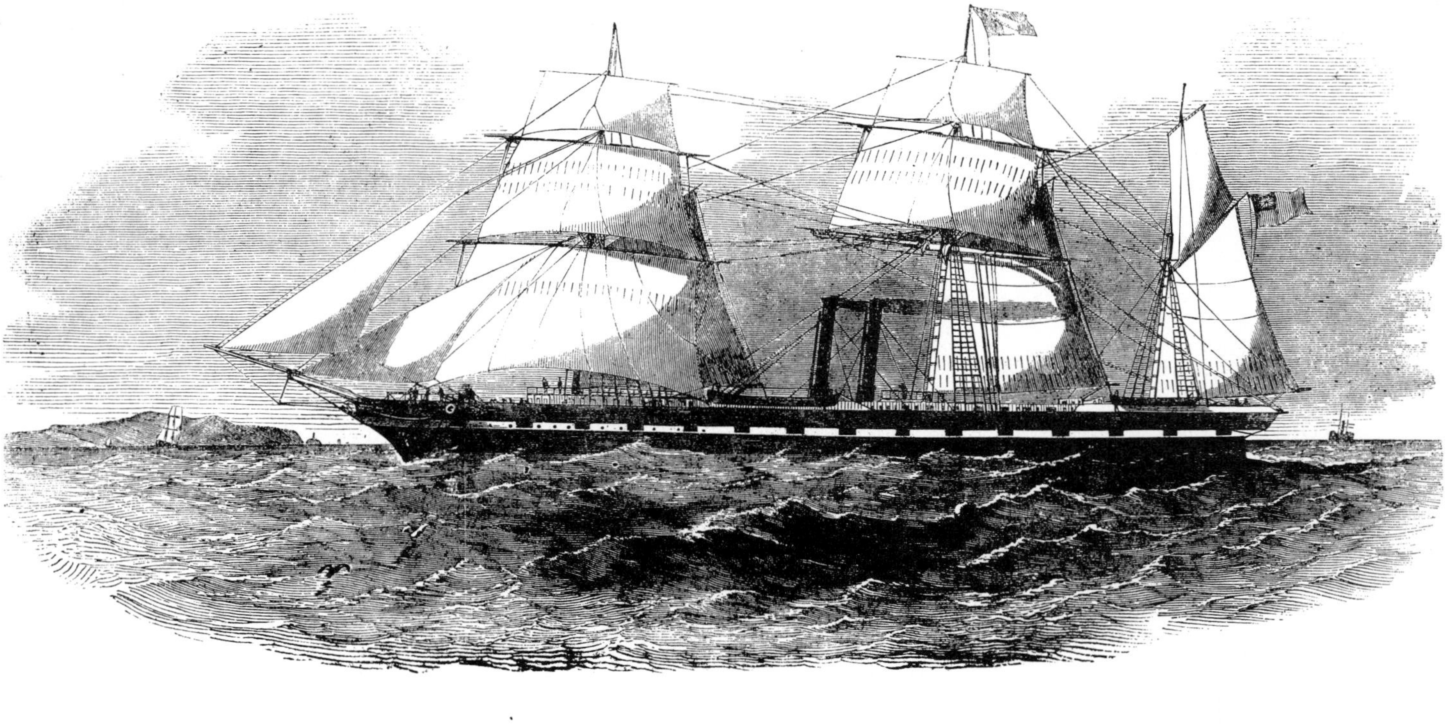

JOHN GRANTHAM

The name John Grantham (1809–74) is so intimately connected with iron shipbuilding at Liverpool in the 1840s and 1850s that some remarks on his career might prove of interest. He must have grown up with iron shipbuilding, as his father superintended the building of the iron steamer *Marquis of Wellesley* in 1823–24. She was a twin-hulled boat and survived for many years in Ireland.[86] The son described his profession as that of a mechanical engineer with an extensive knowledge of iron, but he also worked as a naval architect designing ships of all kinds, superintending their construction in other yards and even building a few himself. By 1830 he had joined the Liverpool firm of Mather, Dixon & Co and soon became both manager and a partner. Within nine years of this date he was a partner in the firm of Page & Grantham, and in 1839 was giving evidence before a Parliamentary Committee of Inquiry.

Grantham's first book, *Iron, as a Material for Ship-Building*, was published in 1842 and has already been quoted. It formed the annual address to the Liverpool Polytechnic Society in the year he was President, and part of it was read to them. Later he produced a much more detailed work, *Iron Ship-Building*, which was first published in 1858 as one volume of text and a separate atlas of plates; ten years later the work was in its fifth edition. His efforts with the *John Garrow* have already been given in detail, but some of his other work is worth listing to show the range of his abilities which were symptomatic of those displayed by the numerous engineers of that era. The work listed here obviously forms but a small proportion of what he undertook.

SOME OF JOHN GRANTHAM'S SHIPBUILDING WORK[87]

1839 Described as a boiler maker in partnership with Page, under the style of Page & Grantham.
1842 Described as John Grantham & Co.
1842 'A new vessel lately built by us. . .' [not named]
1842 Alterations to *John Garrow* [as listed above]
1844 Designed iron barque *Josephine*, built same year at Greenock by Scott Sinclair & Co of 168 tons nm.
1845 Designed and built auxiliary iron steamer *Antelope*, 606 tons, 185.7ft × 24.7ft × 16.7ft; in 1849 machinery removed and converted to a sailing ship; in 1853 lengthened by John Laird of Birkenhead by 42ft which increased tonnage to 778, new engines were installed and rigged as a barque.[88]
1847 Designed auxiliary iron steamer *Sarah Sands*, built by James Hodgson & Co at Liverpool, 218.0ft × 31.8ft × 27.2ft and 818 tons (in 1865); made a sailing vessel in 1864 and listed as having '4 masts'.[89]
1853 Superintended construction of PS *Pacific*, built by John Scott Russell & Co, London, 250.0ft between perpendiculars.
c1854 Superintended construction of iron steamer *The Queen*, 179.0ft length overall.
1854 Superintended construction of iron clipper *Sarah Palmer*, built at Warrington by C Tayleur & Co, 1462 tons om. Plans reproduced in *Fast Sailing Ships* as figures 212 and 213.
1854 Designed iron steamer *Loire*, built same year by Thomas Vernon & Son, Liverpool, 573 tons om.

1855 Designed iron steamer *Empress Eugenie*, 655 tons om.
1857 Designed iron screw collier *James Kennedy*, built same year by Thomas Vernon & Son, Liverpool, 616 tons, 175.0ft length between perpendiculars.
1859 Moved to London.
1861 Founder member of Institution of Naval Architects, and elected to Council immediately; described as 'consulting naval architect, London'; still a Council member in 1871.
c1865 Designed proposed steel paddle steamer for the Channel service, 450ft × 54ft.
1866 Designed steel PS *Scarborough*, built at Blackwall, 142 tons.

Although so much of Grantham's work was connected with steamships, he nevertheless was involved with a number of sailing ships and it is particularly interesting to note his connection with the clipper *Sarah Palmer*. In his book *Iron Ship-Building* he gives the specification for the ironwork of her hull as well as that for the iron ships *Deerslayer* and *Lady Octavia*, and it may be that he was a consultant for the firm of C Tayleur & Co which built all three ships. He was certainly consultant for the Whitehaven Steam Shipping Co.

IRON CONSTRUCTION IN SMALL VESSELS

Some account of the state of iron shipbuilding has already been given, but it remains to be completed by commenting on iron construction in smaller vessels. Prior to 1850 most iron sailing vessels were restricted to craft of under 250 tons, the majority of which were schooner-rigged, whether they were provided with engines or not. The comments in this section are for the most part taken from the Lloyd's Register survey reports, because even if many owners did not desire Lloyd's Register to class their ships, the surveys of those that did provide a good sample of the iron vessels then under construction. The remarks here are designed to describe some of the more interesting features in iron construction which in these years was at an empirical stage.[90]

One of the most prolific yards in building iron ships was Coutts & Co of Newcastle, which was started by John H Coutts of Aberdeen who left his native town soon after the *John Garrow* was launched in 1840; his first ship was the iron steamer *Prince Albert*, launched in 1842. Lloyd's Register classed the following which he built.

SOME IRON SHIPS BUILT BY COUTTS & CO 1843–50

1843   *Flash*, schooner, 139 tons nm 216 om; wire rigging; hollow floors and steep deadrise; in 1848 bottom 'payed with a mixture composed of black lead, arsenic and eggs'.

1844   *Foig a Ballagh*, schooner, 168 tons nm, 246 om; standing rigging of wire rope set up with double screw threads; had considerable deadrise, sharp ends and was so fine aft that the surveyor commented: '... in my opinion will not rise quick from a following sea'.

1844   *Q.E.D.*, auxiliary barque, 271 tons, wire standing rigging set up by a double screw thread, four iron bulkheads; 18 to 20 hp engine fitted in run to drive Smith's patent screw; mizzen mast used as a funnel; built as a collier to carry water ballast.

1846   *Admiral Hood*, schooner, 155 tons.

1846   *Iron Gem*, barque, 355 tons.

1847   *Adonis*, steamer, schooner rig, 374 gross tons.

1850   *Sally Gale*, brigantine, 193 tons m.

By 1850 the firm was styled Coutts & Parkinson. Coutts' naval architect at one time was another Aberdonian, Charles Mitchell (born 1820), who had served his apprenticeship with the Aberdeen Iron Works. By 1862 Mitchell had opened his own yard on the Tyne, and he later expanded the business considerably. He is remembered in Aberdeen as the donor of several university buildings named after him.[91]

While John Coutts was building his first ship in 1842–43, another iron vessel was under construction at Aberdeen in Blaikie Brothers' yard in St Clement Street. John Duffus & Co were the builders and she was a schooner named *Mercury*. 'When ready to be launched the *Mercury* was placed on two large waggons and hauled with crab winches until close to the quay wall, when she was transferred to 'ways' and launched into the harbour, a part of the quay wall having been taken down for the purpose. She entered the water with so great velocity that she went right across the dock, ran into the steamer *Sovereign*, and broke off her own figurehead.'[92]

As Blaikie Brothers made machinery they obviously had the knowledge and equipment for working in iron while John Duffus & Co supplied the shipwright's skill. This venture affords an interesting example of the co-operation required by men of differing skills in the fabrication of an iron hull at a time when iron shipbuilding was still in its infancy. John Duffus & Co's use of Blaikie Brothers' yard was closely akin to a shipbuilder constructing a vessel on a river's bank adjacent to where the timber was to be felled. The imaginary conversation, given by Sir Westcott Abell, between a shipwright, a smith and a boilermaker, could well have occurred during the construction of the *Mercury*.[93]

The *Mercury* measured 165 tons nm and 175 om on dimensions of 84.3ft × 20.2ft × 12.5ft with a flush deck, square stern and 'common bow', and there was a fair amount of structural timber in her construction. The keelson was of wood $14\frac{1}{2}$in × 12in, in two lengths; the beam shelf was also of wood and supported angle iron deck beams; also of wood was the deck, the rudder, and a paint strake planted on the outside of the iron hull and bolted on. The *John Garrow* had been built with a similar type of paint strake which had caused leaks when it sprang off. The *Mercury*'s keel was solid cast iron 7in × 12in in three lengths which were scarphed together as in a wood keel! This was almost a case of outside ballast. The frames were composed of 3in × 3in × ⅜in angles. After survey by Lloyd's Register the timber beam shelf and paint strake were removed and a new iron shelf was inserted.[94]

175

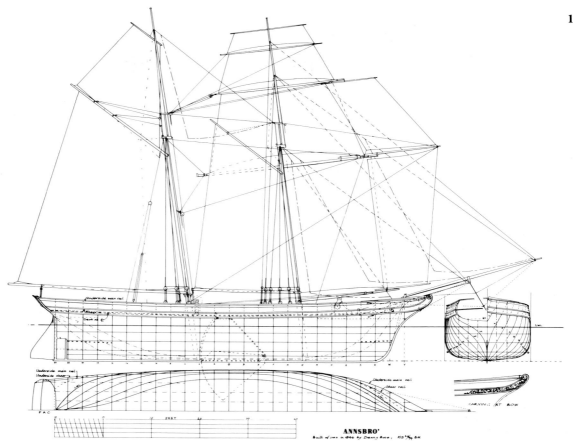

ANNSBRO'
Built of iron in 1846 by Denny Bros., 105 23/94 BM

Fig 175. Two iron vessels afloat in 1843: the John Laird *on the right, built in 1842 at Liverpool of 270 tons nm; on the left the brig* Guide *built for the Hon East India Company. (Parker Gallery)*

Fig 176. Annsbro'. Lines and sail plan redrawn by F A Claydon from two builder's plans in the National Maritime Museum, Greenwich. Built of iron in 1846 by William Denny & Bros at Dumbarton with measurements of 71ft 9in (keel and fore rake) × 18ft 0in × 8ft 9in and 105 tons om. Reconstruction: most of jibboom, as edge of paper ended just outside bowsprit cap; dolphin striker and all bowsprit rigging; all headsails and main topmast staysail; deadeyes and lanyards; hawsepipe; triangular centreplate omitted in favour of the one drawn (alternatives on plan). Stunsails and running rigging drawn by builder.

John Laird of Birkenhead, who built mainly steamers, produced the iron schooner *Proto* in 1841 for the Liverpool and London Shipping Co. She was No 41 on their building list and measured 128 tons nm and 155 tons om. A lithograph of her under sail (figure 123 in *Fast Sailing Ships*) shows a forward raking Aberdeen bow. Three years later Laird built the iron schooner *Dove* of 73 tons, which was originally intended to be a screw steamer. A Lloyd's Register surveyor commented that she was 'a vessel of small capacity very sharp forward and aft' and a tiny sketch he made indicated very steep deadrise.[95]

Plans of British vessels with centreboards are even more rare than a description of vessels fitted with them. One such example was the iron schooner *Annsbro'*, built in 1846 at Dumbarton by William Denny & Brothers for James Marland of Castle Mellon, Ireland. Dimensions on the builder's plan give 71ft 9in length of keel and fore

rake, 18ft 0in beam, 8ft 9in depth of hold and 105 23/94 tons om. A lines plan in the National Maritime Museum has been redrawn by Frederick A Claydon and indicates that the *Annsbro'* has an aperture for a propeller but judging by the large amount of canvas carried, her engine can only have been intended as an auxiliary. The hull-form has a sharp entrance and run of fast-sailing intent, but the floors have little rise and the bilges are kept low. Compared with Denny's schooner *Caledonia* which was built four years later, the *Annsbro'* is 28ft shorter and 3½ft shallower, and is flatter floored. Her centreboard pivotted from a point on her keelson: when raised it was close under her deck, and when lowered it projected 8ft 3in below her keel. A five-sided board is drawn with an ink dotted line but a three-sided one is also added in pencil, presumably at a later date. The actual gear used in lifting and lowering the centreboard is not specified.

The sail plan, now combined with the lines plan, shows a heavily-rigged schooner with a royal yard and two stunsails; the boom of the lower one is extended from the passaree boom used to extend the foot of the foresail. The contract price of the *Caledonia* (1850) was £2900 but the *Annsbro'*, although smaller, had the additional cost of engines.

Not many of these iron vessels were rigged as brigs or brigantines, but amongst the Lloyd's Register survey reports are four sloops: *Tinker* (1839), *Henrietta* and *Clipper* (1844), and *Vulcan* (1846). Like the *Mercury*, the *Tinker*, had a timber keelson; also timber deck beams and timber lodging knees, but iron hanging knees; the plates of the hull were butt-jointed with a covering plate inside over the butts which made her 'remarkably strong'. The *Henrietta* was lengthened in 1846 by fourteen feet and re-rigged as a schooner. The *Clipper* was re-rigged as a schooner in 1847, when her sliding keel was removed; her new masts were now made to lower for going under a bridge, presumably by being stepped in tabernacles.

Several vessels had round sterns, such as the schooner-rigged steamer *Juno*, built in 1841 on the Thames by Fairbairn & Co. In 1848 W Napier & Crighton of Glasgow built some half dozen schooners of about 94 tons each. 'These schooner lighters are built for the purpose of trading through the Canal from Port Dundas to Leith. Have round sterns, are well-finished, strong vessels; are all built, rigged and fitted on the one principle.' They were supplied with a 15ft longboat, a windlass, winch, foresail, mainsail, two headsails and 'other requisite sails'. This description appears under the *Kelvin*'s report. Another round-sterned schooner to use the Forth and Clyde Canal was the *Vulcan*, built in 1841 at Glasgow by Robert Saunderson & Co of 80 tons nm. 'This is a rough, strong-built vessel with round stern; two watertight bulkheads.' It is probable that these canal users had no counter stern but were really double enders with an outside rudder, to achieve the maximum length of hull that would fit within the lock gates.[96]

There were two flat-bottomed schooners for Swansea owners, the *Venus* and the *Tar*, completed in 1848–49. One wonders if they were referred to as 'Beauty and the Beast'. The *Tar* was built by Samuel Hodge on the Thames and measured 190 tons nm. 'This vessel has been constructed for carrying coal tar and has four tanks formed in her bottom by four transverse and one fore-and-aft iron bulkheads, with tight iron covers rivetted to the sides of the vessel about 4ft 0in below the upper deck. She is strong and rather roughly built vessel, well found, and has been specially surveyd while building.'[97] The *Venus* came from the yard of the Seansea Iron Shipbuilders and measured 65 tons nm, being also fitted to carry coal tar. A sketch shows that the floors were quite flat with a sudden urn of the bilge into wall sides. She was fitted with leeboards, and the masts were stepped on deck between chocks; the windlass was fitted as a 'purchase winch'.

In many of these iron vessels, the external plating was fitted like a clinker-built wooden hull with overlapping strakes at the lands. As already observed, many builders at the beginning of the forties employed a considerable amount of timber as structural components in the iron fabric, and although these had been replaced ten years later as engineering knowledge improved, wood was retained for many years for deck planking.

Although Lloyd's Register did not issue any rules for building iron ships until 1855 , an amended survey form for reporting on iron ships was issued in 1846–47. This new form was the result of visits made in 1846 by Augustin F B Creuze to several shipyards to study in detail the constructional methods employed. 'The adoption of this Form has, in a great degree, afforded a guide in assigning character to Iron Ships.'[98] Augustin Creuze was sent by Lloyd's Register in September 1847 to Liverpool to report

on the condition of the steamer *Great Britain* after she had been refloated, following her long standing on the Irish coast. He concluded his report in these words:

> I went to Mr. Laird's iron shipbuilding yard at Birkenhead, partly to see the vessel he is now building, and partly to talk with his foreman who, I consider, one of the best if not the very best ship-smith in the Kingdom. My object was to see whether anything, as a further test of workmanship, could be added to the new Form for iron ships which has been issued, and I was pleased to find that, after a long conversation with him, nothing further suggested itself to me.[99]

A more detailed study of Lloyd's Register's rules for iron ships and of iron as a shipbuilding material can be found in *Fast Sailing Ships*, Chapter Five.

In Germany, the first iron vessel was probably the brig *Hoffnung* which was built in 1844 at Ruhrort on the Rhine by Jacob Haniel & Huyssen for Alexander Seydel. She was fitted with a centreboard. The following year the same yard built the iron barque *Fortschritt* for the same owner. The next iron ship was not built until 1854, which was *Der Orientale* at Rostock.[100]

Fig 177. *Portrait of John Laird from the* Illustrated London News *of 27 July 1861. Together with his brother, Macgregor Laird, he did much to encourage iron shipbuilding as well as building iron vessels of all descriptions. Born at Greenock in 1805, he was later an MP and died in 1874.*

Fig 178. *This picture of the barque* Carmelita *being captured by a Mexican privateer, graphically illustrates one of the dangers lurking on the high seas for all ships during this period. Watercolour unsigned. (Peabody Museum, Salem)*

Fig 179. *With much of her crew aloft reefing the main topsail, the yards of which have been hauled round to spill the wind, the* Idas, *ex-*Augustus, *has dropped her Liverpool paddle tug and is seen passing the Calf of Man outward bound. This ship was built in 1848 at North Yarmouth, Maine, with the name of* Augustus, *and was bought by the Liverpool shipowner Klingender in 1852—53, who renamed her* Idas. *At this date her dimensions were 144.0ft × 32.1ft × 21.9ft and 706 tons. She was wrecked in 1865. The houseflag has the black letters 'KB' on white with a red border. No signature is visible on the painting but it is attributed to Samuel Walters. (Private Collection)*

178

179

Fig 180. Cohota. Lines plan drawn by Michael Costagliola from the builder's offsets in the Webb Institute of Naval Architecture, New York, and from a contemporary model. Built 1843 by William H Webb at New York with measurements of 145ft 0in × 32ft 3in × 20ft 0in and 690 tons.

Fig 181. Cohota. Deck plan and inboard profile drawn by Michael Costagliola from lines plan and from large rigged model of ship made at Canton in c1846. The three mooring pipes ran through centre of cavil rails; no mooring bitts on the model.

Fig 182. Cohota. Sail plan drawn by Michael Costagliola from lines plan and from large rigged model dated c1846. Spar lengths and rigging measured on model. The stunsail booms placed on the lower and topsail yards of the model and also the lower swinging boom, have been omitted on the sail plan.

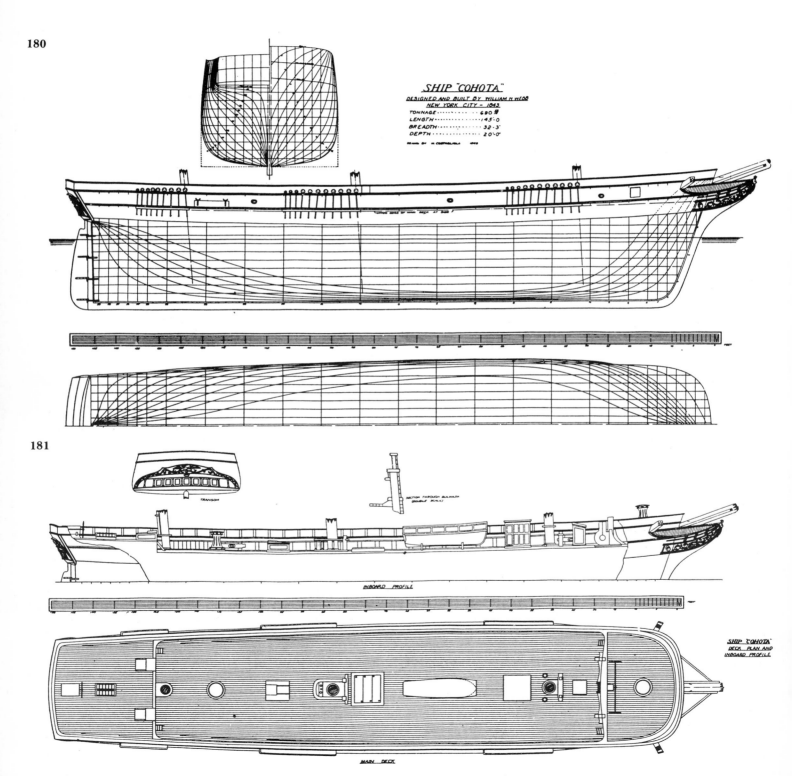

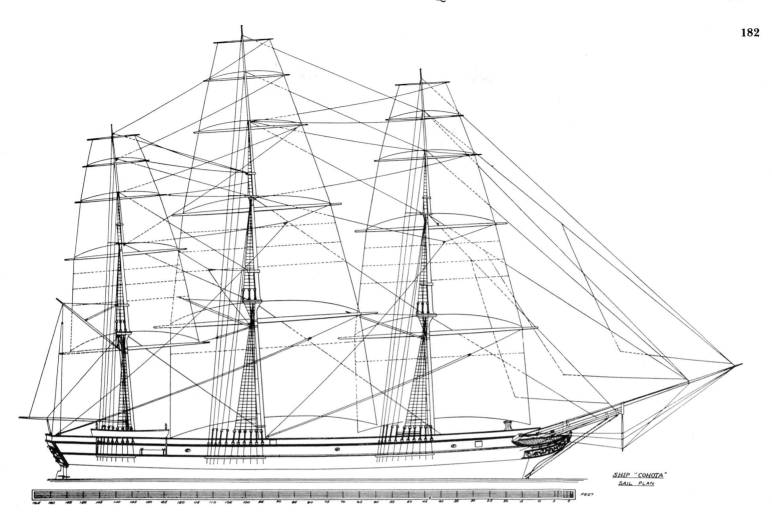

SHIP "COHOTA"
SAIL PLAN

AMERICAN SHIP DESIGN

After the War of 1812 American merchant ships no longer had to rely on speed to avoid capture and so the need for moderately fine-lined cargo carriers ended. Those still afloat continued trading but new ships gradually tended towards full-bodied hulls that would carry the largest amount of cargo without paying excessively large tonnage dues. Out of this was developed the kettle-bottomed hull with its maximum beam at the height of the hull when in light trim, but with the topsides narrowing all the way. Depth was assessed at half the breadth by tonnage rules until 1864. Many kettle-bottomed ships were built at Bath and Boston, but New York was very much taken up with packet ships after 1820 and here sailing abilities outweighed excessive cargo capacity. The China trade and the packet ship were two of the more specialised trades, but American ships were built for general cargo carrying in all oceans of the world. A ship was required to carry double her register tonnage in cargo and although this produced poor sailing abilities it suited the owner admirably and the shareholders even better.

Carrying cotton from New Orleans to Liverpool or France required ships with large holds as did the carriage of lumber, but up to the end of the 1830s many vessels did not exceed a length of 130ft or a tonnage of 500. However there was a gradual move towards the building of larger ships. An early example was the *Washington* of nearly 1000 tons which was built about 1825, although she was an isolated example. Large ships had difficulty in quickly filling their holds with cargo partly because merchants were not organised in this direction and partly because port facilities were poor. During the 1840s, ships of up to 1000 tons were often constructed, although many were packet ships as related in the next chapter.[101]

The general cargo ship was therefore of full hull-form with little deadrise, rounded bilges, full entrance and run, and having a wide square stern and not much sheer. Barque rig became popular in the 1820s, but both ships and barques were usually lofty as in Great Britain, the comparatively short yards being augmented with stunsails set each side. In Teupken's painting of the *Coliseum* (1828) there is a moonsail set and royal stunsails on fore- and mainmasts (figure 26).

But a superior class of merchant ship was developed for the China trade, based on the form of the packet ships, but with greater deadrise and a finer run. Although full-bodied by later clipper standards, these China packets were faster than previous ships in the trade and carried a sizeable cargo. One of the first of these was the *Helena* which William Webb built in 1841 with dimensions for register of 134ft 6in × 31ft 4in × 20ft 0in and 598 tons. Webb followed her with the *Cohota* of 690 tons, built two years later, and Michael Costagliola reconstructed her lines, deck and sail plans from Webb's offsets and a large rigged model of the ship. The deck is almost flush, apart from a short monkey forecastle and a raised quarterdeck which stops just short of the mizzen. The only house on deck is a small galley abaft the foremast. She has a lofty rig, carrying skysails on each mast, but the mizzen is stepped a long way aft. Her fastest passage seems to have been one of 100 days between Calcutta and Boston made in 1850.[102]

Next from Webb's yard came *Montauk* and *Panama* in 1844 which continued the same style of hull-form. However, although the Atlantic packet ships continued to be built and designed as before, there was a rapidly growing desire to build ships for the China trade on clipper lines, with much finer hulls and greater deadrise than were given to the China packets. The *Rainbow* of 1845 was a culmination of this and thereafter sharp hull-forms were required for the China trade.

CONCLUSIONS

The years leading up to 1850 are to many people merely the prelude to the clipper ship era and all that it contained, but clippers constituted but an infinitesimal part of the world's merchant fleet, and carried a fraction of the cargoes shifted across the oceans. A booming freight market allowed uneconomic hull-forms to be built to engage in ocean races and although these ships hit the headlines, there was never a thought of replacing the colliers with Aberdeen clipper brigs. Admittedly, the increasing interest in speed encouraged by railway travel, did rub off onto the mercantile community, and the desire for speedier communication at sea began. New ways of measuring a ship for tonnage in Great Britain, dating from 1836, resulted in vessels being given longer hulls that were also shallower. Greater length provides a higher speed potential so that the ordinary carrier was now capable of faster passages. There must have been some curious contrasts to be seen in the docks and the narrow seas in the late 1840s: long sleek iron schooners with raking masts beside short bluff full-rigged ships with lofty masts, short yards and immensely long jibbooms and flying jibbooms. The medium clipper of 1849 was the extreme clipper of twenty years earlier. But even if cargo carriers did have finer lines than formerly, it was the carriage of cargo and the ways of turning that into profits that exercised the minds of the builders and owners of those days.

4
PASSENGER FRIGATES AND PACKET SHIPS 1815-1850

SUCCESSORS TO THE EAST INDIAMEN

In titling the section thus, the word 'successors' is used in a specific sense to denote ships of first class construction that were built to carry passengers on voyages to destinations eastward of the Cape of Good Hope. To some extent these successors were beginning to establish themselves in the trade to India soon after the Honourable Company lost the first part of its monopoly by the Act of 1813 and the resultant private trade was on such an increased scale that a second Act in 1823 permitted British ships to trade with every country covered by the Company's charter with the exception of China.[1] Trade with the colony of Australia was naturally stimulated. From April 1834 the Company was deprived of its China monopoly and its fleet of large Indiamen was accordingly dispersed.

Some of the East Indiamen were bought for their valuable timber and then broken up: the *Lady Melville*, sold in 1832 for £10,000, was broken up two years later; the *Canning* of 1326 tons fetched £5700 in 1834 and was broken up at once; others fetched similar prices. But some were kept in service by their new owners. These included the *Buckinghamshire*, built in 1816 at Bombay of 1369 tons, which realised £10,550 in 1834; the *Inglis* of 1321 tons, built at Penang in 1811 went for £9150 and was wrecked ten years later; the *Minerva* survived until about 1850; the *Bombay* of 1809 was still owned by Duncan Dunbar in 1860; the *Earl of Balcarres* and the *Java* both became coal hulks.[2]

Before 1813 it had been illegal for a British ship to round the Cape of Good Hope without the Company's licence so that the lifting of regulations caused a minor trade boom. In 1820 *Lloyd's Register* listed 263 ships, none of which was chartered to the East India Company, as leaving Great Britain for India; the average tonnage was approximately 485 tons. But the trade soon became overstocked with tonnage so that five years later only 170 ships

are listed as sailing for Eastern ports, although their average tonnage has increased to approximately 530. The *Thalia* of 357 tons went to Calcutta in 1818 on her maiden passage and in that year there were several ships of her size in the trade, but by the mid-twenties there were few as small as this.

The mantle of the Honourable Company still lay across the trade routes beyond the Cape of Good Hope and many of the merchant ships that now ventured into the Indian Ocean attempted to be minor copies of the lordly East Indiamen. From 1830 many good quality ships of the best construction, built specifically to carry passengers, entered this trade. They were rarely of less than 500 tons and were owned by firms that specialised in the business, such as Richard & Henry Green, Money Wigram & Sons, Joseph Somes, Thomas and William Smith, Duncan Dunbar — names that were household words in their time. Contemporary notices referred to their ships as 'frigates' and as they sailed from Blackwall, twentieth century writers have dubbed them 'Blackwall frigates'.

The British possessions in India produced a steady two-way stream of passengers: officers and troops returning from service and others going out to replace them, governors and their staffs, merchants, wives and families, invalids and many others. These were carried by East Indiamen and other specialist ships, some of which might have been chartered for the purpose.

The discovery of gold in Australia, closely following that found in California, began another vast migration, only this time the participants demanded to be transported as speedily as possible. The clippers that were developed to meet this sudden demand are treated for the most part in *Fast Sailing Ships*, although many passenger frigates were profitably diverted to the Australian trade and others specially built for it. Of course, all sailing ships carried spare cabins in the after accommodation, the passage money being one of the master's perquisites, and these berths provided sufficient space for most people travelling at normal times. No doubt these passengers helped to relieve the bordom of a long passage.

183

184

NORTH ATLANTIC PACKETS

Shortly after the end of European hostilities in 1815, five American businessmen who were textile importers, laid the foundations of a plan to build up New York as a large commericial port by establishing a regular line of trans-Atlantic ships. These ships were to carry exports from America and return with goods from Great Britain. Thus it was that in 1818 the company, which became known as the Black Ball Line, was founded with four ships to run between New York and Liverpool on regular advertised dates 'full or not full'. The newest of these four ships, the *James Monroe*, was of 424 tons and built in 1817, and cabin passengers paid $200 each which included bedding and food. Four years later came the first competition from the Red Star Line of New York with four ships sailing on a regular service, to which the Black Ball Line responded with a further four ships. Later in 1822, the Swallowtail Line was founded, also on the New York and Liverpool run. By 1823, two Lines had been set up to Havre, and in 1824 the Black X Line and the Red Swallowtail Line had been established in London. Others were to follow.

As the years went by, the ships grew in size. By the end of the 1820s, ships on the Liverpool run had reached 600 tons and a decade later the size had increased to 800–900 tons. The first ship of over 1000 tons was the *Roscius*, built in 1838 by Brown & Bell of New York with dimensions of 167ft 6in × 36ft 4in × 21ft 7in and 1030 tons om. By 1845 there were 52 regular ships sailing to and from New York across the Atlantic with three arrivals and three departures per week on average.[3]

At first the number of passengers carried was small, only 10 or 20 per trip on average in the 1820s, and they were all cabin passengers. 25 passengers was about the maximum that could be carried comfortably. The hold and 'tween decks were given over entirely to cargo which was of a mixed nature east-bound, although after 1830 more and more cotton was brought up from the southern ports by coastal brigs and schooners to be trans-shipped to Europe. By 1835, freight on cotton was yielding about $2500 as well as a further $500 from other goods, and the same or a little more on west-bound cargoes. Packet ships made three round trips per year and so the total annual proceeds for cargo totalled about $20,000, while the car-

Fig 183. The Blackwall frigate Madagascar *(left) and* Earl of Balcarres *as painted by Tudgay in a rather stylised scene. The latter's tonnage of 1417 was much larger than Madagascar's 835, but the artist has not made this clear. The* Earl of Balcarres *was built at Bombay in 1815; the other in the Blackwall Yard in 1837. (Parker Gallery)*

Fig 184. The large black circle on her fore topsail below the lowest reef band proclaims this ship as belonging to the Black Ball Line out of New York. This is the Europe *built in 1833 by Brown & Bell at New York with dimensions of 137ft 4in × 31ft 6in × 15ft 9in and 618 tons. A skysail mast is fidded abaft each royal mast. (Parker Gallery)*

Fig 185. The packet ship Roscius *clewing up sail as she gets into soundings. (Parker Gallery)*

185

riage of mails, passengers and specie totalled a further $10,000.[4]

By the mid-thirties, cabin passenger accommodation had increased to 50 or 60 per ship and was now placed in a long poop which extended right forward to the mainmast. It was not until 1838 when the steamers *Sirius* and *Great Western* arrived that the packets began to lose the cream of the business. Thereafter they began to take steerage passengers to America to re-coup monies lost to the steamers, although the packets from Havre had always carried emigrants. An emigrant paid a $20 fare and occupied 80 cubic feet of space or the equivalent of two tons of cargo. Cargo freight was $10 per ton, so the two were about equal, but emigrants caused much more trouble! The regular traders and occasional ships carried the bulk of the emigrants before the packets fell back on this alternative form of earning profits in the 1840s and later.[5]

The North Atlantic trade was a hard one for ships engaged in it winter and summer alike, especially those on regular sailings which had to take their departure irrespective of wind and weather conditions. By degrees a specialised type of ship was evolved: deep and full-bodied with short, sharp ends, that could withstand hard driving and yet, with improved canvas and rigging techniques, could be braced up more sharply to go efficiently to windward with the minimum amount of leeway.

There is a good series of plans to study that were published by William H Webb of New York, whose shipyard, commenced by his father, Isaac, constructed many

of the packets.[6] The size of their ships increased rapidly from that of the *Ohio*, built at Philadelphia in 1825 with a length between perpendiculars of 130ft, to that of the *Oxford*, built at New York by Webb in 1836 with a length between perpendiculars of 147ft 6in. The *Ohio* was similar in hull-form to other full-bodied merchant ships of her day but with a longer and finer run.

Fig 186. The Queen Victoria *endeavouring to get into the harbour at Havre, scrapes against tne bastion on the left-hand side of the entrance. There are only a few more feet to go to get into comparative safety. She has obviously run in before the gale with only a close-reefed fore topsail set and that split up the centre. The starboard anchor is at the cathead ready for dropping. She is presumably the ship built at Bath, Maine, in 1828 of 711 tons. She occasionally sailed for the 'Old Line' of packets and also in the New York to Orleans service. This oil painting is signed: 'Smartly, 1843'. (Peabody Museum, Salem)*

Fig 187. An impression by the Venetian artist, John Luzro, of the ship New England *being dismasted under the command of G W Edge. A ship of 920 tons, built in 1849 at Bath, Maine, she had very little deck space as the poop extended forward of the mainmast, and the big deckhouse was joined to the forecastle. The picture is undated, but Edge was master in the late 1850s. (Peabody Museum, Salem)*

Fig 188. The Stratford, *ex-*Arctic, *at Bristol. Built in 1850 at Williamsburg, New York, she was of 1157 tons. She was in the Red Z Line to Liverpool in 1850. The usual double channels are absent. (Nautical Photo Agency)*

186

A plan of the *Oxford*, drawn by Howard I Chapelle, shows her also to have been full-bodied with a short entrance, a slightly longer run which was full in the quarters, and long parallel sides. There was very little deadrise with high, slightly curving sides, and not much sheer. The topgallant rail ran in one unbroken length and the bulwarks were 5ft 6in high. There was a very short forecastle with just enough space to man the capstan bars, and then the deck was unbroken to the taffrail. There was a short afterhouse with a thwartship alleyway in which the helmsman, when standing at the wheel, was protected from following seas. He could watch the trim of the sails through a skylight above his head. The *Oxford* was of 752 tons, 147ft 6in length, 33ft 6in beam and 21ft 6in depth of hold, and was a consistently good passage maker.[7]

The *Yorkshire*, built by William Webb in 1843, was designed on finer lines and of larger size than the *Oxford*, being almost 250 tons bigger at 996 tons, with dimensions of 166ft 6in × 36ft 2in × 21ft 0in. She had her midship section halfway between the fore- and mainmasts, and from here there was an easy tapering run to the stern. The entrance was short but sharp, and hollow near the forefoot; there was very little deadrise; the bilges were rounded and there was some tumblehome. One noticeable difference compared with the *Oxford* was the long poop now fitted which reached to just forward of the mainmast, and in which were placed cabins for the saloon passengers.[8] She was considered one of the fastest packets built, and her west-bound times, Liverpool to New York,

have been analysed by Robert Albion as follows: shortest 16 days; longest 58 days; average 29 days. These spanned a service of 18 years with the Black Ball Line.[9]

Howard I Chapelle dismisses the claim that the ships especially built for the Dramatic Line in 1836–37 were the first North Atlantic packets to have flat floors, by citing a plan of the *Columbus* and her two sister ships built in 1834–35 which were designed and built by Isaac Webb with just such features.[10]

Most of the packets were heavily rigged with skysails on each mast, and stunsails on fore- and mainmasts waiting to be set in any favourable slant of wind. The ships had to be strongly constructed to carry big cargoes, in addition to passengers. The great problem was to build ships stiff enough to maintain their shape in spite of the hard driving and savage weather, and this was done with iron knees, iron strapping, locking scarph joints, edge-fastened planking, and caulking of the ceiling planks.[11]

Although Webb was not to improve on the design of the *Yorkshire*, he continued to build packets of increasingly larger size, his three-decker *Guy Mannering* of 1849 registering 1419 tons on dimensions of 190ft 6in × 40ft 2in × 28ft 8in. The *Havre*, plans of which are reproduced here from Webb's published drawings, through the assistance of Michael Costagliola, was of 1000 tons and so a little smaller than the *Yorkshire*. Webb usually drew fairly narrow stunsails on his sail plans, particularly the lower ones, although he did include main lower stunsails in many cases.[12]

Fig 189. This engraving of the Devonshire *shows a product from the yard of Westervelt & Mackey of New York, who built her in 1848 with a length of 173ft 6in and a tonnage of 1149. Her shortest westbound passage was 19 days and she sailed under the Black X Line. There is an 'X' on her flag at the main truck. This engraving is from the* Illustrated London News.

Fig 190. Havre. *Lines plan reproduced from plan published by William H Webb in* Plans of Wooden Vessels 1840–69 (1895), *and loaned me by Michael Costagliola. Particulars printed on plan: built 1845; 156ft 0in (length on deck) × 34ft 6in (moulded breadth) × 20ft 6in (depth of hold); 1000 tons cm [customs measurement]. Webb's appraisal of the ship reads as follows: 'Built in 1845 for the regular Packet trade, New York and Havre. Proved an excellent sea boat, made rapid passages, was a handsome and very popular ship.'*

Fig 191. Havre. *Sail plan reproduced from plan published by Webb and loaned me by Michael Costagliola.*

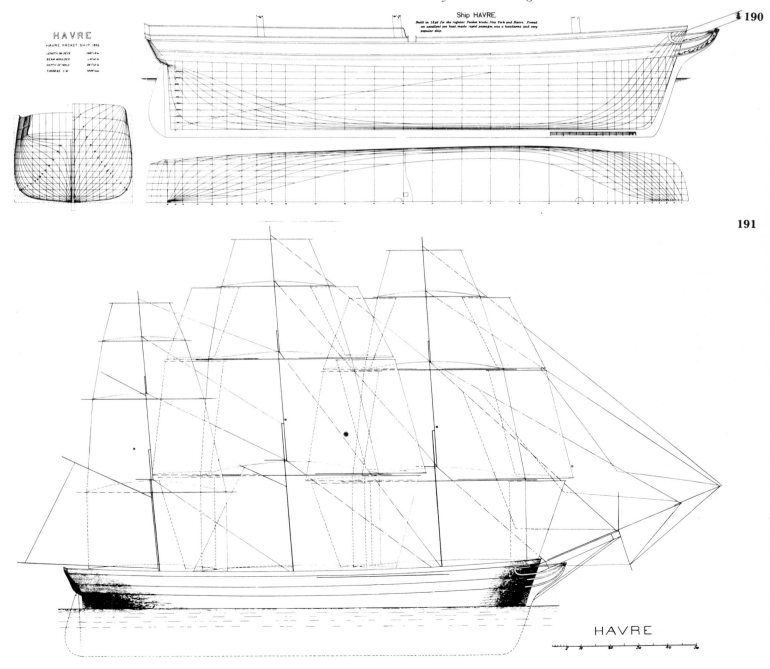

Donald McKay built sixteen packet ships in his yard at East Boston up to the end of 1850, the largest of which were the *New World* (1846 of 1404 tons), *Ocean Monarch* (1847 of 1301 tons), *Daniel Webster* (1850 of 1188 tons), *Cornelius Grinnell* (1850 of 1118 tons) and *Antarctic* (1850 of 1115 tons). Five more packets of clipper category were constructed in the years 1851–56 of which the sister ships *Star of Empire* and *Chariot of Fame*, both built in 1853, were the largest at 2050 tons.[13]

Other prominent builders of packet ships, all at New York, were Brown & Bell, C Bergh & Co, Smith & Dimon, and Westervelt & Mackey.

The vast emigration to America from Great Britain, and the coastal regions of Norway, Germany, Holland and Belgium was principally conducted through the ports of Liverpool, Bristol, London, Havre and Bremen to form the first great exodus in the years 1830–60, which reached its culmination from 1847 to 1854. During the 1840s and 1850s, the average number of people leaving Liverpool each year amounted to 150,000, most of whom were Irish. Continued poverty, an expanding population, famine in Ireland and many other causes continued to swell the numbers of those deciding to leave their native land. But if the American lines of packets could not take them, there were always other ships prepared to do so. Some of them were regular traders in the North Atlantic and were well-found ships, but others were badly-provisioned and over-crowded, and the wretched emigrants were forced to exist,

Fig 192. The Havre *photographed at Arendal, Norway, in the 1870s when owned by T Thommesen & Son. She still carries single topsails, and the stunsail booms on the foreyard are under the yard. (Nautical Photo Agency)*

Fig 193. The Cornelius Grinnell *was one of the packet ships, or 'Line ships' as the Americans called them, which Donald McKay constructed. Of 1117 tons, she had dimensions of 182ft 0in × 36ft 5in × 23ft 6in and was built for the Red Swallowtail Line between New York and London. She served this line until it closed in 1881. The* Illustrated London News *of 31 August 1850 which published her portrait and a scene in the hold, gave sizes of her scantlings. She was built of oak and yellow pine; she had 3 keelsons, 15in square placed on top of each other; she had sister keelsons, as well as 2 bilge keelsons on each side; the garboards were 7in thick but the outer planking was mostly 4½in; the bulwarks were 5½ft high 'surmounted by a monkey rail' [? a topgallant rail]; the poop was 80ft long; the mainyard measured 74ft.*

Fig 194. There were 7 hold beams in the Cornelius Grinnell, *sized 15in × 12in; the lower deck and upper deck beams were sized 15in × 16in, and were all of Southern pine. The knees in the hold were of oak and those in the 'tween decks of hackmatack; the stanchions were 10in square. This engraving from the* Illustrated London News *of 31 August 1850 illustrates the massive timber scantlings.*

192

195

if they could, in conditions little better than a slaver. This was usually at the larger ports where rates were down to 10s per head which might attract the poorest class of person. In 1847, no less than 17,500 persons died on the passage or upon arrival. Vessels only 90ft long might take 300 emigrants. But conditions had improved in the 1850s and Government inspectors in Great Britain ensured that provisions and numbers travelling were in accordance with the law. During all this time, many smaller ports were regularly sending over schooners, brigs and barques with parties of local people, some of whom were of a wealthier class.[14]

Emigration to Australia and New Zealand also suffered during the 1840s from lax supervision at some of the ports of departure, or from epidemics breaking out on board on the much longer passages lasting three or four months. The big Canadian ships chartered for this purpose were especially prone to such problems owing to the vast numbers carried, but by the 1850s health and care of the emigrants had improved.

Some particulars about emigration from Great Britain were given in the *Sydney Morning Herald* of 11 January 1851. Between the years 1825–49 (inclusive) a total of 2,285,184 persons emigrated from Great Britain, and of these 1,260,247 went to America, 808,740 went to Canada, and 185,386 went to Australia and New Zealand. This leaves about 30,000 unaccounted for. Many emigrants were sent out at the Government's expense. During the 1840s various organisations were set up to assist and supervise emigration to Australia such as the Family Colonization Loan Society in which Mrs Chisholm was involved, and the Female Emigration Society. The cost to the Government of sending out emigrants was £17 to £18 per head which was re-couped in London by taxing the colonies; nothing was contributed by the British Government up to the end of 1852.

THE *SERINGAPATAM* AND OTHER EARLY PASSENGER FRIGATES

The decision of the East India Company to abandon the chartering of ships for general trading purposes was virtually inevitable after their China monopoly was revoked with effect from April 1834, for the Company was not geared for trading under competition. This was the province of the privately-owned, privately-run merchant ship, and the Company's decision passed on to them the responsibility for the carriage of the China tea crop and the conveyance of troops and passengers. Some of the Indiamen were indeed purchased and placed in trade again, because the Honourable Company was still chartering vessels for troops, personnel and stores to India. Yet this decision by the Company had to some extent been anticipated, as had been the abolition of its monopoly, and shipowners had had sufficient time to equip themselves with suitable passenger vessels.[15]

During the tenure of the East India Company's monopoly with China in the years 1813–34, the type of merchant ship trading to India and Australia has already been illustrated by the plans of the *Thalia* (figure 31) and by Hedderwick's 500-ton ship (figure 17). In 1833 William Smith, one of the partners in T & W Smith, drew a lines plan which closely resembled Hedderwick's ship although Smith had added double stern galleries.[16] This plan in turn resembles the salient features of a model in the National Maritime Museum at Greenwich bearing the name *Scotia*, which makes her obviously represent the ship of this name built by T & W Smith in 1836 for their own use in the India trade. The *Scotia* was laid down in June 1835 and launched a year later; she measured 132ft

Fig 195. One of five scenes aboard an Australian emigrant ship, from drawings made during the passage by E Skinner Prout and published in the Illustrated London News *of 20 January 1849. The view chosen is from the break of the poop looking forward: on the right is a gallows frame spanning a deckhouse with handspikes for the windlass or capstan bars standing in a rack; forward is a boat, keel uppermost, perhaps with livestock underneath; then comes what may be the galley with emigrants queueing outside with buckets; lastly the foremast. But that is surely not a bentinck boom athwart the ship but the spritsail yard which by this date was rigged at the knightheads and through which the bowsprit shrouds were led. The bulwarks seem broad enough to take odd items but certainly not hammocks.*

Fig 196. Model of the Scotia *with the white-painted animal pens placed on the main hatch and the longboat on top. The forecastle stretches abaft the foremast and the poop extends up to the mainmast, leaving only a small deck space, as in the American packet ships. Tonnage was only measured below this deck which is why the deck was not entirely covered in. The* Scotia *was built in 1836 with a tonnage of 778. (National Maritime Museum, Greenwich)*

196

171

197

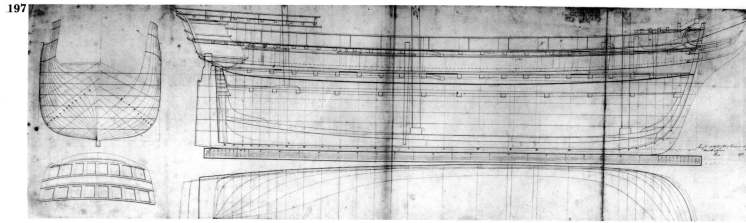

198

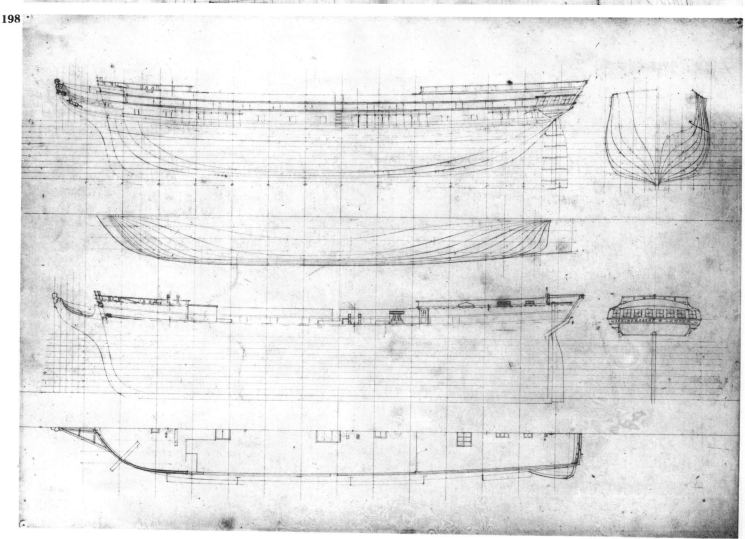

Fig 197. Coromandel. *Lines plan reproduced from plan in the Hilhouse Collection when in possession of Charles Hill & Sons. Built on River Thames in 1820. Measurements given on plan: 128ft 2in length at height of wing transom, 32ft 4in extreme breadth, 576 tons. Another source gives tonnage as 645. She did not set skysails but had fidded royal masts, a flying jibboom, and mizzen topmast stunsails. The* Lady Raffles *had been built to this plan 3 years earlier.*

Fig 198. Seringapatam. *Lines, deck plan, and inboard profile. Measurements taken by William Salisbury from model in National Maritime Museum, Greenwich. Built 1837 by R & H Green at Blackwall Yard, London, and dimensions scaled off plan give: 152ft 6in × 34ft 6in (moulded) × 22ft 0in (approx). Tonnage was 818 om.*

Fig 199. *After the cyclone at Calcutta in October 1864, wrecked vessels lay everywhere, and in the centre of the picture is the old* Southampton *with her foremast gone and her stern windows open. She was built at Blackwall in 1841 and was of 971 tons. (Nautical Photo Agency)*

7in × 29ft 6in × 22ft 0in with a tonnage of 778. Lloyd's Register's surveyor wrote that she was 'more highly finished in workmanship than her sister ship the *Robert Small*' which was launched the previous year. The model of the *Scotia* clearly exhibits the hull-form, deck arrangements and rigging possessed by a passenger ship of this date, including double stern galleries.

T & W Smith of Newcastle were shipbuilders and shipowners of the same standing and calibre as Green or Wigram. After buying William Rowe's yard in 1810, the firm was first known as Smith & Sons and in 1836 became T & W Smith, when Thomas and William succeeded their father.[17]

Enough examples have been cited to show the style of ship being built for Eastern trades and an examination of published pictures confirms that above the waterline the appearance remained very conservative. The only variation of note was the shape of the stern. East Indiamen of a size with the *Farquharson* had double (or 'two-tiered') stern and quarter galleries. Smaller ships, such as the *Coromandel*, copied this practice, although it brought the lower counter dangerously close to the waterline. Illustrations and descriptions during the years 1815–40 usually show vessels with only a single row of stern windows, but there are enough examples of ships with a double row to prove that the latter feature was sometimes used. Another East India trader to have them was the *Lord William Bentinck* of 564 tons, built by Hilhouse, Hill & Co at Bristol in 1828 and chartered by the East India Company on her first voyage.[18]

But the majority of East Indiamen were launched from yards on the Thames and from these same building slips came the passenger frigates which succeeded them, so it is easy to understand how the East Indiamen's style was continued and imitated by builders who had become steeped in the requirements of the trade. Amongst these firms were Green, Wigram & Green, proprietors of the Blackwall Yard, who were in the forefront of producing this new class of vessel, and considerable thought was undoubtedly given to their design and construction. The *London*, launched in 1832, 'may be described as the real pioneer of Messrs Money Wigram and Son's fine fleet of passenger vessels'.[19] A list of ships built at the Blackwall Yard shows that the tonnage gradually increased from 576 in 1831 to 656 in 1836. Then in 1837 the tonnage suddenly advanced with a leap of 160 tons when the *Seringapatam* of 818 tons was launched for Richard and Henry Green.[20]

Writing of the ships built in the Blackwall Yard, Henry Green and Robert Wigram stated in 1881 that the *Seringapatam* was 'the first of a new class and was a great advance in size and form on previous vessels; in her the double stern and galleries were abandoned, which at the time was looked upon as an important stride'.[21] This suggests that several of their ships had been built with double sterns although most surviving illustrations point to the contrary. The plan of *Seringapatam* in figure 198 is drawn by William Salisbury from lines taken off the model in the National Maritime Museum, Greenwich, and he has generously made his plan available. It shows that the new

199

ship repeated the features of previous vessels in retaining the very heavy headworks, the heavy quarter galleries and stern, and a double row of ports along her side.

As to the 'great advance in size and form', the larger size is an accepted fact but the 'form' is hardly an 'advance'; quite the opposite, in fact, to judge by the lines taken from the model, which show a close affinity to a warship. The shape of the midship section has a distinctly naval flavour with very easy curves that suggest they were designed upon arcs of circles, and with flaring topsides above marked tumblehome. There is a shoulder worked into the entrance along the line of the wale, presumably to retard the ship plunging her bows down in rough weather. Two naval designs selected at random which show considerable overall similarity with *Seringapatam* are the privateer *Mars*, built at Bristol by J M Hilhouse in 1779, and the 36-gun frigate, whose plan was published in 1820 by Abraham Rees.[22] The lines of *Seringapatam* bear little relation to the style which we have established as being the model for ships built during the twenties and thirties, although her finer lines, even if they were copying an older model, were undoubtedly a success in the India trade. Her hull-form was also far removed from the style of the American packet ships of the same date.

In *The Chronicles of the Blackwall Yard* it is stated that the *Seringapatam* was 'always noted for her quick and regular passages, and became the model for many succeeding vessels'.[23] Basil Lubbock wrote that twelve ships were built on her lines amongst which were the *Agincourt* and *Southampton*, both somewhat larger ships.[24] Thus was perpetuated the older fashion of a popular ship.

The dimensions of *Seringapatam*, scaled off the lines plan, give 152ft 6in length (foreside of stem under bowsprit to aft side of sternpost), 34ft 6in beam (moulded) and 22ft 0in (approx) depth of hold. Her proportion of beams to length is 4¼ to 1 compared with *Coromandel*'s 4 to 1; but more striking, and the factor which gives her a more modern look, is the great increase in the proportion of depth to length, which has now advanced to 6 to 1, compared with *Coromandel*'s 5 to 1.

Under Captain George Denny, *Seringapatam*'s maiden passage from Calcutta to London occupied 116 days between 15 December 1837 and 10 April 1838. The fast passages made by the passenger frigates averaged 85 to 90 days, pilot to pilot, on either the outward run to Bombay or the homeward one from Calcutta.

A deck scene aboard the *Madagascar* – built at Blackwall in the same year as *Seringapatam* but twenty tons larger – confirms many features to be seen in the model of the latter. The very high bulwarks are clearly discernible with their rounded top above the heads of the men on deck; the squat sheet and halliard bitts at the foot of the mainmast, the large capstan, the small hatchways, and the iron mast hoops are all present. A lithograph by Thomas G Dutton of *Seringapatam* depicts three guns amidships in the main deck ports, and almost concealed in each of the painted ports at 'tween deck level is a scuttle in the bottom right-hand corner which is hinged open.

In the absence of a sail plan, this lithograph illustrates the salient features of her rig. Few Blackwall passenger frigates set skysails and the masthead terminated close above the royal stay, as can be seen here. Nor did they often fit trysail gaffs on fore-and mainmasts. One interesting innovation here is the introduction of a main topmast stay which sets up on deck in addition to the one taken to the fore top; another is that the fall of the main topsail brace leads aft to the bumkin at the stern and not to the mizzen top.

After survey at Blackwall in 1854 when the topsides were caulked, wales re-treenailed and other repairs effected, the *Seringapatam*'s survey report concluded: 'Is in efficient condition; form well-preserved; eligible to carry dry and perishable cargoes to and from all parts of the world and remains at present class'; *ie* 12 AE1.[25]

200

Fig 200. Deck view aboard Madagascar *looking forward to the mainmast. She was said to have been built on the same lines as the* Seringapatam, *being built the same year and 17 tons larger. Note the position of the two yards hanging down the mainmast, and then compare them with the engraving of the* Earl of Hardwicke *(figure 202). Both engravings are done by W H Prior. Could one of them be mis-named? (Parker Gallery)*

Fig 201. The Seringapatam *hove-to, from a lithograph by T G Dutton. The short spar under the bowsprit is the vestigial spritsail yard which is slowly being moved aft, year by year; it acted as a sort of whisker boom to spread the bowsprit rigging. Although there are three guns in the ports of the waist on the main deck, what appear to be muzzles of guns on the lower deck are actually the lids of scuttles which have been hinged-up for light and ventilation. (Paul Mason Gallery)*

Fig 202. This ship is called Earl of Hardwicke *and is in drydock, probably fitting out for her maiden voyage. The position of the two yards — presumably the lower yard and topsail yard — agrees closely with the* Madagascar. *Note the small paddle wheel on its sponson and the tall thin chimney for an auxiliary engine. The* Vernon *and* Owen Glendower *were built with them but the latter had hers removed before her maiden passage. The* Vernon *made at least one voyage to India as an auxiliary, but I have no data about the* Earl of Hardwicke. *Her design is said to have been modelled on the* Seringapatam; *she was built the following year and was 34 tons larger.*

202

One interesting point to be seen in the *Madagascar*'s deck view in figure 200 is the fitting of a form of iron truss to the lowered mainyard in the middle foreground. The use of iron trusses in the thirties is not too well documented at present, but their existence in a Blackwall frigate is to some extent confirmed by a rigged model in the Marlipins Museum, Shoreham, on which a truss is shown on each of the lower yards, although it did not result in placing the yard much beyond the mast. This model is entitled *Seringapatam* and was made in 1840 by Robert Butler. It is a finely executed model to $\frac{1}{4}$in scale but suffers from being much too lofty. A visual examination suggests the typical hull-form of a passenger frigate, but the flush deck is at variance with the full poop and topgallant forecastle of the model in the National Maritime Museum. The introduction of iron trusses enabled yards to be braced further round, thus permitting ships to sail closer to the wind and thereby improve their efficiency and sailing qualities.

Data from contemporary models is acceptable subject to evidence that no later restoration has been undertaken. In the Liverpool Museum is a $\frac{1}{4}$in scale rigged model of the ship *Parker* (built at Liverpool in 1830 for the West Indies trade) and here iron trusses are fitted to the three lower yards. If the model has not suffered restoration, an early example of an iron truss would be authenticated.

The period of the passenger frigates may be said to have commenced prior to the expiry of the Honourable Company's charter in 1834, rather than with the launch of the *Seringapatam*; it was in full flower throughout the forties only to lose its individuality in the next decade.

FRIGATES OF THE FORTIES

The interests of the partners in the Blackwall Yard were tending to diverge so that when the partnership agreement expired in 1843 it was not renewed, the yard being divided between Richard and Henry Green (the sons of George) who took the eastern end, and Money Wigram and Sons who took the western part.[26] Both before and after the division the yard remained as busy as ever and ships of all types were constructed in addition to the passenger frigates. These latter increased in size with each new ship and were soon above one thousand tons. In 1842 there were launched the *Prince of Wales* and the *Queen* of 1223 tons each which were superb examples of the shipwright's art. They closely resembled 50-gun frigates with a flush upper deck and two lower decks. Only two years later they were outclassed by the 1444-ton *Monarch*, built by R & H Green for themselves, and described by a contemporary writer as a 'splendid mercantile frigate ... pierced for 50 guns and capable of carrying a greater number, for besides sixteen ports on a side upon the main deck, there is also an equal number of large scuttles on the lower deck'.[27] There were twelve cabins of an average size of 10ft × 11ft on the main deck, eighteen cabins on the lower deck, and the dining saloon measured 36ft long and 18ft wide. The Tonnage Commission of 1850 examined her and described her as an 'East Indiaman with spar deck, sharp as a frigate but deep in hold'.[28]

A good impression of one of these ships is afforded by a description of Green's *Trafalgar*, built at Blackwall in

Fig 203. The Earl of Hardwicke *was wrecked off the coast of South Africa in 1863. The ship in this picture is not named, but was presumably wrecked somewhere near Durban. Could this be the same Blackwall frigate? She has heavy quarter galleries and a suitable head and hull-form.* (Local History Museum, Durban)

Fig 204. The Queen *at anchor. She harked back to the old East Indiamen. An engraving from the* Illustrated London News *in 1842 in the days before their great marine artist E Weedon enlivened the pages with his brilliant engravings.*

1848, and described by W I Downie, one of her apprentices:

> The *Trafalgar* was a very fine teak-built ship of twelve hundred and fifty tons, like a frigate in appearance, and with a few guns on her main deck. When lying at anchor, with her swinging booms rigged out, and her boats in the water, fast to them, as she did in Madras, she might easily have been taken for a man-of-war. The house-flag, in place of the pennant at the main, would, of course, have told a tale; but, with her painted ports, square yards, and immense whole topsails, she bore a very strong resemblance to one of the sailing frigates of the day. Commanded by an exceedingly clever skipper, and well officered and manned, she was a most comfortable ship. The discipline was very strict. The boatswain and his mates emphasised the orders by the piping of their shrill whistles, and no officer or man addressed a superior on duty without touching his cap.[29]

Contract documents in those days were fairly brief and that drawn up between the shipbuilder James Laing of Sunderland and the shipowner Duncan Dunbar for the construction of the ship *Minden* in 1848 is probably a

Fig 205. *This portrait of the* Sutlej *is an unusual one for Thomas G Dutton as he almost invariably drew a broadside view. This ship was built in 1847 and was of 1105 tons; her apple-cheeked bows are clearly depicted.* (Parker Gallery)

typical example, being apparently set down in the order in which the compiler thought of the items. Due to their comparative scarcity, such documents have now achieved an exaggerated importance.[30]

Agreement with D Dunbar for new ship 742 tons
MINDEN
New ship 1848

Upper deck clamps to be 8in and waterway above. Through metal or copper bolts in wales every 6ft, the same as in the bottom. Planking including butt deck hook and fitting transom to receive the ends of deck forward and aft and *this to be abided by*.

Beams in hold: one at after part of after hatch 6ft 3in down from the deck beam and one at after part of main hatch and one intermediate beam between the one at the fore part of the fore hatch. The between decks to be 7ft from *deck to deck*. The arms of the rudder braces on bottom to square up from the underside keel from the lower one and that is the proper length, and no iron ones; all to be metal, The lower beams to be secured as shown with two iron hanging knees with four through bolts in side arm.

   148ft between the perpendiculars
   rake of stem 7ft
   depth of hold not less than 23ft 6in
   extreme breadth 33ft

All decks to be Dantzic. 8in clamps under and over lower deck beams to have a 5in bottom. Sails to be of best Gourock canvas supplied by Messrs D Dunbar & Sons at 1/2½d per yard and made in London at the price charged for those supplied to the *Camperdown*. To be caulked with good brown oakum. Ship not to exceed 742 tons OM or if she does, not to be paid for extra tonnage; and to be 13 years A1 classed at Lloyd's. Three sheer strakes, timber and fastenings, fittings and everything in other respects to be the same as the *Camperdown*.

   Four orlop beams – 1 in after part of after hatchway
   (to be paid extra) – 1 in after part of main hatchway
                 – 1 in forepart of mainmast
                 – 1 abaft the foremast

Price sixteen pounds fifteen shillings (£16 15s) per old ton, delivered in London. Payable £2500 cash on delivery in the East India Docks in London. Rest as per *Camperdown*. Not to bring coals and to be at Builder's risk until 21 days after arrival in London.

London   15 January 1848   [signed]   D Dunbar
                                        James Laing

The *Minden* was speedily built and was launched on 18 May 1848 and measured 742⁵⁶/₉₄ tons om and 917²¹⁹⁴/₃₅₀₀ tons nm. Her dimensions were: keel 137ft 0in, fore rake 11ft 0in, aft rake 1ft 0in, making a total length for tonnage of 149ft 0in; breadth 33ft 0in, depth of hold 23ft 5in. Her mainyard was 74ft 0in long. No drawings accompanied the contract although some drawings of *Minden* evidently existed. There is a rigged model of the *Camperdown*, mentioned in the above contract, in the Glasgow Art Gallery and Museum.

THE *MARLBOROUGH* AND *BLENHEIM*

T & W Smith had not lagged in the building of new ships and in 1846 and 1848 launched the magnificent *Marlborough* and *Blenheim* as a challenge to Green and Wigram; at the Great Exhibition of 1851 they were declared to be

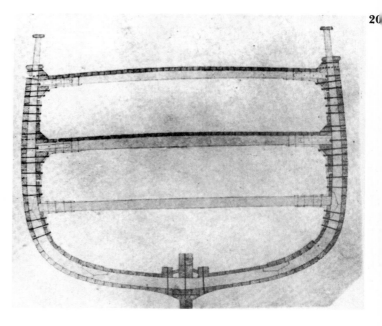

the two finest ships in the mercantile marine. It is difficult to determine if their hull-form is really a logical development from the *Seringapatam* without knowing the design of intermediate ships like Green's *Monarch*, but it is interesting to speculate on the influence exerted by the *Bucephalus* and *Ellenborough* which, according to Basil Lubbock, Charles Laing of Sunderland designed for Smith's in 1840.[31]

There is a rigged model of the *Blenheim* in the Middlesbrough office of Smith's Dock Co, who are successors to T & W Smith, and it was through their courtesy that the lines were taken off by William Salisbury and myself. This model, which is made to ¼in scale, was exhibited at the Great Exhibition of 1851 and was then on view for many years at the museum in North Shields. In 1929 it was rigged or re-rigged for the North East Coast Engineer's Exhibition. A plaque beside the model of *Blenheim* states that it also represents the *Marlborough*. *Lloyd's Register* gives the following comparative figures:

   Marlborough: built 1846; 175.5ft × 41.5ft × 29.1ft, 1387 tons om
   Blenheim: built 1848, 175.0ft × 42.0ft × 29.4ft, 1392 tons om, 1489 tons nm

From these figures it would appear that they were almost sisters.

The plan of the *Blenheim* in figure 207 shows a flush-decked ship having three decks, a round stern with applied quarter galleries, and the heavy head customary in such vessels. The body plan and hull-form are unusual among British merchant ship designs and represent a different line of thought pursued by T & W Smith. There are fractionally more than four beams to length which results in great breadth, but the lines are very easy at every point and resulted in a fast and successful ship. The entrance is short, sharp and convex but the run is longer and somewhat concave. The sections on the body plan appear as if they were developed by using arcs of circles and the marked tumblehome and flaring topsides are very naval in character. This hull is hardly a development of

Fig 206. A midship section through one of Laing's big wooden ships as built in their Sunderland yard. The hold beams were not decked over and were probably only placed occasionally in way of the masts and hatchways. (Copied from booklet issued by Sir James Laing & Co Ltd)

Fig 207. Blenheim. Lines, deck and inboard profile drawn by William Salisbury from measurements taken by himself and the author off a rigged model when in possession of Smith's Dock Co in their Middlesbrough offices in 1957. Built 1848 by T & W Smith at North Shields with dimensions of 175.0ft × 42.0ft × 29.4ft and tonnages of 1392 om and 1489 nm. No reconstruction. Marlborough would be similar.

Fig 208. A photograph taken of the Blenheim showing shores stepped to rig new masts. Probably taken at Calcutta in 1867 when she had been dismasted in a cyclone in the Bay of Bengal. It shows how the painted ports accommodated scuttles hinged top and bottom. (National Maritime Museum, Greenwich)

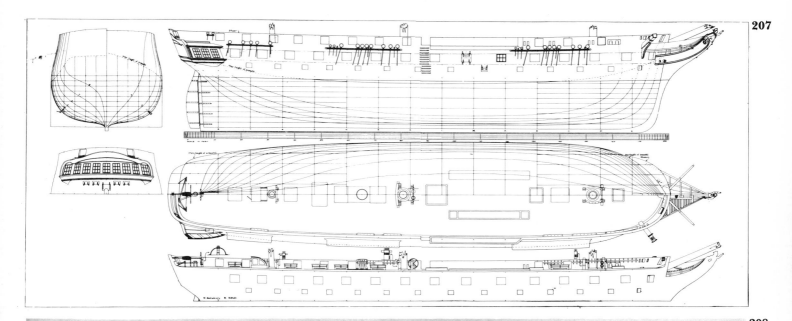

207

208

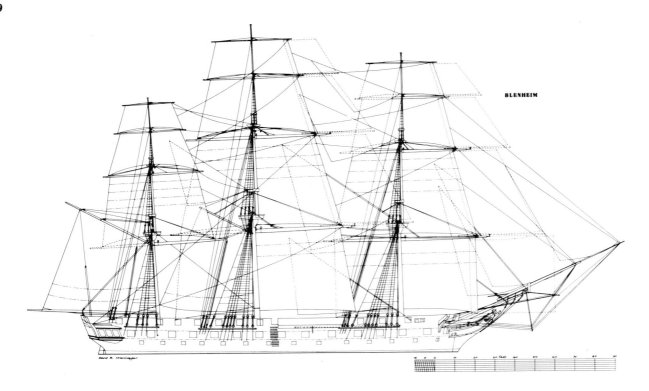

BLENHEIM

Fig 209. Blenheim. Sail plan reconstructed by the author from lines plan, and from sail plan in possession of the late Harold Wyllie. No spar dimensions supplied by Smith's Dock; see text for use made of the various sources for reconstruction. Marlborough *would be similar.*

Fig 210. Blenheim. Sail plan copied about 1961 from original in possession of the late Lt Col Harold Wyllie. This was the chief source for reconstructing the sail plan drawn by the author in 1965. Inscriptions at bottom of drawing read: (on left) 'The Blenheim built by Willm. Smith Esqre. 1848'*; (in centre)* '⅛ of inch Sheer at Tops — a little more at the Bends [?]'*; (on right)* 'The Fore deadeye is equal with the afterpart of the Masts'.

210

the one designed by William Smith 1833, referred to above, but bears similarities to the *Seringapatam*, though like her it is more reminiscent of a warship than a merchantman.

Considering the massiveness of the *Blenheim*'s headwork, it is surprising that it supports only a demi-figurehead, presumably of the Duke of Marlborough. The hull is pierced to carry forty-eight 32-pounders on the upper and main decks, but whereas the ports on the upper deck are open, those on the main deck have closed lids which are hinged top and bottom, and behind each is a

window divided into six glass panes. On this deck the mounting of guns could only take place as a wartime emergency if the ship was requisitioned by the Admiralty. No guns were mounted on the lower deck, but there are small opening scuttles for light and ventilation. The main and lower decks each have a headroom of approximately seven feet which proved very suitable for carrying troops or passengers.

No windlass occurs on the model and it is probable that she hove in her anchor cable on the main deck by means of a capstan and messenger, as done in the Navy. Nor are there any deckhouses on the model but there are numerous deck openings, suitable either for hatchways or for use as companionways. The pumps are situated on the foreside of the mainmast and there is a cargo winch at the foremast. Provision for stowage of hammock nettings in the bulwarks amidships is typical naval fashion. The photograph showing her dismasted at Calcutta, reproduced in figure 208, gives some useful corroborative evidence: there are no deckhouses but there is a big longboat amidships; the lower deck scuttles can just be discerned; there is a bracket for the lower swinging stunsail boom to rest on; the figurehead look a trifle longer in the body than on the model. Considering the fine workmanship that was expended on the head rails and trail boards, it appears sacrilegious to paint straight black and white bands across these curved mouldings to emphasize the gun ports or to achieve the effect if none were present. It gives the effect of being done by callous, unthinking persons and yet all accounts show that the shipwrights and owners evinced a great love and respect for the ships. Many of the illustrations shown here exhibit this method of decoration: 'painted ports' as it has been called.

The sail and rigging plan (figure 209) makes *Blenheim* look a splendid ship and the first impression is the squareness of the sail plan. Although the hull is much the same size as in the *Farquharson*, the *Blenheim* by comparison looks squat aloft with short masts. This illusion occurs because her topgallant and royal yards are much longer than the *Farquharson*'s. The *Blenheim*'s main royal yard is actually the same height above the deck as the former's main skysail. The *Farquharson*'s sail plan is shown as figure 147 in *Merchant Sailing Ships 1775-1815*.

The masts and spars on the *Blenheim*'s model were considered suspect as they were unreasonably lofty, even for a heavily-sparred ship, and so another source had to be found to reconstruct the sail plan. Smith's Dock Co could supply neither sail plan nor spar dimensions, but a sail plan of the ship was discovered in the late Lt Col Harold Wyllie's collection. This is drawn to 1/16in scale and appears to be genuine as the drawing of the hull closely resembles the model. The spar lengths used in the reconstructed sail plan have accordingly been scaled from this drawing. There are some discrepancies between this plan and the model, the chief of which concerns the fore and main topmasts which are about thirteen feet longer on the model; this suggests that the model maker who re-rigged the ship in 1929 forgot to subtract the length of the doubling from the overall length of the topmast. The other principal differences are in the fore and main lower masts which measure six to eight feet longer on the model, and in the main and mizzen topgallant masts which are six to ten feet longer. On the other hand the bowsprit, jibboom, and all the yards are of much the same length as on the model.

As regards the sail plan, no illustration could be found of a contemporary Blackwall frigate with staysails set, so it is impossible to determine if the main topmast and main topgallant staysails were triangular or not. Earlier vessels would have had a spring stay under the foretop to set the main topmast staysail on, but no such stay shows on illustrations of the *Blenheim*. The proportions of the stunsails are those given by Hedderwick and Kipping. The number of deadeyes for the lower shrouds agrees with the number on the model. It is interesting that there are twin main braces shown in pictures of the *Blenheim*: one leads to the foremast below the top, through the usual block on the yardarm; the other, which is a single rope, leads aft to the quarter bumpkin. Other contemporary passenger frigates had a similar arrangement. Robert Kipping, whose books on sailmaking and mastmaking are well known, was sailmaker and foreman to T & W Smith at the time the *Blenheim* was built and his drawings of sails and spars are obviously based on the practice to be found in Smith's ships.[32] (See Figs 21 and 22.)

In 1852 the *Marlborough* was diverted to the Australian trade for one voyage, probably because of the high freights available, and made a very fast passage out and home, besides surviving a hurricane and meeting a large iceberg. The *Illustrated London News* describes the passage home, of which the following is an extract:

> The *Marlborough* (Allen W Young, Commander), weighed from the Port Phillip Head, on the evening of 4th July [1853], and passed out the same night through Bass's Strait to the westward, with a strong north-west gale, which increased until July 6, at 4 pm, when it blew a perfect hurricane, and the ship was in a most perilous position; whilst running with the wind quarterly, she broached-to, from a heavy sea striking her on the quarter, the main topsail blew to ribbons, and the ship was thrown almost upon her beam-ends; the lee side and lee quarter boat being buried in the water. The gusts of wind were also so terrific that it was impossible to stand against them, whilst the tops of the sea were blown completely over the ship ... This happened . . . off the south-west coast of Van Diemen's Land.
>
> So much has recently been said about the *Marco Polo* and other clipper ships, that great credit is due to the *Marlborough* for the efficient manner in which she made her passage out to Melbourne in 78 days; from thence to India and back in 40 days; and now her run home was done in 83½ days – thus making a voyage round the world in five months twelve days, although not successive months. The passengers have expressed themselves highly delighted with the voyage and the kind, gentlemanly conduct of the captain.[33]

The 78 days taken on the outward pasage must be between pilots, as the dates between Plymouth and Melbourne result in 82 days, 3 August to 4 November 1852. On the homeward passage, the crew consisted entirely of Lascars; Cape Horn was rounded on 8 August 1853, and Start Point seen on 26 September.

The two splendid frigates, *Marlborough* and *Blenheim*, marked more than just the end of an era in passenger carrying. Their style and hull-form made them anachronisms in an age hastening towards mechanisation, and the trappings of past grandeurs contrasted strangely with the sleeker lines of the ships being sent afloat as their competitors.

APPENDIX I

Although no specification of the *Baffin* appears to have survived, the following account of the first cost and equipment of the ship helps to complete the picture of this interesting vessel.

FIRST COST OF THE WHALER *BAFFIN**

Tradesmen's Bills

Robert Campion	sail canvas		£ 252	1	4
Brown Logan & Co	chain cable & fittings		189	17	2
John Wilson	crowsnest & spike trough		6	7	1
Ann Patrick	harpoon gun &c		25	0	8
Geo B Highfield	sail canvas		31	17	3
Robt Flinn	harpoon gun &c	6 1 0			
do	harpoons	30 4 0			
			36	5	0
John Christian	sailmaker		98	18	8
Ralph Pearson	best bower anchor &c		40	5	3
James Hurry & Co	ropemakers &c		903	4	8
Edward Laurence & Co for casks, per					

		tuns	gals			
John Beard	80 casks	65	208	213	18	2
Laurence & Whiteside	141 casks	120	150	389	4	6
Smith & Co	61 casks	51	38	164	19	0
Laurence & Co	ale barrels &c			10	3	0
Laurence & Co	butts for beef			11	14	0
				789	18	8

		tuns	gals			
Samuel Lightfoot	14 casks	16	51	53	0	0
Owners *Lady Forbes*	7 casks	7	134	24	5	9
'303 butts contg tuns 262, 77 gallons'†						
Mottershead & Hayes	4 boats & extra bill			118	18	10
T G Molineux	bower anchor			31	17	6
Mottershead & Hayes	cost of hull, spars &c 321½ tons at £16 per ton		5144	0	0
	copper fastening doubling		55 10 0			
				5199	10	0
Joseph Dutton	smith's work &c estimated			150	0	0
David Appleton	blockmaker			112	1	8
William Woods	painting &c			4	5	6
				£8067	15	0

CASH ACCOUNT (SUMMARISED)

John Smith	rigging vessel		£ 28	0	0
W Irving	cooper's wages		6	0	0
22 tons stone ballast			3	8	0
Dockmaster			1	0	0
Allowance for Measurer's men				5	0
Freight on 2 whale boats from Hull			4	4	0
Carpenters' allowance at launch			10	0	0
Dinner &c at launch			29	19	3
Cable junk			19	7	9
Barometer £4 4 0; compasses &c £3 7 6			7	11	6
Azimuth compass £1 1s; boat's compass 7s; spy glass 16s 10d; telescope £4 4s; achromatic telescope £3 13 6			10	2	4
Carpet for cabin £2 18s; curtains £2 7s mats £1 6s			6	11	0

Carriage of harpoons 11s 3d; of ice saws 17s 4d		1	8	7
Bungs for casks £1 16s; parcelling £11 4 4		13	0	4
Glass £6 8 9; muskets £4 12 6; iron buoy £2		13	1	3
100 yds canvas from ship *Lady Forbes*		2	14	0
Hot air stove £12 2s; ship's bell 4s copper pipe for bellows 8s		12	14	0
James Hodson red pine balk			15	0
Michael Ashton pine boards		1	17	0
William Scoresby Jnr for his attendance during the building of the *Baffin* from 25 June 1819 to 15 February 1820 [these dates are from laying of keel to the launch]		100	0	0
Cutting machine and ice saws		21	2	0
2 whale boats		30	0	0
Tin and braziery ware		6	1	6
Small articles and allowances per Capt Scoresby		15	12	3
Thomas Calderbank patent pumps		24	2	5
		£380	16	0

The grand totals for the first account were tabled as follows:

To amount of cash account	£ 380	16	0
Tradesmen's bills for hull, ship's materials, casks and equipment for the fishery	8067	15	0
Balance of interest as per account £152 16 8; Bank commission on £5000 £12 10s	165	6	8
Postages, stamps and incidental expenses for the equipment	4	4	0
Commission on £3199 10s @ 1½% £77 19 10 Commission on £3253 5s @ 2½% £81 6 5	159	6	6
First cost of *Baffin*	£8777	8	2

Before the Baffin *sailed on her maiden voyage from Liverpool on 18 March 1820, additional expenses incurred may be summarised:*

Board wages, advances to crew, general stores provisions (all cash advances)	£ 469	10	8
Provisions: beef, pork, butter, bread, cheese, herrings, groceries, ale, beer, rum &c (all tradesmen's bills)	682	12	5
Total outfit	£1152	3	1

Notes:
* Mystic Seaport, Scoresby Papers 1, account book of *Baffin*, fo 1-14.
† This is a summary of quantity listed above. A tun consisted at this date of 252 'wine gallons' as the Imperial gallon was not adopted until 1824.

APPENDIX II

OUTLINE SPECIFICATION OF THE *JOHN GARROW*
(from Lloyd's Register Survey Reports at National Maritime Museum, Iron Ships, Box 1).

Floors 3in × 3in		[beams apparently
Deck beams (31) 3in sided⎱ rivetted to		consisted of pair of
Hold beams (29) 3in sided⎰ the frames		3in × 3in angles forming a T-bar]
Keel	1in iron	[no sketch of construction given]
Keelson	12in sided, 22in moulded (American elm)	

Space between top timbers	2ft 2in	
Stem and sternpost	¾in iron	
Knightheads and hawse timbers	(English and African oak)	
Plating:		
keel to bilge	¾in (iron)	
bilge	¾in	
bilge to wales	⅝in	
topsides	½in	
sheer strake	4½in (African oak)	[Grantham said this was a band about 2ft deep around ship, bolted to iron plating, and when it sprang off because of sun's heat, ship leaked through bolt holes left unfilled]
Plank sheer	4in (African oak)	
Waterway	10in (Dantzic fir)	
Upper deck	3½in (yellow pine)	
Ceiling	3in (American elm)	
Lower masts	(red pine)	
Topmasts and yards	'good Baltic spars'	
Standing rigging	wire	[see table of sizes below]
Windlass	Bowman & Vernon's patent	[Bowman & Vernon were shipbuilders in Aberdeen]
Pumps	Massie's patent	
Rudder	patent iron	[Grantham said it was on a bad principle; it was too small and thin and because attached to a broad sternpost, half of it was useless]
Boats	carvel longboat, clinker yawl, clinker gig	
Deckhouse	on main deck for crew	[Grantham terms it 'round-house']
'Cuddy abaft'	[this suggests a flush deck, but this is not entirely clear]	
Draft of water	9ft forward, 10ft aft (with 420 tons ballast)	

APPENDIX III

RIGGING SIZES OF THE *JOHN GARROW*

(from Andrew Smith, *Application of Wire for Cables* London 1841, pamphlet)

	Wire rigging as fitted	A Smith's estimated sizes for hemp rigging
Fore and main lower shrouds	3½in	10in [*John Garrow*'s master estimated size of lower shrouds as 8¼in in hemp]
Mizzen lower shrouds	2¾in	7in
Fore and main topmast backstays	3¼in	9in
Mizzen topmast backstays	2⅜in	6½in
Fore and main topgallant backstays	2⅛in	6in
Mizzen topgallant backstays	1⅝in	4½in
Fore and main royal backstays	1⅛in	2½in
Fore and main topmast rigging	2⅝in	6½in
Mizzen topmast rigging	2¼in	6¼in
Fore and main topgallant rigging	2⅛in	6in
Mizzen topgallant rigging	1⅝in	4½in
Fore and main stays	4in	10in
Mizzen stay	2¾in	7in
Fore and main topmast stays	3⅜in	9in
Mizzen topmast stay	2¼in	6in
Fore and main topgallant stays	2¼in	6½in
Mizzen topgallant stay	1⅛in	2½in
Main royal stay [no fore listed]	1⅛in	2½in
Jib stay	3in	8in
Jib guys	3¾in	1½in

The following calculations of weight and cost are added:

Wire rigging as fitted to the *John Garrow*, parcelled and served and ready to go over mastheads		Hemp rigging of equal strength to the wire, based on above estimate	
Weight	4180 lb	Weight	13,204 lb
Surface area	495 sq ft	Surface area	973 sq ft
Cost price: 4180 lb at 60s per cwt	£111 9 4	Cost price: 13,204 lb at 46s per cwt	£271 3 1

APPENDIX IV

ANNUAL TONNAGE LAUNCHED BY ALEXANDER HALL & SONS, ABERDEEN, 1836–1855, DURING THE PERIOD OF 'NEW MEASUREMENT' RULES

The list of Hall's ships as they were launched year by year is given in Appendix 2 of *Fast Sailing Ships 1775—1815*, but this annualised summary presents it in a new light.

Year	**Total tons nm**	**Number of vessels**	**Average tonnage nm**
1836	692	7	99
1837	864	6	127
1838	1388	9	154
1839	1683	9	187
1840	1886	10	189
1841	2211	12	184
1842	2652*	10	265
1843	846	8	106
1844	450	3	150
1845	1674	7	239
1846	703	5	141
1847	714	4	178
1848	1718	6	286
1849	884	3	294
1850	1673	4	418
1851	1985	4	496
1852	1839	5	368
1853	2165	4	541
1854	1498	5	300
1855	4136†	6	689

Notes:

* total tons includes a ship of 530 tons and another of 610 tons

† total tons includes a ship of 2284 tons

REFERENCES
CHAPTER 1

[1] See Roger Prouty, *The Transformation of the Board of Trade 1830—1855*, (London 1957), pp 5–6.

[2] Aubrey F Burstall, *A History of Mechanical Engineering*, (London 1965) paperback edition, Chapter VI.

[3] See W H B Court, *Concise Economic History of Britain* (Cambridge 1954), pp 72–78; C Ernest Fayle, *A Short History of the World's Shipping Industry*, (London 1933), pp 226–68.

[4] Burstall, *History of Mechanical Engineering*, *op cit*, p 204.

[5] PP, *Fourth Report from the Select Committee on Navigation Laws*, June 1847, p 25, item 4583.

[6] Robert S Craig, 'The African Guano Trade', *MM*, 1964, vol 50, pp 25 *et seq*.

[7] W S Lindsay, *History of Merchant Shipping and Ancient Commerce*, (London 1876), vol III, pp 464–66.

[8] B R Mitchell, *Abstract of British Historical Statistics*, (Cambridge 1962), pp 217–18.

[9] Lawrence A Harper, *The English Navigation Laws*, (New York 1939, reprint 1964), p 361.

[10] Richard Rice's figures were compiled for a thesis at McGill University, Montreal. They are used by his courtesy.

[11] *Ibid*.

[12] PP, *First Report from the Select Committee on Navigation Laws*, March 1847, pp 81–83, items 847–50 & 868–69.

[13] PP, *Third Report from the Select Committee on Navigation Laws*, May 1847, p 84, items 3420–21.

[14] For further details of the *Columbus* see: F W Wallace, *Wooden Ships and Iron Men*, (London 1924), pp 14–17 and 324–28 (quoting *The Times* of Nov 1824); and *Mechanics' Magazine*, 18 Sept 1824, pp 433–36; for the *Baron of Renfrew* see: Capt Andrew Henderson, 'Ocean Steamers', *Proceedings of the Institution of Civil Engineers* (reprint), Nov 1853, vol XIII.

[15] PP, *Third Report from the Select Committee on Navigation Laws*, May 1847, p 87, item 3455.

[16] *Ibid*, p 136, extract from item 4063.

[17] Lindsay, *History of Merchant Shipping*, *op cit*, vol III, p 627; see also George Blake, *Lloyd's Register of Shipping 1760—1960*, (London *c*1961), p 12.

[18] *Annals of Lloyd's Register*, (London 1934), pp 19–20.

[19] Blake, *Lloyd's Register*, *op cit*, p 26.

[20] PP, *Third Report from the Select Committee on Navigation Laws*, May 1847, p 81, items 3372–75.

[21] Lindsay, *History of Merchant Shipping*, *op cit*, vol III, p 508.

[22] *Bureau Veritas 1828/1978: a Record of 150 Years*, (nd, English-language edition), pp 5–11, 27–30.

[23] 5 and 6 William IV, c.56.

CHAPTER 2

[1] *Mechanics' Magazine*, 29 Sept 1827, vol 8, pp 161–66.

[2] *Papers in Mechanics*, (*c*1813), pp 98–101.

[3] Peter Hedderwick, *A Treatise on Marine Architecture containing the Theory and Practice of Shipbuilding*, (Edinburgh 1830), in two volumes: vol 1, text with plates I to VIII bound in at end; vol 2, plates only, nos IX to XXIX.

[4] I took the lines off *Brilliant*'s half-model when it was in the possession of James Steele (d.1955).

[5] Thomas Richardson, *Mercantile Marine Architecture: or an Elementary Work on the Art of Drawing the Draughts of Vessels*, (London 1833). There is a slim book of text and 7 plates.

[6] Hedderwick, *Marine Architecture*, *op cit*, pp 351–56.

[7] *Ibid*, p 373.

[8] Darcy Lever, *The Young Sea Officer's Sheet Anchor*, (London 1808), p 61–62.

[9] Capt Sir Henry Heathcote RN, *Treatise on Stay-sails*, (London 1824).

[10] Darcy Lever, *The Young Sea Officer's Sheet Anchor*, *op cit*, p 61.

[11] E W Cooke, *Fifty Plates of Shipping and Craft*, (London 1829).

[12] D B S [?D Bonner-Smith], 'Trysails', *MM*, 1919, vol 4, pp 217–18.

[13] N M M, sketch book by Copley Fielding, (*c*1810–20), Artists 1853–59, size I, p 14.

[14] N M M, sketch book by Edward Gwyn, a coach herald painter of London, *c*1769–80, (Artists *c*1780 size I); see also E A Dingley, 'Gwyn's Book of Ships', *MM*, 1921, vol 7, pp 46–52 for authenticity of drawings. Dingley considers them correct, not imaginative.

[15] Gustaf Halldin and others, *Svenskt Skeppsbyggeri*, (Malmö, Sweden, 1963), plate facing p 204.

[16] Vol 5 of plates (1787) pl 143, fig 1124. An identical plate appears in N C Romme, *L'Art de la Voilure*, (1781).

[17] G C [?Geoffrey Callender], 'Studding Sails', *MM*, 1911, vol 1, pp 186b–187b; and Capt Meuss, 'Studding Sails', *ibid*, p 219.

[18] Hans Szymanski, *Deutsche Segelschiffe*, (Berlin 1934, reprint Hamburg 1972), plates 9–43.

[19] Edmond Paris, *Souvenirs de Marine: Collection de Plans ou Dessins de Navires et de Bateaux Anciens ou Modernes*, (Paris 1884), vol II, pl 62.

[20] Clement Mackrow, *The Naval Architect's and Shipbuilder's Pocket-Book*, (London 1889, 4th ed), p 89. First published 1879, it was still in print this century, being continually revised and enlarged.

[21] Fredrik Henrik af Chapman, *Architectura Navalis Mercatoria*, (Stockholm 1768). See Chapter Two of *Merchant Sailing Ships 1775—1815* for a more detailed description of a flute's hull-form.

[22] Szymanski, *Deutsche Segelschiffe*, *op cit*, pl 33, fig 155.

[23] John C G Hill, *Shipshape and Bristol Fashion*, (2nd ed, Liverpool 1958), pp 94–95.

[24] A J Holland, *Ships of British Oak*, (Newton Abbot 1971), pp 129–42, 153–60, 168–70.

[25] *Ibid*, pp 169–70.

[26] *Ibid*, p 169.

[27] Charles Bateson, *The Convict Ships 1787—1868*, (Glasgow, 2nd ed, 1969), p 362.

[28] N M M, Merchant Ship Plans, no T.1013.

[29] Hedderwick, *Treatise on Marine Architecture*, *op cit*, p 150, citing 13 Geo. III c. 74 and 26 Geo. III c. 60.

[30] John Leather, 'The Shipbuilding Bayleys', *MM*, 1965, vol 51, pp 131–45.

[31] William Annesley, *A New System of Naval Architecture*, (London 1822). He describes the construction and lists the vessels built.

[32] It may be that the *New System* was synonymous with the schooner *Annesley* of 1817; *Lloyd's Register* does not list a vessel called *New System*. Authority for *New System* comes from Liverpool Museum, Shipping Collection, MS notebook by A C Wardle, vol 3, p 43.

[33] See Boyd Cable, 'The World's First Clipper', *MM*, 1943, vol 29, p 66 *et seq*, for fuller details of Alexander Hall's training and his family history.

[34] Hedderwick, *Treatise on Marine Architecture*, *op cit*. There was a separate atlas of 21 plates.

[35] Charles Bateson, *The Convict Ships 1787—1868*, (Glasgow 1st ed, 1959), p 259 and Appendices I and II.

[36] Alexander Hall & Sons, yard book transcribed by James Henderson.

[37] 'Round About Aberdeen, no IV: Shipbuilding', *The Aberdeen Weekly Journal*, 5 Dec 1877, p 6.

[38] Bateson, *Convict Ships*, (1st ed), *op cit*, pp 304–5 and 308–11.

[39] Boyd Cable, 'The World's First Clipper', *op cit*, p 66.

[40] A Hall & Sons yard book, *op cit*, yard No 57.

[41] *Ibid*, yard No 24.

[42] *Ibid*.

[43] 'Round about Aberdeen', *op cit*; and Lloyd's Register survey reports for Aberdeen.

[44] This MS book lists spar dimensions and other work carried out by William Simons.

[45] NMM, Merchant Ship plans, no T.8013.

[46] Smith's Dock Monthly (Newcastle), vol V, p 178.

[47] C Ernest Fayle, *The World's Shipping Industry* (1923), p 224.

[48] Raymond Smith, *Sea-Coal for London*, (London 1961), p 142.

49 *Ibid*, for figures in this paragraph.
50 I am indebted to Robert Hunt of Newhaven for these figures.
51 Michael Bouquet, *No Gallant Ship*, (London 1959), p 121.
52 Richardson, *Mercantile Marine Architecture*, *op cit*, pp 1–2.
53 Hedderwick, *Treatise on Marine Architecture*, *op cit*, p 147.
54 Glasgow Museum, Department of Technology, Spar Book of William Simons & Co, folio E.
55 Hedderwick, *Treatise on Marine Architecture*, *op cit*, pp 360–61.
56 Grahame Farr, *Shipbuilding in North Devon*, National Maritime Museum Monographs (London 1976).
57 Szymanski, *Deutsche Segelschiffe*, *op cit*, pl 26, fig 141.
58 Painting in Altonaer Museum, Hamburg.
59 See Hedderwick, *Treatise on Marine Architecture*, *op cit*, pp 398–401.
60 *Ibid*, p 147.
61 *Ibid*, p 182.
62 A Hall & Sons, yard book, *op cit*.
63 W B W [?W B Whall], 'Double Topsail Yards', *MM*, 1911, vol I, p 155.
64 A Hall & Sons yard book, transcribed by James Henderson.
65 Richard Weatherill, *The Ancient Port of Whitby*, (Whitby 1908), pp 89–178.
66 See no 56.
67 John F. Gibson, *Brocklebanks 1770—1950*, (Liverpool 1953), vol I, appendix I.
68 Szymanski, *Deutsche Segelschiffe*, *op cit*, pl 24, fig 137.
69 Frank G G Carr, *Sailing Barges*, (revised ed, London 1951), p 109.
70 Hervey Benham, *Once Upon a Tide*, (London 1955), between pp 48 and 49.
71 F H af Chapman, *Architectura Navalis Mercatoria*, (Stockholm 1768), pl LIX, fig no 2.
72 *List of Shipping Registered in the Different Ports of Scotland*, (Glasgow 1828), 3rd ed.
73 Page 133; published in Dundee.
74 W A Baker, *Sloops & Shallops*, (Barre, Mass, 1966), pp 138–39.
75 See Grahame Farr, 'Severn Navigation and the Trow', *MM*, 1946, vol 32, pp 66–95.
76 C F Partington, *The Ship-Builders' Complete Guide*; *Theory and Practice of Naval Architecture*, (London 1826), p 108.
77 E W Cooke, *Shipping and Craft*, (London 1829).
78 A Hall & Sons, yard book, *op cit*.
79 *Ibid*.
80 *Ibid*.
81 G A Osbon, 'Ships in William Anderson's Picture', *MM*, 1967, vol 53, pp 290–91.
82 There is an engraving of the *Calypso* by E Duncan after W J Huggins, dated 1826; the *Elbe* is listed in *Lloyd's Register* (1833), (red book); sail plan of *Seagull* at N M M in Admiralty Draughts, plan no 4027 box 64, dated 1833.
83 Capt H Parker and Frank C Bowen, *Mail and Passenger Steamships of the Nineteenth Century*, (London 1928), pl CVIII.
84 Gibson, *Brocklebanks 1770—1950*, *op cit*, vol I, Appendix I.
85 *Gores Liverpool Advertiser*, 25 April 1833. This quotation was sent me by the late W Stewart Rees, but I have not verified it.
86 Gibson, *Brocklebanks*, *op cit*, p 114.
87 David R MacGregor, *The Tea Clippers*, (London 1983), Appendix III, p 244.
88 For a description of construction, see Whitby Museum: Capt William Scoresby, D D, F R S, *Journal*, vol VII, 1818–20; also H B Browne, *Chapters of Whitby History 1823—1846*, (1946), reprint of chapters 16 and 17 (1947). For cost accounts see Mystic Seaport: Scoresby Papers 1, account book of *Baffin*.
89 For a more detailed description of the term 'hull and spars' see David R MacGregor, 'Tendering and Contract Procedure in Merchant Shipyards in the middle of the Nineteenth Century', *MM*, 1962, vol 48, pp 245–46.
90 Whitby Museum, Scoresby's Journal, *op cit*, 15 Feb 1820.
91 *Lloyd's List*, 30 Oct 1830, p 1.
92 Whitby Museum, Scoresby's Journal, *op cit*, 19 Aug 1819.
93 See Basil Lubbock, *The Arctic Whalers*, (Glasgow 1937), p 234.
94 T Sheppard, 'The Hull Whaling Trade', *MM*, 1919, vol 5, p 170; J B Fay, *Catalogue of the Maritime Museum*, *Kingston-upon-Hull*, (Hull 1956), p 6 and pl I.
95 W Oesau, *Hamburgs Grönnlandfahrt*, pp 157–58. I am grateful to John Lyman for drawing my attention to this ship, but I have not examined the work myself.
96 See Lubbock, *Arctic Whalers*, *op cit*; and David S Henderson, *Fishing for the Whale*, (Dundee 1972), pp 11–15.
97 Edouard A Stackpole, *The Sea-Hunters*, (Philadelphia 1953), p 145.
98 NMM, GRN/1, List of Ships Built in Blackwall Yard, fo 124.
99 Stackpole, *The Sea-Hunters*, *op cit*, p 268.
100 *Ibid*, plate between pp 224–25 (from Nantucket Whaling Museum).
101 Oil painting loaned me by a private collector.
102 W J Dakin, *Whalemen Adventurers*, (Sydney 1934), pp 121–22.
103 Frank C Bowen, *The Golden Age of Sail*, (London 1925), plate 23.
104 Howard I Chapelle, *The History of American Sailing Ships*, (New York 1935), p 288.
105 Alexander Starbuck, *History of the American Whale Fishery*, (New York 1964 reprinted from 1878 ed), 2 vols; pp 180–702 consist of voluminous appendices of returns of vessels year by year etc.
106 *Ibid*, p 147.
107 *Ibid*, pp 372–73.

CHAPTER 3

1 Science Museum Sailing Ships Collection, plan press C/17/1 to 29. Plans presented to Museum in 1938.
2 Peter Hedderwick, *Treatise on Marine Architecture*, (Edinburgh 1830), pp 352–56.
3 Yard accounts of Alexander Hall & Sons transcribed by James Henderson.
4 List of gold shipments from Sydney given in *Austrialia and New Zealand Gazette*, 1 May 1852, p 149. Melbourne did not begin exporting gold until 29 Aug 1851. (See *Ibid*, 10 July 1852, p 247).
5 For shipbuilding activities of the Stephen Family see [Sir A Murray Stephen], *A Shipbuilding History 1750—1932*, (Glasgow 1932), p 13 *et seq* and pp 193–94 for list of ships built.
6 A S & Sons, Diary of Alexander Stephen snr.
7 *Ibid*, annual summary for 1850.
8 *Ibid*.
9 *A Shipbuilding History*, *op cit*, p 195.
10 John F Gison, *Brocklebanks 1770—1950*, (Liverpool 1953), vol I, p 122 and Appendix I.
11 Brocklebank Yard Book, Liverpool Museum.
12 *Ibid*, p 56.
13 Information on Lumley Kennedy & Co and a list of ships he built, supplied by Daniel Hay, Borough Librarian, Whitehaven.
14 Sail plan in Whitehaven Library and Museum which is where I traced it in 1961.
15 I am grateful to the late Stewart Rees for particulars of Joseph Steel and some of his ships.
16 I am indebted to Dr Jurgen Meyer for data about the *Tinto*'s last voyage and a cutting showing a picture of the barque under sail; also to the Norwegian Consul General in London in a letter to me dated 22 Feb 1949. The final end of the *Tinto* has not been ascertained.
17 NMM, L R survey reports, Poole, no 39.
18 *Ibid*, Poole No 149.
19 From note in R H Gillis Collection citing *Royal Cornwall Gazette* 19 July 1844; I have not verified this.
20 From logbook of *Admiral Moorsom* in possession of L E Evans of Bray, Co Wicklow.
21 I am grateful to Richard Rice who generously put his list of ships built by George Black at my disposal.
22 Esther C Wright, *Saint John Ships and their Builders*, (Woodville, N S, 1976), pp 11–12.
23 *Ibid*; the book is full of details of the shipyards and there is a list of all the vessels built 1800–92.

24 Reproduced in David R MacGregor, *The China Bird*, (London 1961), pl5. *Countess of Bective* is the vessel on the right, although not named in this plate.

25 R Morton Nance, 'Trows, Past and Present', *MM*, 1912, vol 2, pp 203–4.

26 Adm W H Smyth, *The Sailor's Word-Book*, (London 1867).

27 Hedderwick, *A Treatise on Marine Architecture*, op cit, p 360.

28 Alexander Hall & Sons, yard book transcribed by James Henderson.

29 Henry Hall, *Report on the Ship-Building Industry of the United States*, (Washington 1884, reprinted New York 1970), pp 106–7.

30 *Ibid*, p 108.

31 Howard I Chapelle, *The National Watercraft Collection*, Smithsonian Institution, (Washington 1960) pp 64–65.

32 *Ibid*, pp 65–66.

33 John Lyman, 'Two Canadian Barkentine "Firsts"', *Log Chips*, 1953, vol 3, pp 76–77.

34 *Illustrated London News*, 4 Oct 1845, p 220.

35 I have not seen this painting.

36 Science Museum, Sailing Ship Collection, plan no C/7/5.

37 Hedderwick, *A Treatise on Marine Architecture*, op cit, pp 360–63.

38 Robert Kipping, *Sails and Sailmaking*, (London 1887, 12th ed) p 66.

39 Ryck Lydecker, 'The Mystery Ship of Green Bay', *National Fisherman*, (Camden, Maine), September 1973, p 12C–13C.

40 Vice-Adm Paris, *Collection de Plans ou Dessins de Navires et de Bateaux Anciens ou Modernes*, (Paris 1882), part I, pl 45.

41 Arthur Young, *Nautical Dictionary*, (London, 2nd ed, 1863), p 58. The first edition was published at Dundee in 1846.

42 NMM, L R survey reports, London no 18/886.

43 Vernon C Boyle, 'The Bideford Polackers', *MM*, 1932, vol 18, pp 109–24.

44 Pierre Ozanne, *Diverse Manoeuvres de Barques et Bateaux*, (Paris c1770). Each sketch book contained twelve engravings; there were two bearing this title. The negative numbers in the Museé de la Marine, Paris, are 55101 and 55135 for the two brigs.

45 Robert Craig, 'Polacres Built in Britain', *MM*, 1963, vol 49, p 230.

46 Grahame Farr, 'Polacca Rigs in the Bristol Channel (Statutory) Registers', *MM*, vol 47, 1961, p 304.

47 NMM, Print Room, miscellaneous folder (D size) entitled 'Piracy, Smuggling, Wrecks & Misc. Types'. Engraving published 14 May 1822; neg no A 4348.

48 Basil Greenhill, 'More Light on the Bideford Polacres', *MM*, vol 47, 1961, p 302.

49 Farr, 'Polacca Rigs in Bristol Channel', *op cit*.

50 R W Stevens, *On the Stowage of Ships and their Cargoes*, (London 1869, 5th ed), p 544.

51 Sir Alan Moore, 'Polacres', *MM*, 1956, vol 42, p 339.

52 L A (of Kiel), 'Polacres', *MM*, 1911, vol 1, p 123. For 'fitted' he probably means 'fidded'.

53 Science Museum, neg no 7506.

54 Reproduced in Hervey Benham, *Once Upon a Tide*, (London 1955), p 48.

55 Robert Kipping, *The Elements of Sailmaking*, (London 1851 2nd ed), pp 103–12. In a smaller, narrower format was Kipping's more popular work, *Elementary Treatise on Sails and Sailmaking*, which appeared in 1858 and was in its 12th ed in 1887.

56 George Biddlecombe, *The Art of Rigging*, (London, 1848), pp 105–6.

57 Adm Sir Thomas Symonds, *Naval Costumes*, (c1840). No copy of this work ever appears to have had a title page but as all copies bear an inscription by Sir Thomas Symonds, he has been assumed to be the author. The plates are unnumbered and consist of small lithographs. There is no text.

58 Reproduced in David R MacGregor, *Schooners in Four Centuries*, (London 1982), p 89.

59 B Heckstall-Smith, *Yachts & Yachting in Contemporary Art*, (London 1925), plate XLVII.

60 Chapelle, *Watercraft Collection*, op cit, pp 38–40 and 73–75.

61 Montague Guest, *List of Members of the Royal Yacht Squadron and their Yachts; 1815 to 1897*, (London 1897), p 125.

62 NMM, Admiralty Draughts, plan no 6619 box 65. The *Arrow* had been built in 1823.

63 Adm W H Smyth, *The Sailor's Word-Book*, (London 1867), pp 741–42.

64 NMM, L R survey reports, London no 17,157.

65 *Ibid*.

66 Edgar C Smith, *A Short History of Naval and Marine Engineering*, (Cambridge 1937), pp 97–98.

67 Patent Office, *Abridgements of the Specifications Relating to Shipbuilding, Repairing, Sheathing, Launching &c.*, (London 1862), p 53–54.

68 J Bennett, 'Observations on the Effect Produced by Iron Masts . . .', *Papers on Naval Architecture*, conducted by William Morgan and Augustin Creuze, (London 1826), vol I, p 100.

69 *Annals of Lloyd's Register*, (London 1934), p 80.

70 John Grantham, *Iron, as a Material for Ship-Building*, (London 1842), p 9.

71 *Ibid*, especially pp 43–47 and plates at rear.

72 Andrew Smith, *Observations on the Application of Wire and Hoop Iron . . . for Cables, Standing Rigging, Stroppings for Blocks &c* (a pamphlet, London 1841), p 17, testimonial letter from Anderson, Garrow & Co to Robertson & Co, dated 2 Feb 1841. Andrew Smith had patented a form of iron wire rope.

73 *Aberdeen Journal*, 29 May 1839. Extract made for me by James Henderson.

74 Grantham, *Iron, as a material for Ship-Building*, op cit, p 44.

75 *Ibid*, pp 44–45.

76 *Ibid*, p 45.

77 *Ibid*, p 46.

78 *Ibid*, pp 46–47.

79 *Ibid*, p 62.

80 Andrew Smith, *Application of Wire for Cables, Rigging*, op cit, pp 19–20. In the testimonial referred to, the various ships' names are given.

81 NMM, L R survey reports, Iron ships, box 1.

82 *Mechanics' Magazine*, 1831, vol 14, p 448.

83 Carl C Cutler, *Queens of the Western Ocean*, (Annapolis, Md, 1961), p 551.

84 NMM, L R survey reports, Iron ships, box 1.

85 For fuller list of patents for wire rigging, see David R MacGregor, 'Wire Rigging', *MM*, 1959, vol 45, pp 260–61; also John Lyman, 'Wire Rigging', *MM*, 1960, vol 46, p 295.

86 John Grantham, *Iron Ship-Building*, (London 1868, 5th ed), pp 11 and 101.

87 Except where other references are given, this list of Grantham's work has been compiled from his two books, *Iron, as a Material for Ship-Building*, (London 1842) and *Iron Ship-Building* (London 1868, 5th ed).

88 NMM, L R survey reports, Iron ships, box 1; also *Illustrated London News*, 1853, for report and engraving.

89 Edgar Smith, *Marine Engineering*, op cit, p 103; and *Underwriters' Registry for Iron Vessels*, (Liverpool, Sept 1865 to Aug 1866).

90 NMM, L R survey reports, Iron Ships, box 1.

91 Biographical details on John H Coutts and Charles Mitchell from notes by Mr Melville, an Aberdeen naval architect, as supplied to James Henderson.

92 'Round About Aberdeen, no V: Shipbuilding', *The Aberdeen Weekly Journal*, 12 Dec 1877.

93 Sir Westcott Abell, *The Shipwright's Trade*, (Cambridge 1948), pp 108–10.

94 NMM, L R survey reports, Iron Ships, Box 1.

95 *Ibid*, *Dove*.

96 *Ibid*, schooners *Kelvin* (1848), and *Vulcan* (1841).

97 *Ibid*, schooner *Tar* (1848–49).

98 Lloyd's Register of British and Foreign Shipping, Visitation Committee Reports, conclusion of report for 1853.

99 *Ibid*.

100 John Lyman (ed), *Log Chips*, (Washington), vol 3, November 1951, p 105.

101 Hall, *Ship-Building Industry of the United States*, op cit, pp 66–70.

102 Michael Costagliola, 'The Canton Packet *Cohota*', *American Neptune*,

vol VII, January 1947, pp 5–8 & plans.

CHAPTER 4

[1] Sir Evan Cotton, *East Indiamen*, (London 1949), p 125.

[2] W H Coates, *The Good Old Days of Shipping*, (Bombay 1900), pp 11–13.

[3] Robert G Albion, *Square-Riggers on Schedule*, (Princeton, N J 1938), p 46.

[4] *Ibid*, pp 41–43 and 235.

[5] *Ibid*, pp 247–48.

[6] W H Webb, *Plans of Wooden Vessels . . . Built by William H Webb in the City of New York 1840–1869*, (1895), 2 vols.

[7] Howard I Chapelle, *Search for Speed under Sail*, (New York 1967), plate VI.

[8] *Ibid*, plate VIII.

[9] Albion, *op cit*, pp 276–77.

[10] Chapelle, *op cit*, pp 271–73.

[11] *Ibid*, pp 270–71.

[12] Webb, *Plans of Wooden Vessels, op cit*.

[13] Richard C McKay, *Some Famous Sailing Ships and Their Builder Donald McKay*, (New York 1928), pp 365–73.

[14] Basil Greenhill, *The Great Migration: Crossing the Atlantic under Sail*, (London 1968), pp 5–8; see also Edwin C Guillet, *The Great Migration*, (Toronto 1937), and Oscar Handlin, *Immigration as a Factor in American History*, (Englewood Cliffs, N J 1959).

[15] Henry Green and Robert Wigram, *Chronicles of the Blackwall Yard*, (London 1881), part I, p 58. Part II was never published and Part I terminates in the year 1843.

[16] Smith's Dock Co, *Ships and Men*, (North Shields and Middlesbrough 1949), brochure, p 10. The original plan could not be located in 1965.

[17] Basil Lubbock, *The Blackwall Frigates*, (Glasgow 1922), pp 107–9.

[18] John C G Hill, *Shipshape and Bristol Fashion*, (Liverpool 2nd ed *c*1958), p 15; picture of half-model.

[19] Green and Wigram, *Chronicles of Blackwall Yard, op cit*, p 59.

[20] NMM, *A Memorandum of Vessels built at Blackwall Yard*, compiled 1892 by J F Green; (exhibited as a framed display).

[21] Green and Wigram, *Chronicles of Blackwall Yard, op cit*, p 61.

[22] Half-model of *Mars* at offices of Charles Hill & Son, Bristol, lines taken off by W Salisbury; and 36-gun frigate in Abraham Rees, *The Cyclopaedia or Universal Dictionary of Arts, Sciences, and Literature*, (London 1820), plates vol III, plate no XI.

[23] Green and Wigram, *Chronicles of Blackwall Yard, op cit*, p 61.

[24] Basil Lubbock, 'Merchantmen under Sail', *MM*, 1957, vol 43, p 5; and Lubbock, *Blackwall Frigates, op cit*, p 157.

[25] NMM, L R survey reports, London No 19090.

[26] Green and Wigram, *Chronicles of Blackwall Yard, op cit*, pp 35 et seq.

[27] Lubbock, *Blackwall Frigates, op cit*, pp 161–62, quoting *The Illustrated London News*, 15 June 1844.

[28] George Moorsom, *Brief Review and Analyses of the Laws for the Admeasurement of Tonnage*, (London 1852), pp 93 and 168.

[29] W I Downie, *Resminiscences of a Blackwall Midshipman*, (London 1912), pp 20–1. The quotation refers to a passage in 1862–63.

[30] Contract copied in the offices of Sir James Laing & Co Ltd in 1957.

[31] Lubbock, *Blackwall Frigates, op cit*, p 161.

[32] See Robert Kipping, *The Elements of Sailmaking*, (London 2nd ed 1851), title page and p vii.

[33] *The Illustrated London News*, Oct 1853.

SOURCES

PLANS, MODELS AND RELATED ARCHIVES

These are the principal sources including two printed works where the plans were of major importance. Sources for half-tones and line drawings are not included.

Bristol Museum; plans and models.

Howard I Chapelle; plans of American ships (inspected during his lifetime).

Dundee Museum; models.

Glasgow Museum of Transport; models, including half-models from A Hall & Sons.

Peter Hedderwick; merchant ship plans in his book *Treatise on Marine Architecture*.

James Henderson; reconstructed plans of Aberdeen ships; cost accounts of vessels built by A Hall & Sons.

Charles Hill & Sons, Bristol; Hilhouse plans.

Kronborg Castle, Elsinor; plans of Danish vessels.

Mariners Museum, Newport News; plans by G Hillmann.

Merseyside Maritime Museum, Liverpool; plans of ships built by T & J Brocklebank and Yard Book; models; shipyard lists.

National Maritime Museum, Greenwich; Admiralty Draughts; plans of merchant ships in Longstaff and other collections; Lloyd's Register survey reports.

Vice-Adml Paris compiler of *Souvenirs de Marine*; six volumes containing 60 pages each with plans and data.

Patent Office; Abridgements of Specifications (published in book form)

W Salisbury; plans; shipyard lists; analysis of Hilhouse plans.

Science Museum, London; plans and models of merchant ships, especially Geddie plans.

A Stephen & Sons, Glasgow; diaries kept by Alexander Stephen snr (inspected on firm's premises).

James Steele; half-models and shipyard list (inspected during his lifetime).

Sunderland Museum (now under Tyne & Wear); models.

Whitby Museum (Whitby Literary and Philosophical Society); ship plans including those collected by H W Smales.

Whitehaven Museum; sail plans; shipyard lists.

Author's Collection; plans and shipyard lists.

PRINTED WORKS

The following are the principal books consulted but it is not intended to be an exhaustive list on the period. Articles in journals are given in the References and so are omitted. A number of the books listed were used in reconstructing the plans.

Abell, Sir Westcott, *The Shipwright's Trade* (Cambridge 1948)

Albion, Robert G, *Square-riggers on Schedule* (Princeton, NJ 1938)

Armour, C A, & T Lackey, *Sailing Ships of the Maritimes* (Toronto 1975)

Baugean, Jean, *Collection de toutes les Espèces de Bâtiments de Guerre et de Bâtiments Marchands* (Paris 1814)

Baugean, Jean, *Recueil de Petites Marine* (Paris 1817)

Benham, Hervey, *Once upon a Tide* (London 1955)

Biddlecombe, George, *The Art of Rigging* (London 1848)

Bowen, Frank C, *The Golden Age of Sail* (London 1925)

Brewington, MV and Dorothy Brewington, *The Marine Paintings and Drawings in the Peabody Museum* (Salem 1968)

Burstall, Aubrey F, *A History of Mechanical Engineering* London 1965)

Chapelle, Howard I, *The History of American Sailing Ships* (New York 1935)

Chapelle, Howard I, *The National Watercraft Collection* (Smithsonian Museum, Washington 1960)

Chapelle Howard I, *The Search for Speed under Sail* (New York 1967)

Clark, Arthur H, *The Clipper Ship Era* (New York 1910)

Clowes, G S Laird, *Sailing Ships* (Science Museum catalogues, 2 vols, London 1932)

Coates, W H, *The Good Old Days of Shipping* (Bombay 1900)

Cooke, E W, *Fifty Plates of Shipping and Craft* (London 1829)

Cotton, Sir Evan, *East Indiamen* (London 1949)

Court, W H B, *A Concise Economic History of Britain from 1750* (Cambridge 1954)

Cutler, Carl C, *Queens of the Western Ocean* (Annapolis 1961)

Davis, Ralph, *Rise of the English Shipping Industry* (London 1962)

Falconer, William, (editor William Burney), *A New Universal Dictionary of the Marine* (London 1815)

Finberg, H P R (editor), *Approaches to History* (London 1965)

Finch, Roger, *Coals from Newcastle* (Lavenham 1973)

Fincham, John, *An Outline of Ship-Building* (2 vols text and plates London 1852)

Fincham, John, *A Treatise on Masting Ships and Mast Making,* (2 vols text and plates, London 1st ed 1829 and 3rd ed 1854)

Gibson, John F, *Brocklebanks 1770–1950* (2 vols Liverpool 1953)

Grantham, John, *Iron as a Material for Ship-Building* (London 1842)

Greenhill, Basil, *The Merchant Schooners* (2 vols, London 1951 & 1956)

Hardy's Register of Ships Employed by the East India Co (London 3rd ed 1820 and 4th ed 1835)

Harper, Lawrence A, *The English Navigation Laws* (reprint of 1939 ed, New York 1964)

Hedderwick, Peter, *A Treatise on Marine Architecture* (2 vols text and plates, Edinburgh 1930)

Hill, John C G, *Shipshape and Bristol Fashion* (Liverpool *c*1955)

Kipping, Robert, *The Elements of Sailmaking* (2nd ed London 1851)

Lescaller, Antoine, *Vocabulaire des Termes de Marine* (Paris 1777)

Leslie, Robert C, *Old Sea Wings, Ways and Words* (London 1930)

Lever, Darcy, *Young Sea Officer's Sheet Anchor* (London 1808)

Lindsay, W S, *History of Merchant Shipping 1816–1874* (2 vols, London *c*1874)

Lloyd's Register of Shipping (annually, London)

Lloyds's Register, *Annals of Lloyd's Register* (London 1934)

Lubbock, Basil, *The Blackwall Frigates* (Glasgow 1922)

Lubbock, Basil, *The Arctic Whalers* (Glasgow 1937)

MacGregor, David R, *Fast Sailing Ships 1775–1875* (Lymington 1973)

Marryat, Capt, *Code of Signals for Use of Vessels in the Merchant Service* (London 3rd ed 1820 and 8th ed 1841)

Moorsom, George, *A Brief Review and Analyses of the Laws for the Admeasurement of Tonnage* (London 1952)

Morgan, William, and Augustin Creuze (editors), *Papers on Naval Architecture* (4 vols, London 1826, 1828, 1830, 1832–65)

Morris, E P, *The Fore-and-Aft Rig in America* (New Haven, Conn, 1927)

Moses, Henry, *Sketches of Shipping and Craft* (London 1824)

Murphy, John M, and W N Jeffers jnr, *Spars and Rigging from Nautical Routine* (reprint of 1849 ed, Providence, RI 1933)

Paris, Vice-Adml Edmond, *Souvenirs de Marine* (original 6 vols reprinted as 3, Grenoble 1975)

Parkinson, C Northcote, *The Trade Winds: British Oversea Trade 1793–1815* (London 1948)

Peake, James, *Rudiments of Naval Architecture* (London 1851)

Petrejus, E W , *Modelling the Brig of War 'Irene'* (Hengelo, Holland 1970)

Rees, Abraham, 'Naval Architecture', *Cyclopaedia* (London 1820)

Richardson, Thomas, *Mercantile Marine Architecture* London 1833)

Shields, John, *Clyde Built* (Glasgow 1949)

Smith, J W, and T S Holden, *Where Ships are Born: Sunderland 1346–1946* (Sunderland 1947)

Stackpole, Edouard A, *The Sea-Hunters* (Philadelphia 1953)

Stackpole, Edouard A, *The 'Charles W Morgan'* (New York 1967)

Starbuck, Alexander, *History of the American Whale Fishery* (reprint of 1878 ed 2 vols, New York 1964)

Steel, David, *The Elements and Practice of Rigging and Seamanship* (2 vols London 1794)

Steel, David, *Elements and Practice of Naval Architecture,* (2 vols text and plates, London 2nd 1822; editor John Knowles)

Steel, David, *The Shipwright's Vade-Mecum* (2 vols text and plates, London 1805)

[Stephen, Sir A Murray], *A Shipbuilding History* (Glasgow *c*1932; includes lists of ships built by A Stephen & Sons)

Stevens, John R, *Old Time Ships* (Toronto 1949)

Szymanski, Hans, *Deutsche Segelschiffe* (Berlin 1934)

Underhill, Harold A, *Masting and Rigging, the Clipper Ship and Ocean Carrier* (Glasgow 1946)

Wallace, F W, *Wooden Ships and Iron Men* (London 1924)

Winchester, Clarence (editor, *Shipping Wonders of the World,* (2 vols, London *c*1936)

Wright, Esther C, *Saint John Ships and their Builders* (Wolfville, NS 1975)

Young, Arthur, *Nautical Dictionary* (1st ed Dundee 1846, 2nd ed London 1863)

INDEX

Fig 211. Blenheim's *sister ship* Marlborough *passing icebergs off Cape Horn in August 1853 when homeward bound from Melbourne. An engraving in the* Illustrated London News.